AUTOBIOGRAPHICAL REENACTMENT IN FRENCH AND BELGIAN FILM
REPETITION, MEMORY, SELF

LEGENDA

LEGENDA is the Modern Humanities Research Association's book imprint for new research in the Humanities. Founded in 1995 by Malcolm Bowie and others within the University of Oxford, Legenda has always been a collaborative publishing enterprise, directly governed by scholars. The Modern Humanities Research Association (MHRA) joined this collaboration in 1998, became half-owner in 2004, in partnership with Maney Publishing and then Routledge, and has since 2016 been sole owner. Titles range from medieval texts to contemporary cinema and form a widely comparative view of the modern humanities, including works on Arabic, Catalan, English, French, German, Greek, Italian, Portuguese, Russian, Spanish, and Yiddish literature. Editorial boards and committees of more than 60 leading academic specialists work in collaboration with bodies such as the Society for French Studies, the British Comparative Literature Association and the Association of Hispanists of Great Britain & Ireland.

The MHRA encourages and promotes advanced study and research in the field of the modern humanities, especially modern European languages and literature, including English, and also cinema. It aims to break down the barriers between scholars working in different disciplines and to maintain the unity of humanistic scholarship. The Association fulfils this purpose through the publication of journals, bibliographies, monographs, critical editions, and the MHRA Style Guide, and by making grants in support of research. Membership is open to all who work in the Humanities, whether independent or in a University post, and the participation of younger colleagues entering the field is especially welcomed.

ALSO PUBLISHED BY THE ASSOCIATION

Critical Texts
Tudor and Stuart Translations • *New Translations* • *European Translations*
MHRA Library of Medieval Welsh Literature

MHRA Bibliographies
Publications of the Modern Humanities Research Association

The Annual Bibliography of English Language & Literature
Austrian Studies
Modern Language Review
Portuguese Studies
The Slavonic and East European Review
Working Papers in the Humanities
The Yearbook of English Studies

www.mhra.org.uk
www.legendabooks.com

MOVING IMAGE

Legenda/Moving Image publishes cutting-edge work on any aspect of film or screen media from Europe and Latin America. Studies of European-language cinemas from other continents, and diasporic and intercultural cinemas (with some relation to Europe or its languages), are also encompassed. The series seeks to reflect a diversity of theoretical, historical, and interdisciplinary approaches to the moving image, and includes projects comparing screen media with other art forms. Research monographs and collected volumes will be considered, but not studies of a single film. As innovation is a priority for the series, volumes should predominantly consist of previously unpublished material.

Proposals should be sent with one or two sample chapters to the Editor, Professor Emma Wilson, Corpus Christi College, Cambridge CB2 1RH, UK.

Managing Editor
Dr Graham Nelson, 41 Wellington Square, Oxford OX1 2JF, UK

www.legendabooks.com

Autobiographical Reenactment in French and Belgian Film

Repetition, Memory, Self

❖

Tom Cuthbertson

l

LEGENDA

Moving Image 12
Modern Humanities Research Association
2022

Published by Legenda
an imprint of the Modern Humanities Research Association
Salisbury House, Station Road, Cambridge CB1 2LA

ISBN 978-1-78188-488-1 (HB)
ISBN 978-1-78188-492-8 (PB)

First published 2022

Copy-Editor: Dr Anna J. Davies

CONTENTS

❖

For my parents

ACKNOWLEDGEMENTS

❖

The book you have just opened is the final product of a long and varied process (with a global pandemic also thrown into the mix). Throughout this process, I have racked up a number of debts. These debts might be academic, professional, practical, creative, emotional, financial (or in some cases a mixture of these categories). It is my pleasure to acknowledge these debts here.

This book began life in doctoral research undertaken at the University of Oxford between 2014 and 2018 that was made possible by a Postgraduate Scholarship in the Humanities from the Wolfson Foundation. I would like to take this opportunity to thank the Wolfson Foundation for their support during my time as a doctoral student, and for their investment in Humanities research at postgraduate level. I would also very much like to thank Mary Harrod and Ginette Vincendeau, editors of the journal *French Screen Studies*, for generously awarding me a research bursary that covered the costs associated with producing this book's index. All of this financial support has been very gratefully received.

Throughout the research, writing and production work that went into this book, I have benefited from the help, support, wisdom, skill and generosity of many people in the worlds of academia, arts and publishing. This book would not be what it is without the supervision I received as a doctoral student or without the help and advice my former supervisors have continued to offer in the years that have passed since. I will always be immeasurably grateful for Nikolaj Lübecker's immense patience, unfaltering encouragement, generous guidance, humbling kindness, and intimidating erudition. He has always led me to push my thinking further, to forge new connections, and to make my arguments crisper (even if a few rogue pleonasms may still remain in what follows ;)). Thank you to Dimitris Papanikolaou for having accepted me as an honorary member of the Oxford Greek department. I am indebted to him for his infectious enthusiasm, for the trust and belief he has always placed in me and my work, and for reminding me of the multiple ways in which to understand what happens in Greece is to understand so much of what happens elsewhere. At the end of my time as a doctoral student, I was delighted to talk about my research with two brilliant scholars I admire enormously: my viva examination with Emma Wilson and Sarah Cooper remains one of the highlights of my academic career to date, and this book is far stronger for discussion with them. Emma Wilson was also General Editor of Legenda's Moving Image monograph series when this book was first accepted for publication, and I would like to thank her and her successor J. D. Rhodes for their support for this project. I would also like to thank the other members of the Moving Image Editorial Committee for their very helpful and supportive comments on my proposal. Huge thanks to Graham Nelson, Managing Editor at Legenda, for his very patient guidance throughout the twists and turns that have led up to this book's final publication. He has been a friendly and reassuring presence throughout, and I could not imagine a better or more capable editor. Thank you to Anna J. Davies for her very careful copyediting, and to Susan Tricklebank for her excellent work on the index. At around the time this project moved into its production stage, I began a new job at Newcastle University. I would like to thank new colleagues in the School of Modern Languages – especially Shirley Jordan, Guy Austin, Catherine Gilbert and Carolyn Taylor – for welcoming me so warmly to the department. At Newcastle, I would also like to thank Beate Müller for invaluable German language help with a passage in Chapter 3, and Sandra Salin for linguistic assistance when I had listened to a French voice-over so many times I wasn't sure what I was hearing anymore. For allowing me to access and use certain materials in my research, I would like to thank Vincent Dieutre, Boris Lehman, Stéphane Jourdain at La Huit Production, Dread Scott, Soul Brother, Sarah Pucill and Ming Wong. An earlier version of arguments developed in Chapter 2 appeared in the article 'In/Out: fictionalising autobiography in Vincent Dieutre's *Jaurès*' (2012), *Studies in French Cinema* [now *French Screen Studies*], 17:3 (2017) 265–82 <https://doi.org/10.1080/14715880.2017.1281037>. I am grateful to the publisher (<https://www.tandfonline.com/>) for permission to draw on this material

Debts to friends and family are vast, numerous and far-ranging. For fun, distraction, support, care, love and often life-altering friendship at various points in time and in various places, I would like to thank in particular: Tom Adams, Hayley Barbary, Nick Davies, David Haywood Smith, Joe Horton, Calum Howard, Eddie Knight, Adam Levy, Peter Norris, Avner Ofrath, Alex Paulin-Booth, Carrie Plitt, Melissa Purkiss, Graham Riach, Gordon Ritchie, Kylie Sago, Kate Saunders-Hastings, Ed Still, Adam Tomassi-Russell, Raff Tomassi-Russell, Kate West, Fred Wilmott-Smith. My family has grown a little bit since the last time I had to write an acknowledgements page. I would like to thank my brothers James and Jack Cuthbertson, my sisters-in-law Emma Kastrisianaki-Guyton and Mary Watson, and my little niece Gwen. Most of all, I would like to thank my parents, Bridget and Michael Cuthbertson. For everything, forever, with love. This book is for them.

T.C., March 2022

LIST OF ILLUSTRATIONS

❖

INTRODUCTION

❖

Video Grief Diaries

Reenactment — *The action or process of reproducing, recreating, or performing again; esp. the action or process of acting out a past event.* [oed.com]

Throughout the pages of this book, we will frequently find ourselves confronted with the various ways in which the past can seem to recur in the present, with how time can appear to repeat, change course, double back on itself, and with how such temporal distortions can disrupt and confuse the coordinates of identity, blurring the lines that mark one thing or one moment as fully distinct from another. In the interest of providing a site of anchorage in amongst all of these potentially disorientating twists, turns and returns, I open this Introduction with a word about my book's genesis. Many of the guiding lines of inquiry that work their way throughout what follows first came into focus when watching a film that informs much of the analysis I will go on to develop without ever appearing as its explicit object. This is a film that, in the often unsettling engagements it offers with questions of temporality, affect, intimacy, memory, embodiment, mourning and desire, provided a point of access to begin considering questions that will rise to the surface time and time again in what follows.

In certain ways, Alain Cavalier's (1931–) lyrical, often confessional video diary film *Irène* (2009) is entirely consistent with the other autobiographical works that the French filmmaker has produced in recent years. Embracing the avenues for self–expression opened by the advent of lightweight digital video technology, *Irène*, like films such as Cavalier's earlier *Le Filmeur* [*The Filmer*] (2005) or the later *Le Paradis* [*Paradise*] (2014), inventories and enumerates the minute details of the filmmaker's lived experience — his routines, his thoughts, his hopes, his dreams, his ideas, his associations, his feelings, his regrets. As in these other films, everyday life in *Irène* is laid bare and exposed to continual visual scrutiny, surveyed by Cavalier's ever recording camera. What differentiates *Irène*, however, is the extent to which it thematises the opposition between the abundant visibility of a present moment compulsively captured on screen with the invisibility of a past that has seemingly vanished. *Irène* is a film about the myriad ways in which grief overwhelms and seeps into everything that it touches. It is a film about our experience of different forms and sources of loss and about the sometimes desperate attempts we make to maintain a connection with what has moved out of reach.

A preoccupation with loss is announced right from the opening shots of *Irène*:

Cavalier's camera lingers over the body of his recently deceased mother as it lies, loosely covered in a gold-coloured shroud, at the centre of a funeral chapel. Having appeared in Cavalier's previous *Le Filmeur* as a figure of resilient vitality, responsive and present even on her deathbed, the mother here seems almost transparent, her skin now yellowed and wax-like. These silent images of the filmmaker's dead mother frame Cavalier's film and shape our experience of it. And yet, as Cavalier's video grief diary — this *journal (filmé) de deuil* — develops, it leads us away from the deceased mother, plunging us instead within a larger concatenation of griefs that reveals the extent to which a new loss can often cast us painfully backwards into other losses that preceded it.

After its opening sequence, *Irène* is more markedly concerned with the disappearance of a different female figure — one whose absence is felt yet more gnawingly and whose body, unlike that of the mother, cannot now be filmed. This absence is one that had already exerted a profound influence over much of the director's work, from the austere experimentation of *Ce répondeur ne prend pas de message* [*This Answering Service Takes No Messages*] (1979) onwards. *Irène* explores the haunting, almost palpable absence of Cavalier's deceased wife, the titular Irène, killed in a car accident in 1972. Cavalier's film searches for a means of bringing his wife back to life, of rescuing her from the disappearance and forgetting that threaten her. Cavalier continually seeks an image that might allow him to conjure a presence and provide a remedy to the absence that haunts him and his film. Throughout *Irène*, we accompany Cavalier as he lives through the lens of his camera, trying to draw close a cherished loved one who forever eludes his full grasp.

There is an ineluctable forwards momentum to much of *Irène*, made visible, for instance, by changes of weather and season, and by Cavalier's proximate depictions of his own ageing flesh. This forwards momentum contrasts, however, with the sustained gaze the film casts in the opposite direction towards the past and its relics. At points throughout the film, Cavalier focuses upon a succession of black-and-white photographs of Irène. Zooming in on them, he confesses that he seeks something more than the frozen stillness these images offer. He films pages of his diary from the months leading up to his wife's death, trying to understand her, desperately seeking a trace or glimmer that might alert him to her residual presence, reading for her between the written lines. With dismay, he finds that these words convey only a sense of absence, far removed from the vitality he seeks. In a notable sequence, Cavalier sets fire to one of these diaries on the flame of a camping stove: painstakingly charring its cover, he attempts to reanimate these static words, to turn their morbid fixity into live volatility, to release the past experiences they preserve into the present. Cavalier films the darkened streets of his wife's native city or the various rooms he once occupied with her. In such sequences, he moves in search of a lingering echo or sign, immersing himself in the affective atmospheres of these lived spaces. Elsewhere, he reenacts his angry final words to his wife, filming from the same window from which he saw her alive for the very last time. Throughout his film, Cavalier seeks someone or something who might be able to play the role of Irène in the present, to revive and embody his memories of her. His

FIG. I.1. and I.2. *Irène* (2009), Alain Cavalier
© Caméra One/Pyramide Productions/Arte France Cinéma.

camera repeatedly investigates surrogate bodies and forms seemingly in the hope of reawakening his wife's touch, her sensate and sensuous materiality. It is these increasingly bizarre attempts that give rise to some of the film's most startling, most unexpected images.

Occupying a series of hotel rooms, Cavalier arranges objects in a way that recalls parts of the body he so misses. In such sequences, crumpled blankets on beds assume spectral, corporeal volumes, taking the form of supine torsos and tensed thighs. Elsewhere, shrine-like arrangements of pebbles and balls placed on further hotel beds evoke pubis, breast and belly. Cavalier here both foregrounds the physicality of the connection he once had with his wife and announces his present desire to return to this now lost intimacy. In what is undoubtedly the most bewildering sequence of *Irène*, Cavalier continues to evoke particular parts of his wife's body, but this time with the aid of a slice of watermelon. As Cavalier manipulates it, this hollowed-out fruit becomes fleshy and vaginal. Thrusting a spoon into its crimson interior, he recreates the lacerating violence of the botched abortion that, he implies, once left the teenage Irène infertile; placing an egg inside the cavity he creates in the watermelon's flesh, he also reenacts his own breech birth with a pair of kitchen tongs, apologising to his now dead mother that the bodily damage his delivery caused had prevented her from having further children. Such images are decidedly, deliberately unsettling. Cavalier's fruit-based reconstruction instigates a strange form of conflation between two vaginas, one of which the filmmaker remembers, the other he does not. The sound of metal spoon and tongs tearing through watermelon innards underlines the materiality of acts of violence: violence inflicted on fruit in the present evokes violence inflicted on two female bodies in the past.

In each of his attempts to dispel absence, to actualise something of his memories of Irène, Cavalier reluctantly concedes that none of these methods will ever *really* bring back what has been definitively lost. Initially elated to find an actor able to capture something fugitive but authentic of his lost wife, Cavalier seems dejected at the thought that the resemblance can never be perfect, that the equivalence can never be direct and complete:

> Irène est si vivante, si précise, si unique dans ma tête que... impossible de reconstituer avec elle ou avec d'autres. Voilà, je vais toutes les chasser, m'en débarrasser. *Elles* ne sont jamais *elle*!

> [Irène is so alive, so precise, so unique in my mind that... it's impossible to reconstruct with her or with anyone else. Fine, I'm going to get rid of them all, rid myself of them. *They* are never *her*!]

And yet, as we watch his film, Cavalier's experiments expose us to a subtle, almost uncanny degree of slippage between the visible present witnessed on screen and an invisible past that seems to lurk just beneath the surface. The blankets, stones and fruits that Cavalier arranges in his post-mortem reconstructions are decidedly *not* his wife; but, through a growing form of ambiguity that blurs the line between past and present, presence and absence, reality and imagination, they are *not* entirely *not* her either.

Over the following chapters, we will encounter other, sometimes equally bewild-ering experiments in which a filmmaker attempts to repeat, reproduce or recreate something from an earlier time in the present as a means of exploring aspects of their experiences, memories, emotions, relationships, origins and identities. Through close readings of the autobiographical work of four experimental filmmakers from France and Belgium — Chantal Akerman (1950–2015), Vincent Dieutre (1960–), Boris Lehman (1944–) and Agnès Varda (1928–2019) — this book theorises a radical strategy of self-inquiry and self-representation that I term *autobiographical reenactment*. The films I consider throughout this book are very different, produced by hugely individual artists within a time period that covers the closing two decades of the twentieth century and the opening two of the twenty-first; but they are brought into proximity by the compelling examples of autobiographical reenactment they all contain.

More varied and extensive than those found in Cavalier's film, the instances of autobiographical reenactment that I go on to analyse assume a range of forms. Whilst they do not necessarily or not only entail reconstructing experiences that these four filmmakers themselves lived through (as my chosen vocabulary might at first glance be taken to suggest), there is always a clear autobiographical dimension to them, as was also the case in *Irène*. In this sense, what interests me in this book are multiple, diverse practices of *autobiographical reenactment* rather than just simply the notion of *reenacting autobiography* as more narrowly defined. In certain instances, autobiographical reenactment certainly will entail repeating something that these filmmakers did themselves experience directly: we will watch as they replay earlier moments of their own lives or ask others to do so on their behalf. Elsewhere, the past experiences these filmmakers choose to reenact will lie at a further remove, accrued in the course of lives that are not their own: these may be lives that are known and dear to these filmmakers; equally, they may be lives revived from a much broader span of history that mean something to these filmmakers and in relation to which they seek to position themselves. In yet other instances, the lives and experiences from the past that are reproduced in the present may be decidedly less real: on certain occasions we will witness filmmakers reenact pre-existing artworks (paintings, sculptures, photographs, other films) in which they recognise something of themselves or of how they wish to appear. Sometimes we will observe combinations of these variants. The resources and tools mobilised by these four filmmakers in their respective uses of autobiographical reenactment will be similarly numerous: these might include, for instance, the poses and arrangements of the filmmaker's own body or certain parts of it; the bodies of the other people the filmmakers direct on screen; the inanimate objects with which they surround these bodies; or particular aspects of the technologies, manipulations and representational strategies of the filmic medium.

Through examination of such varied instances, approaches and techniques, I explore how these filmmakers create precarious, fragmentary, often overtly fictionalised, sometimes stridently provocative autobiographical reenactments on screen, reviving and restaging movements, forms, images, gestures and sensations from the past in the present as a means of questioning who they really are, where they come from, their place in the world, what matters to them, their lives, loves, losses, interactions, identifications and attachments. In my analysis of the work of Akerman, Dieutre, Lehman and Varda, I am interested in the distinctive engagements with history, time, reality, memory, identity, subjectivity, emotion, truth, knowledge, proof and archive that are sustained by autobiographical reenactment, and in how such experiments continually prompt us to rethink our understanding of what autobiography can be and can do.

As was the case with the very particular kinds of mourning staged in Cavalier's *Irène*, the varied examples of autobiographical reenactment examined in the following chapters often represent engagements with forms of loss. In certain examples, these engagements will respond to the kinds of grief occasioned by the death of a loved one, as in Cavalier's posthumous search for his wife. Elsewhere, forms of autobiographical reenactment will be used as part of a negotiation with other (though not always entirely unconnected) experiences of loss: memory loss, the loss of youth and health, the diminishment of certain states of being or feeling, the breakdown of relationships, the myriad losses of world history, or the more general kinds of loss associated with the ineluctable passing of time. In the negotiations that they offer with these varied (and frequently overlapping) forms of loss, the works of Akerman, Dieutre, Lehman and Varda test — in a similar way to Cavalier — the access that we can gain to the past and the uses to which this access can be put in the present. These four filmmakers engage with questions raised by *Irène* regarding the function of autobiographical reenactment and the effects that it might produce: What exactly does it mean to repeat something from the past within the filmic present? What kind of relationships across time does this autobiographical repetition permit? What is produced in such repetitions, sameness or difference, and why does this matter? Can we ever *really* return to what is no more?

Surveying the reenactive permutations encountered in the context of documentary filmmaking, Bill Nichols has described what he presents as the 'impossible task' of all reenactment: 'to retrieve a lost object in its original form even as the very act of retrieval generates a new object' (2008: 74). In his exasperated declaration that '*Elles* ne sont jamais *elle*' [*They* are never *her*], Cavalier implicitly acknowledges the difficulty of reenactment's task, reinforcing the irreversibility of loss and the distressing impossibility of making the past return intact, unchanged or identical to the present. This is an irreversibility, an impossibility, that is also often explicitly acknowledged in the autobiographical work of Akerman, Dieutre, Lehman and Varda. From this perspective, we might be led to ask whether, in its use as a strategy for the negotiation of loss, autobiographical reenactment always tends inevitably towards the ceaseless, pathological repetitions that Freud saw as the defining, all-consuming symptoms of melancholy (1957: 243), foregrounding only the definitive irretrievability of what once was and standing as a recurrent index of loss's irrecoverability. In the strange forms of temporal slippage that it depicts, Cavalier's film itself offers an incipient answer to such questions, one I explore throughout this book. As it experimented with the surprising, disorienting effects that can be unleashed through reenactment, depicting Cavalier's often excited and hopeful responses to them, *Irène* also offered possible alternatives to melancholic responses to loss. As Nichols indeed goes on to suggest in his account: if reenactment generates new objects, it can also generate new pleasures (2008: 74).

The varied uses of autobiographical reenactment found in the filmmaking of Akerman, Dieutre, Lehman and Varda generate their own new, distinctive pleasures. Whilst their films frequently announce the pain, disappointment and frustration encountered in the impossibility of reversing loss and of fully recapturing what is no more, their respective autobiographical experiments with reenactment simultaneously explore the possibility of other, more positive relationships with the past, ones that can potentially be a source of pleasure, enjoyment, hope, optimism, comfort and joy. This book examines a range of creative, imaginative, intensely personal engagements with the past and with what has been lost that remain held in various ways within this tension between reenactment's pleasures and pains. The works of Akerman, Dieutre, Lehman and Varda recognise that autobiographical reenactment might not be able to regain an absent original and bring back the past as it really was *then*; but as we will see, their films also repeatedly explore how, through the development of often strange modes of cross-temporal negotiation, autobiographical reenactment can sometimes create new pleasing versions of the past as these filmmakers want or need it to be *now*.

Living in Reenactive Times

The films of the four artists that constitute this book's corpus are by no means unique in their use of reenactment as a strategy of autobiography. Forms of auto-biographical reenactment resembling aspects of what we will go on to see in the films of Akerman, Dieutre, Lehman and Varda are indeed discernible in the work of other filmmakers from around the world. This is the case, for instance, for much of the filmmaking of British artist Sarah Pucill, whose varied uses of reenactment correspond to certain of those overlapping typologies outlined above. Her 2004 film *Stages of Mourning* in particular responds to a comparable impulse to Cavalier's *Irène*, though does so through different means: we watch as she carefully recreates and reframes several of her own earlier artworks in an attempt to reach out to her deceased partner, artist Sandra Lahire, and to mourn her death. More recently, Pucill's companion pieces *Magic Mirror* (2013) and *Confessions to the Mirror* (2016) have staged reenactments of photographic self-portraits originally created by French surrealist Claude Cahun. These reenactments seek to revive and reappropriate the disruptions of gender, identity and subjectivity that once propelled Cahun's work, whilst opening an extended meditation on the movements of artistic identification, inspiration and influence across media and time.

A use of reenactment that seeks to remake and rework pre-existing artworks, to use them as ambiguous tools of self-exploration, appears very differently in the work of an artist such as Ming Wong, who has increasingly adopted forms of reenactment as a dominant creative methodology. The 2007 film *Lerne deutsch mit*

FIG. I.3. *Magic Mirror* (16mm, bw, 75min, 2013), Sarah Pucill © Sarah Pucill.

Petra von Kant [*Learn German with Petra von Kant*] — made whilst the Singaporean artist was preparing to relocate to Germany — remakes a climactic sequence from Rainer Werner Fassbinder's *Die bitteren Tränen der Petra von Kant* [*The Bitter Tears of Petra von Kant*] (1972), with Wong assuming the eponymous role originally played by actor Margit Carstensen to explore the sexual and racial politics of representation and to ask what it might mean to be a queer, Asian artist in Europe. As a means of resurrecting this gesture of queer homage and of commemorating ten years spent in Germany, Wong has more recently chosen to revisit this earlier source material in *Lehre deutsch mit Petra von Kant* [*Teach German with Petra von Kant*] (2017), refracting Carstensen's original performance across a much wider range of modern interpretations with the help of his students from the Berlin University of the Arts.

In further corroboration of reenactment's ongoing consolidation as a recurrent strategy within contemporary queer filmmaking, Kaori Oda's 2010 film *Thus A Noise Speaks* obliged the Japanese filmmaker's family to reenact their own earlier reactions to her coming-out, asking them to reflect upon the emotional impact their original responses once had. Looking elsewhere, family (with its affections, tensions, misunderstandings and concealments) has provided fertile ground for reenactment in the work of further artists. Highly stylised reenactments brush up against various archival traces (childhood home videos, handwritten prison diaries) as part of a hampered struggle for rememoration in David Achkar's *Allah Tantou* [*God's Will*] (1992), for instance, with the filmmaker seeking answers to the uncertain death of his incarcerated father that might help him to fill in painful gaps in tightly intertwined public and private histories. In producing wholly convincing counterfeits of childhood home movies, Sarah Polley adopts a contrasting approach to filling in the gaps in her own story in *Stories We Tell* (2012). As neatly resumed by

Nein, hier ist nicht von Kant
No, this is not von Kant

FIG. I.4. Still from *Lerne Deutsch mit Petra von Kant / Learn German with Petra von Kant* (2007), Ming Wong. Digital video installation, 10 mins. Courtesy of the artist.

her film's title, Polley's self-consciously speculative uses of reenactment foreground the extent to which truth so often depends upon exactly how we tell the story. This is something that applies equally to the very different engagements with family and origins found in films such as Alejandro Jodorowsky's *Poesía sin fin* [*Endless Poetry*] (2016), Guy Maddin's *My Winnipeg* (2007) or Manoel de Oliveira's *Porto da Minha Infância* [*Porto of My Childhood*] (2001): in each instance, autobiographical reenactment serves to resurrect aspects of these filmmakers' youths in the cities in which they grew up, continually treading the line between past and present, fact and fiction, reality and desire, and orchestrating curious encounters between selves.

When we begin to look for instances of autobiographical reenactment, remaining attentive to the wide variety of their possible appearances, we are sometimes led to approach very familiar films in unfamiliar ways. This is the case, for example, for that stalwart of university documentary and autobiography courses, Ross McElwee's *Sherman's March* (1986). Along what can be read as a meandering retracing of the trajectory followed over a century earlier by the titular General William Tecumseh Sherman on his 'March to the Sea' during the American Civil War, McElwee here questions his ideas of success and ambition as he traverses America's southern states. Reenacted movements and journeys in which individual and collective histories merge also lie at the heart of the work of an artist such as Sarah Turner: her 2009 film *Perestroika* mourns the death of a friend through the reenactment of a Trans-Siberian train journey that allows the artist to explore the ambiguous and unstable interactions of experience and landscape — an inquiry that was itself revisited in

Turner's follow-up film *Perestroika: Reconstructed* (2013). As her works explore the elements of fiction and imagination that inescapably bleed into the act of giving an account of oneself, Turner offers interlocking reflections on the uncertain mechanics of memory and of filmic representation.

This brief cross-section of international examples watched or rewatched during this book's preparation should suffice to demonstrate, on the one hand, the extent to which considering autobiographical filmmaking from the perspective of reenactment leads us to productively seek connections between hugely different works and to develop new readings of sometimes well-known texts. On the other hand, this survey should also illustrate how the heterogeneous strategy of self-inquiry and self-representation that I term autobiographical reenactment amply exceeds the films of Akerman, Dieutre, Lehman and Varda. So why these four filmmakers? The extensiveness, prominence and variety of examples found in the work of Akerman, Dieutre, Lehman and Varda make them particularly instructive case studies for exploring how and why filmmakers use autobiographical reenactment in their work, the different forms such reenactments can assume and the effects they can produce. These filmmakers' experiments with autobiographical reenactment also exist usefully in dialogue. As we will see, this is particularly the case with the work of Dieutre and Lehman, both of whom position themselves in different ways, formally and thematically, in relation to the determining influence of Akerman. This is also true — albeit less obviously so — of the work of Varda as it offers very different responses to some of the questions that animate the work of the filmmakers who precede her in this book. Over the following chapters, I draw out and amplify such connections, bringing the films of these four artists and the distinctive instances of autobiographical reenactment they contain into generative conversation.

As the cursory survey of British, Singaporean, Japanese, Guinean, Canadian, Chilean, Portuguese and American filmmakers offered above should similarly remind us, autobiographical reenactment is also by no means restricted to the French and Belgian context that provides the cultural-linguistic framing of this book's corpus. Examining the work of Akerman, Dieutre, Lehman and Varda will certainly bring us into contact at various points with a number of debates, discourses, other artists and their texts that often have a particularly Franco-Belgian flavour to them; however, the more we explore the forms and functions of autobiographical reenactment, the more we are simultaneously compelled to look elsewhere, towards other cultural developments and phenomena that readily traverse such regional delimitations. This shifting of our gaze leads us first to the work of other contemporary filmmakers who make autobiographical use of reenactment in their work, as I have shown; but it also carries us much further. The varied autobiographical uses of reenactment found in the filmmaking of Akerman, Dieutre, Lehman and Varda can be profitably situated and indeed sometimes better understood within a much larger cultural context.

Something that became repeatedly apparent during the research and writing of this book was the extent to which we currently live in what we might think of as *reenactive times.* Recent decades have indeed been indelibly marked by a pronounced proliferation of various uses of reenactment, one discernible across multiple cultural contexts and activities. The spread of the domains in which this proliferation is most apparent combined with the fact that these domains frequently build upon and respond to earlier, often well-established practices leads us away from identifying a coherent or singular, even entirely new cultural turn; what is certain, however, is that within a timeframe that overlaps with this book's central corpus of films, uses of reenactment have gained growing visibility, diversity, urgency and momentum. In such a way, reenactment today appears as an ever more widespread cultural means of investigating, commemorating and representing the past, called upon for a variety of reasons, by a variety of practitioners and with a variety of effects.

In popular imagination, reenactment remains perhaps most forcefully bound to those activities that fall under the capacious rubric of 'living history' — practices that, from the spectacular entertainments of Ancient Rome, to the 1920 (re)storming of the Winter Palace, via countless popular, religious or civic rites and rituals, rest at least partially upon often lengthy precedents. The connected term of 'historical reenactment' immediately brings to mind the undertakings of those individuals who descend upon muddy fields at weekends to replay the violent skirmishes of the past (with regionally variable preferences for conflicts such as the American Civil War, English Civil War, World Wars I and II, or those of the Medieval period, for example). With their carefully researched costumes and replica weaponry, such practitioners seek temporary immersion in the affective intensities of the past, striving to establish a direct experiential connection with history. The label might also suggest those resurrected Victorians, Edwardians, Tudors, Vikings, Celts, Cowboys, Romans (etc.) who greet visitors to museums, preservation societies and sites of historical interest, or who appear in a variety of more or less educational audio-visual content, all eager to share 'their' experiences of what life was really like in the historical moment they are there to represent. Both within these most recognisable of manifestations and in further activities, the labels of living history or historical reenactment cover an ample spectrum from hobbyist to professional to officialised to activist modes, incorporating significant degrees of variation in form, context, content, intent and audience. Across such variations, reenactment is today used widely as a tool to depict, explain, explore, mark, interrogate, contest, reframe, teach and communicate the past in the present.

Such functions have been called upon in sometimes contrasting ways as the methodologies of historical reenactment have been adopted and tested in other domains. This is notably the case in areas of contemporary creative arts, with particularly dense constellations having appeared in recent decades in performance, dance, choreography, dramaturgy, body-based, site-specific, installation and video practices. Such uses of reenactment are visible in the work of figures as varied as Alison Smith, Jeremy Deller, Mark Tribe, Rod Dickinson, Milo Rau, Harun Farocki, Pierre Huyghe, Sandra Davis, Ion Grigorescu, Artur Zmijewski, Trajal Harrell, Omer Fast, Mark McGowan, Candice Breitz, Dread Scott, with certain examples having rapidly achieved privileged status within the still developing canon

FIG. I.5. *Slave Rebellion Reenactment* (2019), Dread Scott, performance still 1. Photo: Soul Brother. Courtesy of the artist.

of 'reenactment art' — something most obviously true of Deller's influential *The Battle of Orgreave* (2000). The steady emergence of a wide range of such works attests to the continuing spread of artistic uses of historical reenactment, with the events of the near and distant past both painstakingly replicated and radically reimagined in the present through art.

Many of these creative works explore in particular how the occurrences of history and the memories that surround them are mediated, with reenactment contributing an extra layer or frame of (re)mediation to our present experiences of the past or intervening within ongoing chains of historical representation. In the burgeoning field of reenactment art, a preoccupation with investigating varied histories of representation has also seen artists excavate a diverse range of earlier images, artworks and performances to then recreate these in the present, both self-reflexively questioning the status and origin myths of their own artistic disciplines and looking elsewhere across the archives of visual culture. We see this in the reenactments produced of and in varied media by artists such as Marina Abramović, Diane Borsato, Wu Tsang, Edgar Arceneaux, Elizabeth Subrin, Jill Godmilow, Brice Dellsperger, and duos Pauline Boudry and Renate Lorenz or Iain Forsyth and Jane Pollard, for instance, with works like Abramović's much-cited *Seven Easy Pieces* series (2005) having rapidly achieved levels of institutional and scholarly canonisation to rival Deller's artistic battle reenactment. Whether they aspire to close mimetic resemblance, to conspicuous reframing, to explicit transformation or to creative appendage, such creative interventions lead us to examine what stays the same and what changes when a pre-existing artwork is remade, occupying a sometimes uncanny space of reverberation between original and copy, the art of then and the art of now.

A concern with how the past, along with the varied events, images and actors it contains, is to be represented inheres within another cultural domain in which a contemporary proliferation of uses of reenactment is particularly felt, namely documentary film and television. Right from the origins of the form, reenactment has of course featured prominently in the documentarian's toolkit, tightly entangled as it is within foundational tensions that lie at the heart of the documentary image: between aspirations to capturing the real in its authentic and objective truth, on the one hand, and providing inevitably partial, imperfect, subjective representations of reality and lived experience, on the other. These tensions have been variously enlivened and tested by reenactments offered in a number of recent documentaries: here we might think of Clio Barnard's *The Arbor* (2010), Carol Morley's *Dreams of a Life* (2011), Kitty Green's *Casting JonBenet* (2017), Joshua Oppenheimer's *The Act of Killing* (2012) or Rithy Panh's *S-21: The Khmer Rouge Killing Machine* (2003) and *The Missing Picture* (2013), to name but a small selection of prominent examples. As seen in the work of scholars such as Stella Bruzzi (2020), such films issue a powerful and fruitful challenge to theorists of the documentary image, urging them to think in nuanced ways about what a documentary is and does.

As reflected in the emphasis on acts of violence discernible in certain of these examples, the use of reenactment as a tool for exploring and potentially adjudicating on conflicting and contingent truths is perhaps most explicit in documentary treatments of crime. Alongside the instances of 'living history' discussed earlier, such documentary reenactments are undoubtedly amongst the most immediately identifiable and culturally widespread manifestations of the proliferation I am seeking to outline. Reenactment has of course long been a staple of television series such as *Crimewatch* (1984–2017) in the UK, *America's Most Wanted* (1988–2012) in the USA and *Aktenzeichen XY...ungelöst* [*Case Number XY...Unsolved*] (1967–) in Germany — programmes in which crimes are reenacted as a means of establishing their circumstances and of assigning guilt to their perpetrators. Similar guiding aspirations have informed much of the pronounced 'true crime' media boom of recent years, encouraged in particular by the deliberate acquisition strategies of platforms such as Netflix, that has significantly contributed to reenactment's growing cultural prominence. Such uses of documentary bolster broader cultural associations of reenactment with crime and its punishment, or with the criminal justice system and its representations. At least as far back as pathologist Bernard Spilsbury's involvement in the notorious 'Brides in the Bath' murders of the early twentieth century, reenactment has long been used as a key strategy of forensic investigation and proof-making and remains solidly anchored as such in sectors of the popular imaginary. Such associations (also tapped into by works in certain of the other cultural domains surveyed above) have been reinforced by the fact that modes of reenactment continue to be called upon today in legal systems around the world, with new applications increasingly offered by developments in reconstructive VR/AR technologies. As encountered in the gallery, in the courtroom, at the crime scene, or on screens both big and small, reenactment is used in the context of crime as an investigative tool to navigate fraught horizons of truth in search of those often elusive fragments of proof that might allow us to say with certitude *this is what really happened*.

Covering cultural domains as disparate as techniques of forensic investigation, recurrent methodologies in contemporary visual art, multiple modes of documentary representation and various approaches to doing history in public, the contemporary proliferation of reenactment practices I have sought to describe would appear to be characterised first and foremost by dizzying variety. Writing in the introduction to a 2009 special issue of the journal *Framework* dedicated to contemporary uses of reenactment, Jonathan Kahana indeed acknowledged this when he hazarded that: 'It would seem to strain credibility to use the same name — reenactment — for such a methodologically, institutionally, and geographically diverse cultural phenomenon' (2009: 50). Kahana is of course right to express reservations: both within and across the porous categorisations I trace above, cases of reenactment so often seem impossibly far removed one from another. After all, are we really talking about the same phenomenon when available examples include, for instance:

- videos on the English Heritage YouTube channel where costumed versions of Victorian domestic servants demonstrate how to churn butter, make pigeon pie, wash clothes and perform countless other historical gestures;
- the course plotted along Australia's eastern coast for a replica of HMS Endeavour as part of commemorations initially planned for 2020 despite protests from descendants of those who were the first to suffer at the original arrival of James Cook and the commencement of European colonialism;
- artist Dread Scott's 2019 restaging of the 1811 German Coast uprising where hundreds of reenactors retraced the path of the largest rebellion of enslaved people in United States history along a two-day march through modern-day Louisiana;
- the undertakings of the Moore's Ford Memorial Committee activist group in Wallon County, Georgia, who annually restage the eponymous 1946 lynchings as a means of keeping its memory alive in the present and of fighting against forces of often deliberate historical forgetting, reenacting events slightly differently each time;
- Stanley Schtinter's resolutely absurdist 2018 recreation of the funeral of Princess Diana — *Funeral of Diana, Princess of Wales 2.0* — in which mourners and bystanders in a venue in Salford were greeted with incongruous performances from a live Mariachi band as well as an additional reconstruction of the murder of British television presenter Jill Dando;
- choreographer Trajal Harrell's counterfactual history of contemporary dance in *Twenty Looks or Paris is Burning at The Judson Church* (2014), with the encounter it imagines in 1963 New York between early exponents of postmodern dance aesthetics and the Harlem voguing ball scene;
- provocative theatrical works programmed by the International Institute of Political Murder under the direction of Milo Rau, whether these reproduce a

homophobic murder in Belgium, the Ceaușescu genocide trial, the Eldorado do Carajás massacre, the Van Eyck Ghent Altarpiece, or numerous other sources;

- consecutive instalments of Marina Abramović's *Seven Easy Pieces* series in the rarefied space of the Guggenheim rotunda, where a much-mythologised period in the history of European and American performance art was revisited, with the emphasis placed firmly on the 'straight' and untainted retransmission of seminal pieces;
- the markedly more reinterpretive approach to similar source material adopted by artists Iain Forsyth and Jane Pollard that has seen them update and reimagine canonical works in video and performance art by Vito Acconci and Bruce Nauman;
- Pauline Boudry and Renate Lorenz's interventions into very different histories of performance in installations such as *N.O.Body* (2018) where drag artist Werner Hirsch restaged a black-and-white photograph of Barnum Circus 'Bearded Lady' Annie Jones, asking the viewer to question the politics of bodily difference then and now;
- the high-camp remakes of films by Brian De Palma, David Lynch, Alfred Hitchcock, Stanley Kubrick, Andrzej Żuławski and many others that Brice Dellsperger has created as part of his ongoing *Body Doubles* video series (1995–);
- Andrew Jarecki's hugely successful Emmy-winning true crime miniseries *The Jinx: The Life and Deaths of Robert Durst* (2015), with the surprise murder confession it seemingly captured and the real-life arrest and trial that followed;
- the conflicting crime scene reconstructions of Errol Morris's documentary *The Thin Blue Line* (1988) with its influential critique of documentary regimes of truth-making;
- the 2016 trial of former SS guard Reinhold Hanning where VR headsets allowed judge and jury to explore 3-D models of Auschwitz-Birkenau and adopt the perspective of a man eventually charged with 170,000 counts of being an accessory to murder;
- research agency Forensic Architecture's cutting-edge investigations into the deaths of Harith Augustus, Zak Kostopoulos, Pavlos Fyssas, Halit Yozgat or Mark Duggan, where modes of reenactment have been used to scrutinise police, state and corporate violence and to contest the truth claims sustained by competing forms of evidence.

By the same token, what could these disparate, bulleted activities possibly have in common with a film in which, as we saw, a widower reimagines both a birth and an abortion with a slice of watermelon or, indeed, with the very different autobiographical films produced by the four French and Belgian filmmakers that I go on to examine in the chapters of this book?

Reenactment in the work of Akerman, Dieutre, Lehman and Varda will sometimes appear in yet other contexts and assume yet further forms, only some of which will resemble the examples listed above. In certain films, Akerman uses the movements of her recording camera to belatedly retrace the trajectories of bodies from history; elsewhere, she stages overtly fictionalised performances of past experiences — both her own and those borrowed from unknown others — that seem to foster a strange degree of affective seepage across time. In a very different approach, Dieutre uses his own body to produce imperfect copies of both seventeenth-century paintings and twentieth-century films, before experimenting with participatory, reenactive modes of film spectatorship through which he asks the viewer to bear witness alongside him to an ambiguous reconstruction of a lost moment of intimacy from his romantic past. Dissatisfied with the various archival traces that he excavates in a faltering search for self-knowledge, Lehman will begin by directing unknown children in reenactments of his youth in an attempt to investigate the circumstances of his early life. He will then physically retrace the forced movements of victims of genocide across Eastern Europe, following directly in historical footsteps, and will use similar effects to pre-emptively imagine what his own death might look like. Varda will use her own body and the bodies of others to reconstruct images from art history (both her own and those created by artists she admires) before reenacting episodes from her early life and doing the same on behalf of her dying husband. As Kahana's strained credibility urges us to ask, what do we gain by speaking of such different examples (whether found in contemporary autobiographical filmmaking from France and Belgium or in the countless other cultural domains in which a proliferation of reenactment practices is today most keenly felt) in the same breath?

Cultures of Againness

As indicators of the marked proliferation I have sought to identify, I of course could have chosen any number of further cultural examples, all equally different. We may well live in reenactive times, but the reenactments that surround us are not one, fixed thing. Reenactment is a mode, a mood, a tool, a technique, a strategy, a form of interrogation and investigation, that seeks in differing ways to reproduce, reconstruct or repeat something from an earlier time in the present and that explores what is unleashed when this happens. Reenactment is used for varying reasons and with varying effects in a wide range of often very separate cultural domains; and yet, wherever and in whichever forms they are encountered, contemporary uses of reenactment reliably confront us with overlapping questions, challenges, tensions, ambiguities, provocations and possibilities. These may, of course, shift in prominence, intensity and focus depending on exactly how and why reenactment is used; but they nevertheless encourage us to look for connections and resonances between all of reenactment's many manifestations, be they found in the diverse areas surveyed above, or in the very different autobiographical experiments of Akerman, Dieutre, Lehman and Varda.

I am particularly guided in this view by performance theorist Rebecca Schneider, whose 2011 book *Performing Remains: Art and War in Times of Theatrical Reenactment* moves continually back and forth between American Civil War reenactment societies, photography, statuary, experimental theatre and performance art, as well as the multiple other forms of 'againness' that, she argues, weave their way, blatantly or surreptitiously, throughout our public and private lives. In drawing together activities that preceding scholarship had often treated separately and combining these with insights from a diversity of scholarly discourses, Schneider in many ways set the agenda for the then incipient field of 'reenactment studies' — a site of dispersed interdisciplinary inquiry that, as reflected in the more recent publication of prominent titles such as *The Routledge Handbook of Reenactment Studies* (2020), continues to gain exposure, adherence and institutional clout. In terms of my own contribution, what I am certainly *not* arguing for in this book is the conscious or calculated participation of the four filmmakers who provide my corpus within a particular cultural trend. Nor, indeed, do I consistently use those varied cultural works and practices surveyed above as points of direct comparison to the close readings I develop of the filmmaking of Akerman, Dieutre, Lehman and Varda in this book's chapters. Rather (and in a way that is strongly informed by interventions such as Schneider's), I suggest, on the one hand, that the diverse instances of reenactment discernible in the films I examine engage with qualities and ideas that we also find elsewhere; and, on the other, that maintaining a broad, elastic view of what reenactment can be and can do, as well as of the different ways in which it can be approached, is most helpful in thinking about the specific filmic case studies I assemble.

Considered in this agglomerative way — receptive to the possible variants it allows and to how these variants speak to one another — reenactment appears as an often politically charged means of dealing with the past (and with what it means to us) in the present. Reenactment is concerned with the relationships that might exist between different temporal moments and the texts, artefacts and experiences they contain. It investigates the possibility of passage across time, be that in the form of dialogue, of influence, or in the movement of feelings, sensations and contacts. It questions the knowledge of the past that we can gain from within the present, its completeness and reliability, and tests the various forms that this knowledge can take. It experiments with the viability of different modes of historical understanding, ones grounded in the ambiguities of recall, the distortions of fiction, in the surfaces, substance and shapes of the living human body, in evidence both material and immaterial, in the intensity of affective experience. It is concerned with what is produced by repetition — sameness or radical difference — and questions the status of a later copy relative to an earlier original, of a representation relative to a prior reality, along with the stakes of truth, authenticity and interpretation that this status entails. Through reenactment's varied manifestations run a number of common threads that relate particularly to themes of memory, time, archive, knowledge, mimesis and transformation. These threads lead us to the heart of what reenactment is and does, and in so doing help us to think further about the distinctive uses I identify in the work of my four chosen filmmakers.

Whether in the witness statements of true crime, recreations of historical events based on contemporary written accounts, or indeed in any of the varied autobiographical uses I go on to explore, so many forms of reenactment confront us with questions of memory. The contemporary proliferation of reenactment practices I have identified in many ways participates in what Andreas Huyssen has described as a 'memory boom of unprecedented proportions' that in recent decades has ushered in widespread cultural debates over the nature of memory as well as our experience of it (1995: 5). For Huyssen, if human memory can be accepted as an 'anthropological given', it is nevertheless closely linked to the ways a culture constructs and lives its temporality; as a consequence of this, he suggests, the forms memory takes are contingent and subject to change (2). Questions of memory are thus always aligned with equally pressing questions of *representation*: 'rather than leading us to some authentic origin or giving us verifiable access to the real, memory, even and especially in its belatedness, is itself based on representation' (2–3). Memory does not, he maintains, grant access to the real, unmediated past itself, but, rather, imagines, articulates and represents anew in the present. Even if all memory is in 'some ineradicable sense' dependent on past events and experiences, the temporal status of any act of memory is, Huyssen writes, always the present (3). For Huyssen, the 'tenuous fissure' that opens up between experiencing an event and belatedly remembering it in representation is unavoidable; crucially, however, instead of lamenting or ignoring it, this split should, he suggests, be understood as a stimulant for cultural and artistic creativity that makes of memory something so much more powerful and vital than a mere system of experiential storage and retrieval (ibid.).

Huyssen's account of memory's creative *presentness* recalls the Freudian notion of 'screen memories'. In his influential text, Freud underlined the extent to which memories of an earlier time do not emerge, but are instead continually formed in the present, whilst also acknowledging that a variety of motives (beyond exclusive concerns for historical accuracy) shape both this formation process and the selection of the memories themselves (1962: 322). Describing, in terms that complement Freud's presentation, how history endlessly returns to and rewrites the story of the past, Matt Matsuda suggests:

> The past is not a truth upon which to build, but a truth sought, a re-memorializing over which to struggle. The fragmentary, disputatious, self-reflexive nature of such a past makes a series of 'memories' — ever imperfect, imprecise, and charged with personal questions — the appropriate means for rendering the 'history' of the present (1996: 15).

As a belated representation of something from an earlier time, reenactment can make the mechanisms of memory with the recurrent struggles they entail yet more apparent, laying bare the active, deliberate processes of rememorialisation. Reenactment can grant physical, visible form to the present labour of remembering the past, foregrounding the choices, obstacles and desires that inflect it, as well as its ready openness to the lure of revision, of fiction, of partiality, of omission or addition. Reenactment highlights the extent to which, as curator Robert Blackson suggests, 'memory, like history, is a creative act' (2007: 31). Such phenomena are discernible in so many of those reenactive domains surveyed above, be that in battle reenactors literally fighting over how the past is to be remembered; the conflicting testimony of biopic, crime and historical-based documentaries; or the work of artists who revive moments of (art) history. Such intricacies of memory will also appear in the work of filmmakers who seek their own imperfect answers to the deeply 'personal questions' they ask.

In light of the present mechanisms of formation and selection he identifies, Freud pondered whether the most we might ever say of memory is that it *relates to* the past, rather than properly being *of* or *from* it. And yet, something so often foregrounded by reenactment is how the embattled fissure between past and present can be manipulated, made to expand but also to contract. This is hinted at, for instance, in certain of the interviews Schneider conducted upon the recreated Civil War battlefield for *Performing Remains*: 'For many history reenactors, reenactments are more than "mere" remembering and are in fact the ongoing event itself, negotiated through sometimes radically shifting affiliation with the past *as* the present' (2011: 32). When asked whether they believed the historically accurate arrangement of bodies, costumes and props could ever *really* cause the past to recur in the present, Schneider's reenactors were often divided, offering as many yes's as no's. Between the poles of these responses, however, participants also described a more uncertain form of temporal experience: 'I found a far more consistent sense across participants that whether or not time actually recurred, time did seem to bend, and almost all acknowledged a kind of touch or whisper or "shiver" of time seemingly gone ajar' (51). Immersed in the enveloping intensity of affects that seemed, disorientingly, to come from an earlier time, Schneider's interviewees often found reenactment to be, if not the past itself, then somehow also *not not* that past (8) — an ambiguous scrambling of time's stable coordinates found in so many forms of reenactment.

Certain of those battle reenactors who professed to experience this bending confusion of temporality claimed to be 'touching time'. For Schneider, the exact status of this 'touch' is problematic: on the one hand, 'to touch is not to become coextensive, to fully become that which is touched or which touches', but on the other, to touch is 'to (partially) collapse the distance marking one thing as fully distinct from another thing' (35). There is, of course, a pronounced queerness to this affectively charged, desiring touch, to this ambiguous experience of time shivering and going ajar, of modern and historical bodies partially merging across (temporal) difference. Such touches have, Schneider acknowledges, featured heavily in queer theory's destabilisation of identitarian politics, 'helping to unsettle approaches to the social that tend to sediment "identity" into solid-state positionalities' (36). For Schneider: 'To be touched and to be moved indicates a level of libidinality in affective engagements in the social, suggestive of shift and slip' (ibid.). Her words evoke prominent scholars of queer temporalities and historiography that also influence my own analysis in this book. Alongside postcolonial critiques of modernity and informed by the denormativisations of linear time operated by scholars such as Walter Benjamin and Jacques Derrida in texts that resist developmental teleologies of progress, important work in queer and sexuality studies has sought to account for experiences and encounters that challenge the stable separation of past, present and future, exploring modes of anachronism, lag, drag, spectrality, uncanniness, as well as the possibility of contacts, exchanges, identifications and conversations across temporal divisions (see particularly Dinshaw 1999; Fradenburg and Freccero 1996;

Freccero 2006; Freeman 2010; Love 2007). The autobiographical uses of reenactment I go on to study so often explore what Carla Freccero refers to as 'affect's persistence through time and its force as that which compels past-, present- and future-directed desires and longings' (2011: 20–21). Amidst the ambiguities of Schneider's historical double negative, her indeterminate *not not*, forms of reenactment — both those explored in the chapters of this book and those found elsewhere — test borders, be they temporal, identitarian, or a combination thereof, asking what happens if one time, one thing is no longer entirely separate from another.

Reflecting upon the uncertain slippage across time she witnessed and heard described on the recreated battlefield, Schneider questions whether in such reenactments 'something other than the discrete "now" of everyday life can be said to occasionally occur — or recur' (2011: 14). Whilst, Schneider recognises, this excessive *something other* is abundantly familiar to practices linked to theatre, art, and ritual, it is decidedly more alien to practices such as historiography that 'profess to privilege "hard" facts or material remains over "softer," ephemeral traces such as the affective, bodily sensations or (re)actions of those living too far into the future for proper, evidentiary recall' (ibid.). Vanessa Agnew in many ways resumes such hard/soft oppositions and the suspicions that adhere to them when she suggests that if reenactment is to 'gain legitimacy' as a method of doing history, it must undergo a number of stabilising reforms that involve 'disambiguating experience and understanding and determining the extent to which affect can indeed be considered evidentiary' (2007: 309). Whether in investigations of crime, the documents and remains drawn upon by practitioners of living history, or the source materials modern artists extract from earlier points in histories of representation to then recreate in the present, reenactment so often engages important questions of archive, proof and evidence that will be particularly relevant in my exploration of reenactment's autobiographical uses.

Key to my analysis will be the notion that, as a technique of research that both responds to and creates documentation and evidence of varying kinds, reenactment simultaneously accesses and contributes to archive. So much of Schneider's *Performing Remains* is concerned with rethinking the archival logic that dictates that if something does not leave discrete, visible, saveable traces behind, it is destined to vanish forever: in her engagements with reenactment she asks, crucially, whether our habituation to this logic might in fact lead us to ignore 'other ways of knowing, other modes of remembering' (2011: 98). In my examination of the work of Akerman, Dieutre, Lehman and Varda, I am interested in what these other possibilities of knowing and remembering might be: whether the reenactive body itself might offer a living, breathing, changing tool or technique of archiving (Lepecki 2010); whether the potentially evidentiary force of affect makes of reenactment a reliable method of knowing and understanding the past (Agnew 2004, 2007); whether the repetition of gestures, movements and forms might offer a platform for the storage and transmission of historical knowledge in ways that direct a potent challenge to other kinds and contexts of record-keeping (Taylor 2003); whether reenactment's repetitions ultimately encourage us to see in the archive not so much 'excavation sites' as possible 'construction sites' (Foster 2004: 22).

Cristina Baldacci has questioned whether in certain circumstances reenactment might help to deliver 'a counter-history where archival documents are revived or, if necessary, recreated *ex novo* (through fiction) as witnesses and personal devices of memory and resistance' (2019: 64). In the context of such possibilities for alternate, resistant forms of archiving, I am particularly interested in the extent to which, through the affective seepage across borders it can encourage, reenactment might offer what José Esteban Muñoz referred to as 'a kind of evidence of what has transpired *but certainly not the thing itself*' (1996: 10; emphasis mine), and in so doing challenge us to rethink the very meaning of evidence in relation to truth, authority, authenticity, stability and doubt. As it constructs a new version of something from the past that is not entirely, not exactly that earlier thing itself, reenactment disrupts what Schneider frames as the 'pristine ideality' of the artefactual originals so valued by the archive (2011: 99–100). Whether in documentary, crime, art, living history, or indeed in autobiographical filmmaking, as a belated representation of an earlier reality, reenactment is inextricably bound up in anxieties around mimesis that concern the relationships between originals and copies as well as the extent to which it is possible to capture and replicate what something or someone from an earlier point in time was really like. Representing earlier images and occurrences belatedly, reenactment inevitably repeats the past in difference; but as Schneider asks, fully aware of the millennia-old charges of theatricality, imitation, forgery that swarm around the question, why does this difference necessarily have to cancel out authenticity? (30).

The copy's uncertain status is of course a recurrent preoccupation in postmodern and poststructural critiques of authorship, originality and essence. Identifying a tendency in contemporary choreography for modern dancers to recreate sometimes well-known, sometimes obscure twentieth-century dance works, André Lepecki explores how reenactment unlocks and activates untapped possibilities held in earlier works into the present. Such reenactments, Lepecki suggests, bypass both a nostalgic lens and the 'arresting force of authorial authority', refusing that a work should be permanently fixed within its singular originating version. In so doing, they create copies that actively participate in the 'virtual cloud' of alternate possibilities surrounding the pre-existing work itself but that are also entirely new (2010: 31, 35). Towards the opening of *Performing Remains*, Schneider urges us to examine what she terms the copy's 'curious inadequacies', but also to question '*what inadequacy gets right* about our faulty steps backward, and forward, and to the side' (2011: 6). What, she asks, 'does the error, the missing, the not-quite-right get right about that which it strives to replay?' (156). This 'not-quite-right' could designate, for instance, the distortions introduced by historical reenactors certain of how, to their mind, history *should have been*. It could also describe the work of artists such as those surveyed by Lepecki, who rework earlier images or performances, often seeking to speak directly to modern concerns. It could equally apply to the films of Akerman, Dieutre, Lehman and Varda, where autobiographical experiments continually push them back and forth between poles of sameness and difference in the repetitions they stage. Considered in this way, the *inadequacy* of reenactment's mimetic copies does not necessarily entail the loss or corruption of some 'prior, purer actual', but sometimes also offers important tools for critical dialogue and negotiation across time (18).

As Amelia Jones reminds us, scholars as varied as J. L. Austin, Jacques Derrida or Judith Butler lead us to understand all representations as performative 'redoings of one kind or another' (2012: 16). The analysis proposed by scholars such as Schneider is indeed anchored in the fundamental idea that such reiterative redoings offer both a vehicle for sameness and a vehicle for difference or change (2011: 10). Faced with the fraught 'struggle' of rememorialisation identified by Matsuda in the continual writings and rewritings of history, there are obviously risks attached to the transformative possibilities opened up by reenactment's repetitions. These risks concern, perhaps most pressingly, those revisionist uses that would seek to deny the suffering inflicted by the atrocities of history on still vulnerable groups, or that would instrumentalise the past in service of regressive political agendas in the present. Commentators — particularly those who have sought to evaluate reenactment against other models of historical knowledge — have questioned whether certain forms of reenactment might offer merely a form of fantasy role-play that, through the elastic appropriation of pasts both real and imagined, comes provocatively close at points to a model of ideologically led historical wish fulfilment as what is missing from lives *now* is forcibly reclaimed from lives *then* (Agnew 2004: 328; 2007: 307). The editors of the recently published *The Routledge Handbook of Reenactment Studies* indeed stake a still developing disciplinary identity precisely on the mitigation of such risks when they close their Introduction with the suggestion that: 'By rigorously scrutinizing the operations of the historical echo chamber and by trading in its main currency, conjecture, reenactment studies can help us to revive and conserve notions of fact, truth, and objectivity' (Agnew, Lamb, and Tomann 2020: 10).

The potential threats that attach to certain (mis)uses of reenactment are all too real. But I maintain that there also remains room for conjectural, speculative, imperfect, interrogative, fantasy-driven, deeply subjective forms of reenactment to perform important cultural and political work. Jones is right to suggest that today's increasing investigations of the possibilities of repetition might be seen to be 'sparked by (and eliciting of) openness and hope, by way of presenting new possibilities of intervention and by activating fresh ways of thinking, making, being in the world' (2012: 14). Surveying forms of historical reenactment found in contemporary art, Sven Lütticken suggests in comparable terms that these experiments can throw open a space within which to reconsider, even reimagine, past realities: 'Art can examine and try out — under laboratory conditions, as it were — forms of repetition that break open history and the historicist returns of past periods; it can investigate historical moments or eras as potentials waiting to be reactivated'. For Lütticken, such artistic uses of reenactment can stage small but significant acts of difference that create a space for 'possible and as yet unthinkable' historical performances (2005: 60). For Blackson, rather than a treadmill-like going over the same ground, reenactment in art and elsewhere can instead assume a powerful 'emancipatory' agency, transforming our relationships with the past (2007: 29). As will frequently be apparent in the work of Akerman, Dieutre, Lehman and Varda, transforming our relationships with the past can both alter our lived experience of the present and inflect the varied futures we are moving towards.

Understanding reenactment in such terms — as a belated, always imperfect representation that does not grant a route back to an unchanged earlier reality, or as a copy that exists in a continually shifting relationship of sameness and difference to the original it 'inadequately' riffs upon — leads us once again to ideas that will return throughout this book and that first appeared in connection to Alain Cavalier's search for his wife in *Irène*: ideas around loss and how we respond to it. Guided by effects seen in Cavalier's video grief diary, I questioned earlier whether reenactment's inability to restore the past intact and selfsame to the present imbued it with a melancholic force, redoubled each time an attempted repetition or recovery seemingly falters and fails. As Bill Nichols underlined in a text quoted in relation to *Irène*, to recognise something as a reenactment is indeed to recognise it as something other than a genuine return to lost object, something other than the real past itself. Guided again by Cavalier's film, I suggested that when used in response and in relation to loss, if reenactment foregrounds (and sometimes painfully so) the definitive irretrievability of what once was, it can also potentially generate often strange new pleasures. Nichols acknowledges reenactment's implication in the protracted work of mourning, in those attempts to make good a trauma, a death, a catastrophe, or any number of further losses as varied as the objects to which desire might flow (2008: 74). Cristina Baldacci and Stella Bruzzi similarly situate reenactment as an important tool of *Durcharbeitung*, of working through (Baldacci 2019: 64; Bruzzi 2020: 200–04); as they investigate both reenactment's pains and pleasures, the labour of mourning undertaken by my four filmmakers tests multiple possible ways of coming to terms with and living with loss.

Schneider encouraged us to see in the mimetic repetitions of reenactment not the corruption or loss of a more authentic actual, but platforms for dialogue and negotiation across time where getting the past wrong might also get something right about the present longings, fantasies and identifications that drive the pursuit of *againness*. In such ways, reenactment forges what Nichols refers to as a critical 'mise-en-scène of desire' (2008: 76). Considered from this perspective, the autobiographical reenactments I explore staunchly and knowingly resist the pull of nostalgia, certainly in its most immobilising, fetishising guises — a phenomenon that, as scholars such as Svetlana Boym (2001) have convincingly shown, shares a great deal with melancholy's investment in the attempted repetition of the unrepeatable and in the impossibility of returning to lost origins and originals. Akerman, Dieutre, Lehman and Varda recognise — gleefully or begrudgingly — that to repeat something from the past in the present is inevitably to repeat it differently. But they also see in this difference, in the fact that what returns through repetition is not *entirely*, not *exactly* the same as what came before, an opportunity: to explore why it is that they are drawn to this past and what it means to them; to reimagine, reconfigure, supplement, extend, expand, reactivate this past, or perhaps turn it into something new altogether. The labour of mourning that reenactment performs is an often precarious one. Throughout the chapters of this book, pleasures and pains, fulfilments and frustrations will indeed coexist and interact. But as this book develops, reenactment will increasingly offer ways of dealing with loss that can be positive, constructive, reparative, hopeful, pleasurable, comforting, joyful and fun.

Autobiography/Reenactment/Film

Via the combined perspective adopted up to this point, I have framed reenactment as a technique, tool, strategy, platform or method that, as it appears in a range of forms and domains, generates questions, challenges, tensions, ambiguities, provocations and possibilities that reliably overlap to some degree. These generated effects of course assume specific inflections depending on exactly how and why reenactment is used, as I indeed acknowledged earlier and as comes through in many of the varied commentaries referenced above. Such inflections might relate to the fact that levels of tolerance for fiction, fantasy, transformation, error and 'inadequacy' are perhaps generally greater in art than in certain of the activities that fall under the rubric of living history or that relate to crime and the criminal justice system, for instance; they might also arise from the possibility that different stakes conceivably confront those who recreate, say, canonical works of art from centuries past or still traumatic events from recent history.

Specific inflections also attach to the autobiographical uses of reenactment I identify in the work of four filmmakers from France and Belgium. These inflections concern, in particular, how reenactment leads us to think in certain ways about autobiography, how autobiography does the same in turn for reenactment, and how the filmic medium offers specific resources for developing such engagements. As four filmmakers stage fiercely individual inquiries into who they are as people and artists as well as the multiple connections that link them to others past and present, the autobiographical charge and relevance of the reenactments explored in this book will vary: it will be more immediately apparent in certain case studies than in others, but it will always be there. The centrality and range of the autobiographical in what follows is one of the things that distinguishes my corpus and my analyses from other recent studies of reenactment's uses in film (see particularly Margulies 2019; Bruzzi 2020; Carrigy 2021). Indeed, I maintain that reenactment can lay bare some of the fundamental anxieties that lie at the heart of the autobiographical, anxieties that are sometimes actively embraced in pursuit of unexpected avenues of self-inquiry and self-representation.

Such anxieties concern, for instance, the coherence and solidity of the autobiographical self. It has by now become almost a convention of scholarship on autobiographical film to quote, then refute, an influential 1980 essay from Elizabeth Bruss that questioned the viability of film as a possible medium of autobiography in contrast to supposedly more viable literary models. Much of Bruss's criticism hinges on what she presents as autobiography's fundamental 'identity-value'. This value designates the illusion — so richly sustained in Bruss's understanding of literary autobiography — that past and present selves, the individual who lives and the individual who later tells the tale, are necessarily experienced as one and the same. Film, Bruss suggests, struggles to carry off the same illusion, the same elision with such ease (1980: 307–09). Reenactment amplifies the opportunities so many filmmakers have resiliently found in what Bruss identifies as medial deficiency. Many of the instances of autobiographical reenactment I examine deliberately foreground the essential otherness and division inherent to the act of self-scrutiny. Such uses plunge us within the 'gulf' that opens up between past and present as soon as we turn our attention inwards, forcibly alerting us to autobiography's doubling (multiplication, even) of selves (Sheringham 1993: vii–viii). As we will see particularly clearly in Lehman and Varda, in producing reenactments with other bodies, these filmmakers literalise the essential alterity of the autobiographical encounter with oneself, refusing to conceal the distance separating perceiver and perceived (ibid.), often making it visible, physical, three-dimensional, denying conflation or elision. In certain instances of autobiographical reenactment, a filmmaker will share the frame with a version of themselves that really *is* other and that is enthusiastically announced as such.

Through the different forms of autobiographical reenactment they mobilise, these filmmakers do not necessarily seek to retrieve a totally accurate version of them-selves, but rather explore conspicuous forms of self-staging. This autobiographical mise-en-scène revealed by reenactment frequently allows them to indulge their own desires, fantasies and curiosities, to offer a version of themselves not as they really are but as they choose to picture themselves. In such a way, reenactment offers a particularly clear demonstration of models of subjectivity that Michael Renov has identified in much autobiographical filmmaking from recent decades: as a site of permanent instability — of 'flux, drift, perpetual revision' — rather than of coherence (2004: 110). As it allows Akerman, Dieutre, Lehman and Varda to endlessly reimagine and revise themselves, embracing the flux and drift of subjectivity, to script and stage themselves in difference, autobiographical reenactment makes explicit the extent to which giving an account of oneself functions as a continual process of exploratory self-fashioning and self-editing.

The otherness that inheres in the act of self-scrutiny is one that, through auto-biographical reenactment, is often made to interact with much more extensive forms of otherness in ways that unsettle the boundedness of identity and experience, their stability in space and time. As they explore the temporal and spatial mobility of affect, reviving feelings and sensations from other moments and places, many of the instances of autobiographical reenactment explored over the following chapters confront us with how modern lives are subject to the affective pressure exerted by other lives, often ones that come from a much earlier time, from outside the span of a filmmaker's own living memory. Foregrounding how identities and experiences in the present can be shaped by identities and experiences from the past, autobiographical reenactment explores a model of subjectivity as very much *in history*, where the story of an individual is implicated in the emotional reverberations of much larger histories that dwarf them. We will see this particularly clearly in the work of Akerman and Lehman. As it grants access to affects from a different time and place, autobiographical reenactment holds out the possibility of reliving experiences that we ourselves did not originally live through, that do not belong to us, to 'remember' them as if they were our own, in a way that expands the limits of autobiography, rendering porous the borders separating one person's lived experience from the lived experience of another. These revived experiences can be the real, verifiable experiences of world history; but, as we will see particularly clearly in Dieutre, for instance, they can also be borrowed from elsewhere — from art, from fiction and from other histories of representation. As it allows the mobility, multiplicity, libidinal attachment and intensity of *identifications* to supplant the solidity of a singular, fixed *identity*, autobiographical reenactment encourages strange forms of merging between lives, past and present, real and unreal.

Making clear the extent to which what it brings to the present is not the real, unmediated past itself, autobiographical reenactment manifests the distorting transformations of memory. Approaching the 'fissure' that Huyssen identifies between prior event and belated representation not as a failure of reliability but as a spur to artistic creativity, autobiographical reenactment leads us to see in memory very present acts of creation through which the past is opened up to the ongoing struggle of rememorialisation. In such ways, autobiographical reenactment reminds us that there is *always* fiction in autobiography. The memories reenactment recreates openly announce their imperfections, but also ask us to see in them a certain *realness*, to accept that in getting the past wrong they might actually get something right about the desires and fears of the subject of autobiography. Through their status as fragmentary fictions, as products of imagination, the memories crafted through reenactment expand the range of experiences available to autobiography, filling in its zones of unknowability: earlier in this Introduction, we saw Cavalier restage his own birth with a watermelon, an egg and a pair of kitchen tongs; elsewhere in this book, we will encounter other equally improbable, equally bewildering autobiographical experiments.

There was, of course, a conscious provocation at work in Cavalier's fruit-based reconstructions as in other moments of his film, just as multiple provocations will emerge from those autobiographical uses found in the work of Akerman, Dieutre, Lehman and Varda. The provocative is indeed far from unfamiliar territory for contemporary reenactment considered more broadly, where numerous examples demonstrate a power to spark debates over whether certain things from the past should be left alone, or if they should only ever be treated in particular ways. With such debates tightly bound to specifics of subject matter, content, intent, and context, reenactment frequently stands upon complex ethical ground. These complexities arise and are explored in particular ways when reenactment is used autobiographically, with the subject of autobiography becoming the ultimate arbiter of what is accurate, desirable or acceptable, even if this is sometimes decided in cooperation with others or left partially up to the viewer to decide. Indeed, our experience of watching many of the films I assemble will equate to being continually challenged to keep up as filmmakers negotiate who and how they want to be, or their own personal understandings of the truth.

In the films I go on to examine, we will find ethical challenges as varied as the filmmakers who elicit them. These can relate to, for instance, issues of authority, authorship and ownership engaged when a filmmaker copies something previously made by someone else; the relationships of power and responsibility maintained between filmmaker and the other lives they represent or evoke, as well as how such relationships shape the parameters of identification, knowledge and control; how the filmmakers respond to the pain and suffering of others and how they choose to commemorate atrocities both past and present; whether a historical duty to remember dictates 'appropriate' ways of remembering (ways that perhaps enjoin us sometimes to forget); frictions of scale and focus foregrounded by the interactions of the individual with the politico-historical; the shifting contracts of trust and credulity struck between those who create and those who consume autobiography; ambiguous questions of spectatorship and what it means when a filmmaker asks or forces their viewer to bear witness to the imperfect return of something obscene.

This last ethical provocation in particular hangs over some of the most striking instances of reenactment considered in this book. As we will see in selected works by Akerman and Dieutre, these are instances where it gradually becomes apparent that in watching filmed footage on screen we are being led to adopt a viewpoint once held by someone else, and so to expose ourselves to the memories and feelings that attach to this recreated position of viewing. These feelings and memories may well be pleasant, as will be the case in Dieutre; but they can equally be ugly and haunting, connected to experiences we might, given a freer choice, be tempted to look away from (or at least within which we might not choose to immerse ourselves so deeply). In the effects that they produce as well as in the means through which they produce them, these sometimes unsettlingly immersive reenactments share something with certain examples found in the other cultural domains I have surveyed; but as will also be true for the other case studies I explore, such examples simultaneously lead us to question what might be specific about film as a medium of reenactment. Throughout the following chapters, I remain particularly attentive to how cinema's representational resources — whether manifested in decisions of format, mise-en-scène, framing, montage, structure, editing, SFX, interactions of image and sound or in other formal and aesthetic choices — can support reenactment. In such a way, this book is alert not only to the relevance of other cultural areas to the filmic experiments I examine, as argued throughout this Introduction, but also to possible forms and formats of reenactment that have not always yet been explored by existing scholarship.

Whilst I remain attentive to these specificities and to how they might expand reenactment's possible scope, another thing I am deliberately *not* making a case for in this book is autobiographical reenactment's status as a new, distinct or unified cinematic genre. I am once more guided in this by Renov who, whilst recognising the enlargement of critical vernaculars that inevitably occurs when a diversity of autobiographical practices is considered, nevertheless resists the fixity of new orthodoxies that would seek to durably (re)define the autobiographical (2004: xii). I remain convinced that such reifying, stabilising temptations are unhelpful when, as Renov suggests, autobiography has always been boundary defying and when new practices persistently move into its purview (ibid.). What I present in this book as autobiographical reenactment does not designate a fixed or exhaustive taxonomy; rather, it names a varied, hybridised site of experimentation that invites us to continually revisit our understanding of autobiography's limits and possibilities, of what *counts* as autobiography.

The sheer variety on display in the films I have selected should of course lead us away from seeing in autobiographical reenactment a single, fixed thing. Each of the following four chapters is dedicated to one of the filmmakers of this book's central corpus, and to the deeply personal autobiographical experiments they undertake. For each filmmaker, I develop close readings of between three and six main films, generally organised in thematic rather than strictly chronological terms. These chapters are organised under headings — *Haunting* for Akerman, *Queerness* for Dieutre, *Archives* for Lehman, and *Stillness/Movement* for Varda — that announce the specific terms within which I analyse how and why autobiographical reenactment is used. My chosen headings resume qualities broached at various points in this Introduction and that lie at the heart of so much reenactment: the disruptive, disorienting movement of affects both pleasurable and painful across borders separating timeframes and identities; the sometimes embattled encounter between competing modes of remembering, knowing and understanding; the possibility of reciprocal dialogue across time between different media and forms; the ongoing transformations of mimesis and the reframings and revisions they permit; the question of whether repeating the past brings it back as it really was, or uses it as the source material to create something else instead. The ideas my headings foreground are not necessarily exclusive to the work of any one of the filmmakers; but they do provide particularly relevant axes around which to explore very different films, and to bring these films into conversation, amongst themselves, with others, or with larger cultural contexts. Such headings also hint at how the instances of reenactment I identify and the stakes that define them are embedded and participate in the wider work of each of the filmmakers. In such a way, even when encountered in relatively 'minor' works or in instalments that make up a mere fragment of much larger filmographies, reenactment offers a key to understanding these filmmakers' respective creative practices and the dominant logics that drive them. This will certainly be the case for the haunting effects of temporal denormativisation I identify in the varied uses of reenactment found in Akerman's filmmaking, to which I now turn.

CHAPTER 1

❖

Chantal Akerman — Haunting

Introduction — Ghosts, Doubles, Repetitions

Marianne Lambert's documentary *I Don't Belong Anywhere: The Cinema of Chantal Akerman*, released less than two weeks before its subject's suicide in October 2015, offers a particularly sensitive study of one of cinema's most tireless innovators, a filmmaker whose remarkable career repeatedly crossed stylistic, generic and media boundaries. Speaking at the opening to the documentary, standing on the upper deck of the Staten Island ferry with the Manhattan skyline visible behind her, Akerman frames her life's work in a way that immediately unsettles the terminology I have just used to present it: 'Je pense que le mot *carrière* n'est pas adéquat à ma vie, parce que quand tu as une carrière tu as un plan, et j'ai toujours fait ce qui me plaisait et ce qui m'intéressait' [I don't think the word *career* is adequate to describe my life, because when you have a career you have a plan, and I've always done what I liked and what interested me]. Lambert accompanies Akerman as she revisits these motivating pleasures and interests but also the pains, fears and anxieties that exist alongside them. The documentary represents a valuable attempt at constructing an adequate portrait of an artist whose work has so frequently proven difficult to definitively pin down.

The sensitivity of Lambert's documentary is born from familiarity with Akerman as a person and as a filmmaker, Lambert having worked as production manager on films such as *Demain on déménage* [*Tomorrow We Move*] (2004) and *La Folie Almayer* [*Almayer's Folly*] (2011). There is an easy intimacy conjured between documentary maker and documentary subject, as Lambert evacuates her own scrutinising presence and allows Akerman to speak, spontaneously and openly, for herself, avoiding the temptation to confine the filmmaker within the schematic logic of the 'plan' she so rejects. In extended sequences, Akerman reflects in a meandering and non-chronological manner on her life and films, as well as on the porosity of the border between these two intertwined halves. These sequences are interspersed with extracts from Akerman's many films; with images of Akerman working alongside her long-time collaborator Claire Atherton on the montage of *No Home Movie* (2015), her final film; with interviews from actors and other filmmakers who acknowledge the inestimable influence Akerman exerted over their own artistic practices. There is a pronounced spatial dynamic to many of these reflections as Akerman revisits sites and locations, the abundant familiarity of which is evidence

FIG. 1.1. and 1.2. *I Don't Belong Anywhere: The Cinema of Chantal Akerman* (2015), Marianne Lambert © Cinémathèque de la Fédération Wallionie-Bruxelles/Artémis Productions/RTBF/CBA. Lambert's extract is taken from *Les Rendez-vous d'Anna* (1978), Chantal Akerman © Paradise Films/Hélène Films.

of their insistent recurrence within the filmmaker's work: the streets and cafés of Brussels; the urban landscapes of New York; the very different urban landscapes of Paris; arid, limitrophe deserts — those of America's southern borders and of the Middle East.

One such spatial revisitation stands out in particular for the reenactment it occasions. This revisitation concerns Akerman's *Les Rendez-vous d'Anna* [*The Meetings of Anna*] (1978), a film in which the titular Anna, a Belgian filmmaker of Polish-Jewish descent strikingly played by Aurore Clément, traverses increasingly drained European landscapes to promote her new film, occupying a series of anonymous hotel rooms, train stations and carriage compartments. The extract that Lambert chooses from this film shows one of the extended, static takes so familiar from this film in particular and from much of Akerman's work more generally, plunging us within the sharply receding perspective lines of a very ordinary interior space. Clément walks slowly away from the camera along the windowless corridor of one of the many hotels her character occupies, the regular percussive sound of her heels cutting through the silence. As Clément nears the end of the corridor, walking past pairs of shoes left out by their owners for shining, the shot changes and Lambert provides the reverse angle that is famously so often withheld in Akerman's films. This frontal shot shows Clément still walking slowly down a hotel corridor, the sound of her heels still echoing in this empty space; however, in the transition between shots, something has clearly changed. The original extract that Lambert chose from *Les Rendez-vous d'Anna* showed Clément as she appeared in 1978; the reverse shot that Lambert's documentary adds shows Clément as she appeared in 2015, visibly older, the same but different, continuing a trajectory started many years previously.

Lambert's documentary goes on to introduce another extract from Akerman's original film: shown in a lateral pan, the Clément of 1978 opens the blinds of her hotel room then stands immobile, staring out of the window over nearby railway lines. Moments later, Clément replays these actions in 2015 and in reverse, closing the blinds of her modern hotel room and staring outwards through them, motionless. As they remake, invert and expand an earlier film, these sequences share something with works such as Pierre Huyghe's *L'Ellipse* [*The Ellipsis*] (1998) or Deimantas Narkevicius's *Revisiting Solaris* (2007). Through the belated supplement that it offers, Lambert's documentary confronts us with the ambiguous spectacle of Clément as she reenacts her own gestures from four decades earlier, replaying the past in the present across her own, transformed body.

In the interview that Lambert goes on to conduct with Clément, sitting on the hotel room bed in 2015, she reflects on her own career and on the extent to which it was moulded by Akerman. She also reflects on the feeling she had throughout her first collaboration with Akerman that playing 'Anna' was really to play a version of the filmmaker herself:

> *Lambert*: C'est un peu le rôle de Chantal que vous jouiez.
> *Clément*: C'est Chantal. C'est elle, c'est Chantal. On sent que c'est... il faudrait arriver à ce que ce soit elle qui parle.

[*Lambert:* You were kind of playing the role of Chantal.
Clément: It's Chantal. It's her, it's Chantal. You feel that it's... you have to get to the point where it's her who's speaking].

The autobiographical resonances of Akerman's *Les Rendez-vous d'Anna* — a film that dwells upon cinematic vocation, bisexual desire, childlessness, the movements and trajectories of diaspora, the bonds of mothers and daughters, the place of the individual in history, the ever-present shadow of mass destruction — are clear and manifold and have been acknowledged by commentators and by the filmmaker herself. As Akerman wrote tellingly in *Chantal Akerman: Autoportrait en cinéaste* [*Chantal Akerman: Self-Portrait as a Filmmaker*], the photo-textual self-portrait produced to coincide with the 2004 retrospective of her work at Paris's Centre Pompidou, growing up she had for a long time thought of 'Anna' as her real name (2004: 44).

As they are inflected by such resonances, these sequences of Lambert's documentary study leave us with the sensation of witnessing a curious chain of doublings and repetitions — ultimately of watching Clément reenact herself reenacting Akerman. In the wake of the death of Akerman, the uncanniness of this sensation is multiplied, introducing a certain ghostliness into Lambert's images. As Clément reprises her earlier role, playing herself playing Akerman, the deceased filmmaker seems to haunt this reenactment, certainly not entirely present but not entirely absent either. Clément's reenactment stands as an embodied index of the passing of time but also seems to trouble the stable separation of *then* and *now*, as it stages the uncertain return of something seen in an earlier time. *Les Rendez-vous d'Anna* once crossed European landscapes that seemed haunted by the traumatic events of recent history, encountering a succession of lost, damaged figures whose individual lives were ensnared with broader historical processes that exceeded them, and who seemed horrified by the past but fearful for the future. As Clément reenacts her own past gestures in 2015 for Lambert's documentary, she seems to revive these ghosts of history once more, but now Akerman herself is counted among them.

A great deal of the success of *I Don't Belong Anywhere* lies in the way in which Lambert manages, without mimicry or direct reproduction, to evoke something recognisable of Akerman's filmmaking, to mobilise certain aesthetic and thematic qualities that we experience in a comparable way to qualities found in the filmmaker's own work. Lambert does not seek to explain or define Akerman and her films, to lay them bare and schematise; rather, her documentary finds a means of gently teasing out and amplifying certain textures, logics and approaches that are discernible throughout the works produced by Akerman herself. In the slippages they instigate between spaces, identities and temporal moments, the reenactments described above are a particularly clear example of this mode of evocation. As Clément reenacts her own previous movements and stances, she introduces ideas that rise resiliently to the surface in Akerman's own filmmaking: an intense emotional engagement with sites and spaces and with the feelings, memories and associations that attach to them; endlessly repeated but often faltering attempts to mourn interlocking forms and scales of loss; an uncertainty around what exactly is produced through such acts of repetition — sameness or difference, identicality or rupture (or maybe something in between); the ambiguous interplay of autobiographical fact and fiction, truth and (re)invention; the relationship of self and other, identity and identification, and the possibility of reliving experiences that are not our own; a pervasive effect of ghostliness that blurs the lines between past and present, presence and absence, real and unreal.

It is this last idea in particular that informs my approach in this chapter. Attentive to the kinds of effects revived by Lambert's evocative reenactment, this chapter considers a pronounced spectral quality to Akerman's filmmaking, presenting her work as deeply invested in dynamics of *haunting*. Such an approach helps us to understand the specific ethical and temporal preoccupations that Akerman's work engages. Haunting in Akerman's filmmaking represents a means of exploring the sometimes uncomfortable affective weight that the experiences of the past exert on lives and subjectivities in the present. It is a form of memory work through which Akerman seeks her own place in time and space, questioning how her identity is moulded by things that came before and what her responsibilities to these things might be. Akerman's deeply political art of historical haunting recalls the words of Wendy Brown when she writes that:

> We inherit not 'what really happened' to the dead but what lives on from that happening, what is conjured from it, how past generations and events occupy the force fields of the present, how they claim us, and how they haunt, plague, and inspirit our imaginations and visions for the future (2001: 150).

In the case studies that I examine in this chapter, reenactment emerges as the tool through which the haunting that suffuses Akerman's films is intensified and foregrounded, through which certain lingering affects are kept mobile and vivid. It is the means through which Akerman turns haunting into an active, interrogative stance, opening herself up to the affective pressure of the past, allowing herself to be haunted, staging a deeply personal investigation into the challenges of remembrance and historical knowledge. It is a technique of mourning through which the ghosts of history, both personal and collective, are revived and called forth into the present without ever fully being exorcised.

The analysis of Akerman's work that follows is developed through four distinct case studies. In the films that I examine, we will encounter very different kinds of reenactment adopted in response to very different kinds of haunting: we move from an engagement with the reverberations of histories of racial violence in the southern states of America (*Sud* [*South*]), to considerations of the failures of intergenerational memory in the wake of the Holocaust (*D'Est* [*From the East*] and *Histoires d'Amérique: Food, Family and Philosophy* [*American Stories: Food, Family and Philosophy*]), to an exploration of the intimate traumas of growing up queer (*Portrait d'une jeune fille de la fin des années 60 à Bruxelles* [*Portrait of a Young Girl at the End of the 1960s in Brussels*]). The non-chronological ordering of case studies that I offer in this chapter in many ways moves steadily from darkness into light, from inescapably negative to comparatively more positive relationships with the past and with what has been lost. This is not done through a desire to impose a linear, developmental, redemptive logic onto a filmmaking practice that decidedly resists such an imposition. As other studies of the spectral qualities of her work have similarly insisted (Youmans 2009), the forms of haunting that Akerman here amplifies and interrogates through reenactment are ones that staunchly refuse the possibility of definitive redemption, forgiveness or healing through communion with the past. Akerman's work is much more ambiguous, much more hesitant than this. Rather, engaging with case studies in this way allows me, on the one hand, to establish how each of the reenactments Akerman stages oscillates continually between poles of pleasure and pain, optimism and pessimism; and on the other, to draw out the exact extent to which the pitch and amplitude of these oscillations is modulated from film to film. This approach helps me to think in a nuanced way about what is specific about the compulsive repetitions, revisitations and returns her work contains as well as the incomplete processes of working-through that they operate.

The varied reenactments considered in this chapter are staged through the technologies of filmic representation (choices of montage, movements of cameras, arrangements of mise-en-scène), through the appearance on screen of bodies that seem to channel the past directly into the present, or through a combination of these approaches. Certain of the instances that I identify in this chapter will appear subtler than many of those found elsewhere in this book. I indeed recognise that, taken alone, some of these examples might seem to improbably stretch stable categorisation as reenactment. Mindful of this, I open this chapter with what undoubtedly constitutes the clearest (and most unsettling) instance of reenactment encountered anywhere in Akerman's work. Through a close reading of this film, I establish the defining characteristics of Akerman's use of reenactment as an investigative tool of haunting that I will then go on to locate in subsequent — sometimes less clearly marked — case studies. I ask the reader to follow with me as I test the shuttling chain of these definitional connections. In return, I will show how this distinctive engagement with Akerman's diverse filmography encourages us to approach certain films in new ways and alerts us to the forms of dialogue that exist between works that might otherwise appear wholly unconnected. Bringing these very different texts into inhabitual but generative conversation reveals how thinking Akerman in terms of reenactment distils a logic of repetition and imperfect return that lies at the very heart of her filmmaking.

Atmospheres of History: *Sud*

The four case studies examined in this chapter lead us to think about the dynamics of haunting at play in Akerman's filmmaking in strongly spatial terms. In exploring the haunted and haunting spaces with which Akerman's work confronts us, my analysis is influenced by a number of critical discourses that have gained increasing traction over recent decades in the fields of human and cultural geography around the conception, practice and production of geographical knowledge. As part of a broad and ongoing reorientation of geographical analysis, many of these discourses interrogate experiences of space in terms of affect, materiality and embodiment in ways that are helpful for thinking further about Akerman's films. Particularly instructive within this context is the work of Ben Anderson around what he terms 'affective atmospheres'.

As an affective force, atmosphere is a slippery concept to define accurately or comprehensively. As Anderson suggests, both in everyday speech and in aesthetic discourse, the word atmosphere is often used interchangeably with any number of other ways of naming collective affects: 'mood, feeling, ambiance, tone' (2009: 78). The possible referents for the term are, he recognises, similarly multiple: 'epochs, societies, rooms, landscapes, couples, artworks, and much more are all said to possess atmospheres (or be possessed by them)' (ibid.). For Anderson, it is precisely because atmosphere remains so fundamentally ambiguous that it is appropriate as a concept for investigating the myriad ambiguities of affective and emotive life. Atmosphere's close proximity to the meteorological indeed alerts us to associations with that which is 'uncertain, disordered, shifting and contingent — that which never quite achieves the stability of form' (ibid.). But, as Anderson argues, approaching affect in terms of a resemblance to the instability and ephemerality of weather simultaneously reminds us of how such phenomena may well remain indeterminate 'even as they effect':

> Perplexingly the term atmosphere seems to express something vague. Something, an ill-defined indefinite something, that exceeds rational explanation and clear figuration. Something that hesitates at the edge of the unsayable. Yet, at one and the same time, the affective qualities that are given to this *something* by those who feel it are remarkable for their singularity (ibid.).

Though (or perhaps because) vague, uncertain, unclear, ungraspable, ephemeral, impossible to exactly put a finger on, atmospheres exert an enveloping, pressurising force that is actively if disorientingly felt. For Anderson, the concept of atmosphere is ultimately so compelling and so good to think with precisely because, in this shifting indeterminacy, it holds a series of opposites — 'presence and absence, materiality and ideality, definite and indefinite, singularity and generality' — within a perpetual relation of tension (80).

The spaces filmed by Akerman in this chapter's four case studies indeed condense the kinds of atmospheric opposites Anderson described above; but these opposites emerge as a function of another, larger tension resiliently at play in her work. The atmospheres of affect that Akerman plumbs are pervaded by uncertainties of temporality — by a strange impression that something recalled from an earlier time (events, experiences, sensations) is making itself felt, disconcertingly, *hauntingly*, in the affective textures of the present. In his description of atmosphere as an affective force able to 'interrupt, perturb and haunt persons, places or things' (78), Anderson certainly hints at atmosphere's possible haunting charge; but it is important to recognise how, in the work of Akerman, this charge develops through a specific tension between past and present. As it explores the temporal indeterminacy of the affective atmospheres that adhere to a number of very different spaces, Akerman's work moves into proximity with accounts of the spectral aspects of spatial experience. Geographer John Wylie — a key figure in the interrogation of such 'spectral geographies' — has discussed in markedly atmospheric terms the search for adequate ways of exploring and expressing 'the physicalities and haunting tangibilities of memories [...] as these precipitate into, disperse throughout and linger within landscapes and objects' (2009: 279). This is something that is keenly felt in all of the films by Akerman examined in this chapter, and with particular force in the example to which I now turn, where traumatic memories spread and hang across landscapes and the objects they contain, pressing down on the present with a physical, tangible force.

Akerman's 1999 documentary *Sud* evokes the racist torture and murder of James Byrd Jr in the American town of Jasper, Texas that occurred in June of the preceding year. Byrd had been viciously beaten by three white supremacists before being chained to the back of the assailants' truck and dragged along a remote stretch of country road, dying when his body struck a protruding drainage pipe, his head and arm severed in the impact. Byrd's decapitated and dismembered body was then dumped in front of the cemetery of one of Jasper's predominantly Black churches. This infamous hate crime was shocking through its sheer brutality and in the way that it appeared to mark the hateful re-emergence of the Jim Crow era's violent lynching traditions into the closing years of the twentieth century. Despite a subject matter that would at first glance appear extraneous to the filmmaker's own autobiography, this opening case study confronts us with ambiguities that also dominate the more obviously autobiographical examples I go on to analyse in this chapter. This is a film in which to attend to affective atmospheres is to agree to be haunted by the past, to be engulfed by the sometimes oppressive weight of history. *Sud* confronts us with how opening ourselves up to the resurgence of history's affects troubles clear distinctions of past and present whilst offering us a way of 'remembering' things we did not necessarily directly experience ourselves. It is a film where reenactment concentrates these atmospheres, amplifying their haunting charge, whilst refusing to resolve the tensions that structure them.

Akerman had planned to make a film about the southern states of America before Byrd's horrifying death. *Sud* grew out of Akerman's interest in the interactions of landscape and memory, and in how this interaction has been variously mediated through cultural representation. Specifically, the film's genesis reflects Akerman's attraction towards what we might understand as the 'mythology' of the American 'Deep South' — an imagined geography depicted by countless works of film, literature, painting and song in which a certain pervasive atmosphere of beguiling stillness, humidity, languor, torpor, lethargy reigns, but one that is permanently shadowed by the thinly concealed threat of danger and violence. Akerman's first access to the American South was, she suggests, primarily literary. She confesses in her *Autoportrait en cinéaste* to having been particularly struck by the renderings offered by James Baldwin and William Faulkner — writers who extensively examined and indeed propagated the mythology of the South as a site of great natural beauty that had borne witness to centuries of violence threatening to re-erupt at any moment. She recalls in particular Baldwin's depiction in his *Harlem quartet* [*Just Above My Head*] (1979) of an unsettling quietude that barely covers the still raw traumas of American history: a leaden, enveloping 'silence du Sud' [silence of the South] that holds within it anxious fear of the coming day with the untold fresh terrors it might bring (2004: 116–22). Akerman's film project was initially motivated by a desire to map this mental geography onto the physical geographies of America's southern states, to examine their correspondences. Rather than viewing her film as an investigation into the precise circumstances of Byrd's death, Akerman conceived of *Sud* as an evocative, reflective meditation on how this particular act of racist violence fits into the combined mental and physical landscapes of the region (233).

Arriving in Texas, Akerman was drawn to the temporal depth she found in these southern landscapes, a depth that can produce slippages between past and present. The South that she sets out to explore is one that is inscribed by the marks of history, in which the often beautiful landscapes that we encounter in the present constantly recall past histories of enslavement and racial persecution. In making *Sud*, Akerman suggests that she was motivated by a desire to explore whether these southern landscapes themselves could 'remember' something other than their own beauty, something much uglier that lay just beneath the surface of the limpid images she filmed in the present (2004: 164). She describes how when she first travelled through America's southern states to begin her film, within landscapes that could not, for her, be mentally dissociated from the bloody past they once housed, it was impossible to look at an empty cotton field without remembering that there were once enslaved men, women and children working there under the whip, or to look at a tree without remembering that, not that long ago, Black bodies hung from branches in what Billie Holiday referred to ironically as the 'gallant South' (36–39). As she films these southern spaces in duration, delving ever further within the atmospheres that fill them, Akerman exposes the spectator to this same temporal seepage, confronting us with something horrendous at the edge of the unsayable, something both there and not there, both of then and of now.

Writing about *Sud* in her *Autopotrait en cinéaste*, Akerman presents this relationship between a surface present and the past that lurks beneath in terms of a distinctly Benjaminian form of 'dialectical' interpenetration, where present images receive the lingering imprint of past images (2004: 44). However, the kind of incendiary discharge through which a connection between past and present is suddenly, *explosively* illuminated — 'allume[r] la mèche de l'explosif qui gît dans ce qui a été' [light the fuse to the explosive latent in what has been] — that Akerman, via Benjamin, identifies in her own film (ibid.) is not really corroborated by our experience of watching *Sud*. The unsettling imprint of the past in the present in Akerman's film is instead much better understood in terms of the sustained kinds of haunting I have been describing so far, as the filmmaker herself indeed elsewhere recognises. In the production notes to her film, Akerman establishes the questions that preoccupied her as she headed through these landscapes: 'How do the trees and the whole natural environment evoke so intensely death, blood and the weight of history? How does the present call up the past? And how does this past, with a mere gesture or a simple regard, haunt and torment you as you wander along an empty cotton field or a dusty country road?' (Akerman quoted in Capp 2000). The communication between past and present that so fascinated Akerman

FIG. 1.3. *Sud* (1999), Chantal Akerman © AMIP/Paradise Films/INA/RTBF.

in the dazzling, languorous landscapes of the South is felt nowhere more potently, nowhere more hauntingly, than in the notable instance of reenactment contained in *Sud's* closing sequence.

Akerman's film ends with an unbroken, seven-minute-long tracking shot, filmed backwards from the rear of a moving vehicle, that traces the route along which James Byrd Jr was dragged to his death. At intervals along the road, we see blue, spray-painted circles on the tarmac that signal where the victim's possessions and severed body parts were found. Within this reenactive mise-en-scène, Akerman confronts us with disorientating oscillations between presence and absence, past and present, living and dead. As Marion Schmid suggests, although not in any way graphic, the closing sequence of *Sud* is arguably unmatched in Akerman's work for its sheer violence (2010: 113). Though Byrd's wounded, dismembered body is wholly absent from our screen, the bone-shattering, flesh-wrenching violence to which it is subject makes itself unavoidably felt. We see no physical presence, but we feel Byrd's return with an affective materiality that disconcerts us. What we 'watch' in *Sud's* closing sequence is clearly not the very same racist murder that occurred several months earlier on this stretch of Texan roadway; and yet, as the journey of Byrd's body is retraced, a degree of ambiguity seeps into these images and we momentarily question what exactly we are seeing.

Akerman's reenactment resembles other investigations into how memories embedded in landscape might be drawn out and amplified in ways that implicate, even engulf the viewer. Even if they lack *Sud's* explicitly reenactive force, certain sequences filmed from moving cars in James Benning's *Landscape Suicide* (1986) stage similarly intense and durational inquiries into how acts of violence fit into their environments (see also MacDonald 2005: 264). As it retraces the trajectory taken by an individual framed in political and media discourse as a perpetrator rather than a victim of violence, Eric Baudelaire's *Also Known as Jihadi* (2017) learns clear lessons from *Sud* as well as from the case study explored in this chapter's following section (a comparison strengthened by the fact that Claire Atherton was responsible for the montage of all three films). But the recreated viewing perspective Baudelaire leads us to assume is subject to a lesser degree of slippage than what we see along the roads around Jasper — a slippage that contributes significantly to the unsettling effects of Akerman's film. Through the arrangements of filmic mise-en-scène and the movements of a recording camera, *Sud* reenacts the dying moments of a victim of racist violence and asks us to witness, *participate* even. Commenting on this closing sequence in a way that acknowledges its uncomfortable ethical charge, Akerman suggests that, through this closing reenactment, she wanted us to put ourselves (at least partly) in the position of the victim: 'By using that very long shot, I was trying to capture maybe a very, very, very, very tiny bit of what Byrd went through' (MacDonald 2005: 266). And yet, plunged within this reconstructed viewing perspective, we wonder at moments whether we are simultaneously being led to occupy the viewing position of perpetrator. Throughout this extended sequence and the mobile identifications it sustains, Akerman refuses to let us look away from the rapid scrolling of verge, trees and tarmac, as well as from what its implications for all of us might be.

Writing on *Sud*, So Mayer warns against framing the murder of James Byrd Jr itself as a reenactment of something past, as an atavistic citation of atrocities otherwise consigned to an earlier chapter of history: 'There is no drag; this is not baggage or belatedness' (2019: 110). For Mayer, this murder instead was and remains part of a constitutive continuum of white supremacist genocidal violence on which America is founded (ibid.). In reenacting Byrd's murder and in retracing a forced trajectory followed shortly before her arrival in Texas, Akerman performs such a refusal to historicise, immersing us within this continuity of violence, within the *presentness* of racial hatred. Through a specifically cinematic form of reenactment, we are led to access individual experiences that are not our own, and from there to access much wider (ongoing) experiences; we are forced to position ourselves in relation to these experiences, to feel them as our own and to be haunted by them.

Many of the interviewees who appear in *Sud* talk of socio-historical progress, promising that the community of Jasper can overcome the trauma of Byrd's murder, that it can learn from it and be redeemed by the suffering it brought. In this context, it is far from insignificant that the non-profit organisation established in 1999 to remember this act of violence and the life it extinguished, as well as to prevent future atrocities, was called the Byrd Foundation for Racial Healing.[1] In contrast, Akerman's reenactment explicitly refuses the possibility of definitive closure and healing, of the redemptive march into a glimmering future. In its disruption of the hopeful reassurance of 'we shall overcome' and in the resilience of the gaze it casts upon this dusty road surface baked under a relentless sun, Akerman's ending echoes that of Lucille Clifton's poem 'Jasper Texas 1998', another striking engagement with the death of James Byrd Jr.[2] The reenactment that concludes *Sud* offers an instance of mourning for the dead but one that refuses to let painful feelings subside and to let the dead fully rest or return. Akerman's reenactment amplifies the queasy, haunting charge of the affects of the past, forcing us to question the ethical imperatives to which they expose us. *Sud* explores how, as Wendy Brown wrote, the dead can claim us and how they haunt, plague and inspirit our imaginations and visions for the future. The film draws us forcibly into the unhealed wounds of history, ensuring that these wounds continue to fester and occupy the affective force fields of the present.

When we begin to attend to the spectral qualities of Akerman's filmmaking, we are quickly confronted with how one form or site of haunting can overlap with or open onto another. Tracing these adjacent hauntings alerts us to a perhaps unexpected autobiographical valency to *Sud*, whilst bringing it into closer proximity with my next (chronologically earlier) case study. We have seen how Akerman's first exposure to the landscapes of America's southern states was through works of literature, with Baldwin's descriptions of atmospheres of unsettling quietude having strongly shaped her perceptions of the region. Writing in her *Autoportrait en cinéaste*, Akerman confesses that the heavy silence of the South that she found in such texts inevitably recalled the other, equally weighty silences that she, as the daughter of East-European Jews who had fled pogroms and endured the Nazi death machine, heard growing up: 'Chez moi à la maison, ce n'est pas du silence du Sud dont on parlait quand on parlait enfin de quelque chose, mais du silence du camp, et là c'était la même peur du jour qui vient, parce avec le jour qui vient, il n'y avait que le pire qui pouvait arriver' [At home, it wasn't the silence of the South that we spoke about when we finally spoke about something, it was the silence of the camp, and there it was the same fear of the coming day, because with the coming day only the worst could happen] (2004: 122). Nikolaj Lübecker has described how, as such autobiographical associations infiltrate apparently distinct subject matter, *Sud* crafts a space for Black and Jewish experiences to resonate: 'a space where vulnerability — respectfully and almost beyond the level of representation — is met with vulnerability' (2019: 49). For Lübecker, this resonance takes place in a 'ghostly' register that is difficult to map and in which, importantly, no precise claim is made about the relation between these affective experiences (ibid.).

The subtle space of resonance in which different experiences of persecution are brought into contact in this indeterminate, almost imperceptible manner allows us to grasp the extent to which *Sud* is itself haunted by a film that preceded it and by the autobiographical search it operates. The scrutinising gaze Akerman casts over the landscapes of the South is indeed haunted by memories of landscapes she had filmed before, several thousand miles away at another point on the compass. If empty cotton fields, spindly trees and dusty Texan roads summon the spectre of the whip, the noose, the man dragged to his death, yet further behind these images there lingers the faint imprint of other atrocities — ones which, for Akerman, seemed closer to home. As she confesses: 'Je pensais bien en avoir fini avec cette histoire de *D'Est* et avec toutes ces obsessions. Mais le film que je viens de tourner dans le Sud des Etats-Unis me semble bien faire écho tant au film *D'Est* qu'aux obsessions qu'il a mises en relief' [I thought I was done with this *D'Est* business and with all of these obsessions. But the film I've just made in the South of the US seems to echo as much *D'Est* as the obsessions it brought out] (Akerman quoted in Liénard 2006: 132). As we move from the haunted landscapes of the American Deep South at the threshold of a new millennium to the haunted landscapes of the European East depicted in the immediate aftermath of the fall of the Berlin Wall and the collapse of the Soviet Union, the more recognisably autobiographical reenactments found in *D'Est* offer the means through which Akerman revives and interrogates other continental histories of suffering, seeking her own place within them.

Reversing Exile: *D'Est*

Anderson opens his reflection on the concept of 'affective atmospheres' by exploring the atmospheric qualities of certain socio-political moments (2009: 77). To illustrate his point, Anderson quotes from a speech delivered by Karl Marx in 1856 at a meeting to mark the fourth anniversary of the Chartist *People's Paper*. In a now famous passage, Marx invokes the 'revolutionary atmosphere' that, he suggests, surrounded the wave of republican revolts that had swept across European society just a few years earlier in 1848, 'enveloping and pressing it from all sides'. Addressing his audience directly, Marx inquired: 'the atmosphere in which we live, weighs upon every one with a 20,000-pound force, but do you feel it?' (1978: 577). Marx's question eloquently summarises the strange way in which, as Anderson recognises, atmospheres can seem to adhere to certain contexts and junctures, exerting a considerable if ambiguous pressure on events, lives and imaginations.

   With the eventual demise of European communism and the rise of triumphalist discourses proclaiming the end of ideology, a very different kind of revolutionary atmosphere had of course descended upon Europe by the time Akerman made *D'Est* in 1993. In Akerman's film, this is an atmosphere that once again entails a certain temporal depth, accommodating disruptive forms of spectral return. *D'Est* explores how — as Jacques Derrida suggested in his *Spectres de Marx* [*Spectres of Marx*] in that same year — when we arrive at the apparent end of history the past begins to make renewed demands on the present in a way which unsettles the futures we are supposedly marching towards. Time in *D'Est* is decidedly out of joint: within the period of radical transformation the film depicts, the persistence of history disrupts linear narratives of progress and the denizens of Eastern Europe are shown to live with ghosts. As Akerman journeys across the homelands of her parents, moving from Eastern Germany to Poland and on to Russia, she discovers the extent to which the uncertain atmospheres of radical change hanging over these landscapes are still haunted by the spectre of the pogrom, the gulag, the death march, the camps. Moving amongst these spectres, Akerman explores those nagging obsessions that would not be resolved by the conclusion of her journey eastwards and that would go on to make themselves felt afresh along the haunted roadways of Jasper: 'l'Histoire, la grande et la petite, la peur, les charniers, la haine de l'autre, de soi, et aussi l'éblouissement de la beauté' [History with a big and a little H, fear, mass graves, hatred of other people, of yourself, and also dazzling beauty] (Akerman quoted in Liénard 2006: 132).

D'Est exists in two different, though interlocking, forms: on the one hand, the 1993 documentary film that here provides my object of study; on the other, the 1995 video installation *Bordering on Fiction: Chantal Akerman's 'D'Est'* in which the images of the documentary are refracted and unpacked across multiple screens and accompanied by additional recorded texts from Akerman. In terms of their genesis, execution and critical reception, it is impossible to entirely disentangle the two versions and my reading of the documentary film will at points be strongly influenced by texts written by Akerman and by other commentators more directly in association with the multi-screen installation piece. Akerman was initially approached in 1989 by a curatorial team drawn from galleries in France and America with the project of creating a multimedia installation that would consider the contemporary coming together of the European Community. We are told that Akerman was immediately enthusiastic about the project and proposed integrating a focus on 'what was left out of the union as well', turning her attention to the rise of nationalism and antisemitism registered across the European continent in these years of socio-political upheaval (Halbreich and Jenkins 1995: 8). As curator Catherine David writes, the project began to take shape 'in the aftermath of impressions, memories and emotions' that Akerman brought back with her from a journey she had taken to prepare for an unmade film about the Russian modernist poet Anna Akhmatova (1995: 58). Two subsequent journeys — to the former East Germany and Poland in the summer of 1992 and then to Russia in the winter months of the same year — allowed Akerman to gather the footage for her film and to consolidate the resonant impressions, memories and emotions that she found inscribed in these eastern landscapes.

Writing in a fragmentary text originally produced in anticipation of her two eastern journeys, but subsequently republished in her installation's exhibition catalogue, Akerman reflects on the motivations behind her film, focusing particularly on the timeliness and urgency of her intervention: 'While there's still time, I would like to make a grand journey across Eastern Europe [...] I'd like to film there, in my own style of documentary bordering on fiction. I'd like to shoot everything. Everything that moves me' (1995: 17). Faced with the apparently unstoppable encroachment of international capitalism across Europe that promised to sweep away all that lay before it, Akerman sought to offer an avowedly subjective survey of a rapidly transforming region. But, as she acknowledges later in the same text, for this daughter of displaced Polish Jews who eventually resettled in Belgium, there are also clear 'personal reasons' for making her journey across Eastern Europe that exist alongside the 'obvious historical, social, and political reasons' presented by a critical juncture of regional regime change (20).

We have seen how Akerman's early life was dominated by what she presents as the crushing 'silence du camp' and by what this silence covered — most pointedly her mother's internment and loss of her own parents. Akerman grew up, she suggests, within a domestic context of enforced forgetting and under the permanent, if unnamed, shadow cast by the mass destruction that had violently interrupted her extended maternal line like that of so many others. So much of

Akerman's work attempts to investigate the troubled afterlives of the experiences of her parents' generation — of persecution, hiding, deportation, internment, loss, uprootedness — and to remedy the painful failures of memory transmission as well as the severance from cultural rituals, traditions and identities that occurs as a result. Writing towards the opening of her *Autoportrait en cinéaste*, Akerman imagines a parental dialogue that foregrounds this desire to the fill the gaping holes that perforate her personal history, as well as the resistance this desire encounters:

> *Arrête de ressasser disait mon père et ne recommence pas avec ces vieilles histoires, et ma mère tout simplement se taisait, il n'y a rien à ressasser disait mon père, il n'y a rien à dire, disait ma mère. Et c'est sur ce rien que je travaille.*

> [*Stop going on about it my father would say and don't start with those old tales again, and my mother would just be quiet, there's nothing to go over said my father, there's nothing to say said my mother. And it's on this nothing that I work*] (2004: 12–13).

Here as elsewhere in Akerman's work, this compulsion is figured as a constantly renewed process of *ressassement*. The French verb *ressasser* suggests both repetition on the one hand and intensity or duration of focus on the other: it is both to return obsessively to certain themes and to think upon them at length, dedicating heightened levels of attention and affective energy to these extended instances of brooding, ruminative reflection. Continuing the labour of *ressassement*, *D'Est* undertakes this same difficult task of filling in the *rien* that lies at the heart of so much of Akerman's life and work, attempting to return to a past from which she feels cut off. In embarking upon this grand journey across Eastern Europe *while there's still time*, Akerman scours landscapes thrown suddenly into uncertainty for the material that might allow her to repair the blanks and missing links in her own story before this material is erased forever or changed beyond recognition.

Certain of the extended sequences found towards the opening of *D'Est* resemble images of the sun-baked landscapes of rural Texas. Journeying through the eastern regions of Germany at the height of summer, Akerman shows stretches of country road drenched in the same kind of oppressive, buzzing heat seen in *Sud*. In these images of stillness and light we detect something of the 'éblouissement de la beauté' the filmmaker described above. As Akerman's journey eastwards develops, we are escorted away from summer and further into winter, into scenes that retain a dazzling beauty but of an increasingly austere kind. In sequences that have clearly influenced other regional depictions such as Sergei Loznitsa's *Portrait* (2002) and *Landscape* (2003), *D'Est* moves from German side roads to beach resorts, to apartment buildings, to music halls, to Polish potato fields, to the snow-covered streets and avenues of Moscow. Akerman records anonymous figures standing in line for early-morning buses, moving silently inside their homes, sitting numbly in crowded train stations. Through the scrutinising force of Akerman's slow, scanning pans and extended static takes, our attention is entirely focused on these figures' bodies and faces and the spaces that surround them.

It is as Akerman's camera scours these (by turns beautiful, austere, banal, strange, funny) scenes at length that something ugly from history seems to press upon the affective textures of the present — something that again hesitates at the edge of the

FIG. 1.4. *D'Est* (1993), Chantal Akerman
© RTBF/RTP/CBA/Lieurac Productions/Paradise Films.

unsayable, detectable but never fully defined. The images of a rapidly modernising Eastern Europe that Akerman captures at a very specific moment of socio-political transformation may well include such emblems of the apparently unstoppable march of progress as Pepsi cans and Panasonic bags; but remnants of an earlier time still make themselves insistently felt. Just as the landscapes of the American South appeared haunted by a history of racial violence that threatened to erupt at any minute, so too do the landscapes of the East hold within them the memory of the atrocities that they once housed, the reverberations of a different regional history of suffering. Enveloped in these reverberations, the unknown bodies that Akerman films seem to provide the site around which the physicalities and haunting tangibilities of memory coalesce. As she suggests in one of the audio-texts written to accompany the installation version of her film, this haunting charge excavates

> old images that are barely concealed by other, more luminous, even radiant ones: old images of evacuation, of people with packages marching in the snow toward an unknown place, of faces and bodies placed side by side, faces that vacillate between a strong life and the possibility of a death that would come to strike them without their having to ask for anything (Akerman quoted in David 1995: 63).

As we watch groups trudging slowly through the snow, waiting endlessly in sites of arrival, transit and departure, bending stiffly to unearth potatoes from frozen furrows, we are assailed by the uncanny sensation of witnessing modern bodies *reenacting* movements from history perhaps thought confined to the past. Through what Rebecca Schneider refers to as 'the residue of the gesture or the cross-temporality of the pose' (2011: 2), these historical 'reenactors' confront us with possible images of what *new* death marches, *new* deportations, *new* struggles for survival might look like.

In a film that sees a Western–European artist cast her gaze over Eastern–European bodies and that has previously been read convincingly through an ethnographic lens

FIG. 1.5. *D'Est* (1993), Chantal Akerman
© RTBF/RTP/CBA/Lieurac Productions/Paradise Films.

(see particularly Russell 1999: 163–69), we might, of course, question the use of such modern individuals as the (unwitting? unwilling?) site around which to channel memories they might rather forget. But it is precisely as a warning against forgetting that Akerman uses these images: such 'reenactments' once again issue a potent warning against overlooking the perpetual *presentness* of violence's threat and our global vulnerability to it. Within a film project that sought from its outset to cast light on those dark forces 'left out' of European unification, we are reminded that death might today still strike unbidden and without warning, both in this region and elsewhere. As Derrida indeed warned, amidst rampant evangelising around the putative end of history, no amount of 'progress' can make us forget that never before in the history of mankind have so many around the globe been enslaved, starved or exterminated (1993: 141).

Writing in her *Autoportrait en cinéaste*, Akerman describes the associations and reactions such images awoke in her: 'Ces visages *D'Est*, je les connaissais, ils me faisaient penser à d'autres visages [...] Et ces files d'attente, ces gares, tout cela résonnait en moi, faisait écho à cet imaginaire, à ce trou dans mon histoire...' [The faces from *D'Est*, I knew them, they made me think of other faces [...] And those queues, those stations, it all resonated within me, it echoed that imaginary, that hole in my story...] (2004: 42). Alongside the instances suggested above, *D'Est* also stages another, much more extensive, form of reenactment — one that subtends the film's entire montage, conditioning everything that we see. Tackling *D'Est* non-chronologically, after the explicitness of *Sud*'s closing sequence, helps us to see the diffuse reenactment it contains more clearly, and to recognise how Akerman here once again retraces the forced trajectory of bodies through space. It is through this sustained reenactment that Akerman questions where she, as a second-generation Holocaust survivor, might fit in these haunted landscapes, corralling spectres into her autobiographical search.

A number of commentators have identified how, in moving from Germany to Poland to Russia, *D'Est* retraces in reverse-direction the westward migration of Jews fleeing antisemitic persecution. As Alisa Lebow suggests, *D'Est* is to be viewed as a 'reenactment, in reverse, of displacement, a homecoming to a land that the filmmaker herself never called home' (2008: 8). As the film's eastwards movement continues through pans, pauses and the transitions of montage, we are left with the sensation of watching with Akerman as she makes this recreated journey herself from behind the camera. For Lebow, allusions to Nelly and Jacob Akerman's exile that exist just beneath the surface of *D'Est* make its reversed retracing of a much larger exilic march into a sort of 'embodied rehearsal', allowing the filmmaker to make it her own (2016: 57). In reenacting this trajectory, Akerman turns haunting into an active, interrogative stance, deliberately opening herself up to the ghosts of the past, seeking her place amongst them.

But *D'Est* stages a homecoming that never arrives at its final destination. Akerman refrains from filming in the actual locations where her parents had grown up, just as she refuses to show specific, identifiable sites of historical atrocity. The syntax of Akerman's film is, as David suggests, structured around a rigorous set of formal and thematic oppositions, where interior scenes alternate with exteriors, where we move suddenly between night and day or between individuals and crowds, where static frames give way to steadily moving lateral tracking shots, silence to blaring noise, long takes to short (1995: 59). Through such oppositions, the successive sequences of *D'Est* create an almost hypnotic rhythm that seems to sit constantly on the verge of implosion, foregrounding 'ruptures, frustrated attempts and an infinitely deferred resolution' across the images we watch — an impression of instability which is amplified yet further by the disjunctions, disorientations and discontinuities introduced by the film's desynchronised soundtrack (ibid.). The constantly shifting rhythms of the montage of *D'Est* resist any definitive closure in what Rina Carvajal refers to as the 'mesmerizingly inconclusive effect of the film' (2008: 16).

D'Est is, as Ivone Margulies suggests, emphatically a series without telos (1996: 202). The images that appear in one of the film's final extended sequences of a concert cellist acclaimed by her adoring audience in the Moscow Conservatory, so different from the various other images that precede them, initially seem to hold out the promise of some resolution; but this scene of artistic finale is far from the end point to Akerman's search. These images give way to a final tracking shot of yet more frozen figures standing in the snow, figures that both evoke an unresolved past in which the filmmaker still struggles to find her place and that await a now uncertain future. The pleasure of catharsis is denied. The 'embodied rehearsal' that is undertaken along this reenacted journey stirs up the ghosts of history, exposing Akerman to them without being able to exorcise them. As Akerman suggested in the audio-text to her gallery exhibition:

> There's nothing to be done; it's obsessive and it obsesses me.
> Despite the cello, despite the cinema.
> The film finished, I say to myself, *that's* what it was; once again *that* (Akerman quoted in David 1995: 63).

In recalling the opening line to *Waiting For Godot* (1954), Akerman's *nothing to be done* frames her as a reluctant inheritor to Vladimir and Estragon, awaiting a resolution and a release that never comes. Throughout *D'Est*, Akerman attempts to fill in the holes in her own autobiography, whilst always foregrounding the impossibility of ever definitively doing so.

Akerman's words above bespeak, as Sandy Flitterman-Lewis suggests, 'the anxiety that arises from knowledge of the insufficiency of representation' (2019: 17). Akerman would here appear to acknowledge how, as Michael Renov wrote, 'in the face of staggering epochal loss, art can only hope to signify the limits of its healing powers' (2004: 120). Renov made this stark assessment in relation to Claude Lanzmann's *Shoah* (1985), a film where very different forms of reenactment are similarly unable to attain redemptive catharsis (Margulies 2019: 141–81). How indeed could a film ever remedy the scale of loss that lies at the heart of Akerman's work and the gnawing obsessions this loss generates? The obsessions that propelled Akerman's grand journey across Eastern Europe are not resolved by the end of *D'Est*: we have seen how they resurfaced in the gaze Akerman would go on to cast over the southern states of America, and they have resurfaced in other films both before and since. As these compulsive repetitions confront her each time anew with the impossibility of restoring what has been lost and with the growing risk of diminishing returns, Akerman's *ressassement* and the forms of reenactment that participate in it would seem to tip over inevitably and painfully into the cycles of melancholy.

But this is not the whole story: compulsive repetition coexists in Akerman's work with conscious and dogged determination, with courageous experimentation. The functioning of Akerman's *ressassement* in many ways exemplifies aspects of the important response to Freudian melancholy offered by Julia Kristeva. This is a response that, as it shapes Kristeva's presentation of a Durasian literature of anti-catharsis, offers ways of engaging with the work of another artist who repeatedly staged unsettling confrontations with the unresolved 'silence of horror in oneself and in the world' (1992: 225). For Kristeva, melancholy's impeded processes of working-through can sometimes provide a vital spur to creativity, to a search for new expressive forms (42; see also Rushworth 2016: 6–7, 56–57). Akerman's labour of *ressassement* entails a similar search for original forms of representation that might prove *sufficient* to the recurrent questions that she asks — to *that*, once again *that*. Her filmmaking foregrounds the painful impossibility of making the past return intact and simultaneously announces a desire to examine the ambivalences of human longing and belonging, seeing in these ambivalences ethical and creative challenges. Akerman heeds Svetlana Boym's (2001) call to explore 'reflective' rather than 'restorative' forms of nostalgia: she interrogates the imperfect, always fragmentary processes of remembrance and explores both the desires that motivate remembering and the obstacles that perpetually stand in its way. In the incomplete homecoming that it stages, *D'Est*, like so many of her other films, represents Akerman's attempt to show through art the generative resilience of her desire to remember, and the ways in which this desire is continually undone.

Writing in her *Autoportrait en cinéaste*, Akerman frames her cyclical attempts to remedy the stalled transmission of intergenerational memory in a way that acknowledges this potent creative dimension whilst foregrounding the determination which drives it:

> Un enfant avec une histoire pleine de trous, ne peut que se réinventer une mémoire. De ça je suis certaine. Alors l'autobiographie dans tout ça ne peut être que réinventée. Elle est toujours réinventée, mais là, avec cette histoire pleine de trous, c'est comme s'il n'y avait même plus d'histoire. Que fait-on alors? On essaie de remplir ces trous, et je dirais même ce trou, par un imaginaire nourri de tout ce qu'on peut trouver, à gauche, à droite et au milieu du trou. On essaie de se créer une vérité imaginaire à soi. C'est pour ça, on ressasse. On ressasse et on ressasse.

> [All a child with a story full of holes can do is reinvent memories. Of that I am certain. And so autobiography in all that can only be reinvented. It's always reinvented but in this case, with a story full of holes, it's as if there's no story left. So what do you do? You try and fill these holes, I'd even say this hole, with an imaginary powered by whatever you can find, to the left, to the right and in the middle of the hole. You try and create your own imaginary truth. That's the reason why you keep going over it all. You go over it over and over again] (2004: 30).

This drive to reinvent memory and autobiography through the crafting of a personal space of imaginary truth is seen yet more clearly in the following case study — an earlier instalment in the sustained work of *ressassement* that offers a very different negotiation of the anguished obsessions that propel Akerman's work. This is a film that, as it grapples with connected experiences of loss, reinventing Akerman's story, proposes pleasures that appear slightly more durable than those seen above (albeit not durable enough to entirely preclude this grand journey across Eastern Europe just a few years later). What Akerman here pursues resembles the tentative process of creation that Laura U. Marks finds in responses to loss from so much intercultural media: 'the movement from excavation to fabulation, or from deconstructing dominant histories to creating new conditions for new stories (2000: 5). Whilst *D'Est* inverted European trajectories of Jewish exile, here they are replicated and extended, offering a broader reflection on diasporic memory where the ghosts of history are more explicitly marked. In summoning these ghosts, Akerman combines elements of the different forms of reenactment we have seen so far.

Reinventing the American Ghost Story: *Histoires d'Amérique: Food, Family and Philosophy*

The very opening images of Akerman's 1988 film *Histoires d'Amérique: Food, Family and Philosophy* (henceforth *Histoires d'Amérique*) bear the marks of reenactment. These images at first hover at the edge of decipherability, lent consistency only by the faint gradations of blue-grey they contain. Before long, however, an object enters into the frame that instantly renders these images legible. The unmistakable sight of the Statue of Liberty outlined hazily in the distance betrays the location of this introductory sequence; it explains the gentle rocking mobility of the camera, mounted on the deck of a boat moving slowly towards land across the waters of New York's Upper Bay — the same harbour to which Akerman returned in Lambert's *I Don't Belong Anywhere*, as we saw at this chapter's beginning. As Akerman's camera continues its movement shoreward, other recognisable forms enter the frame and details of the Manhattan skyline captured at dusk come into view. For a modern viewer, the sight of the twin towers of the World Trade Centre appearing on the horizon is still inescapably uncanny; indeed, despite the concrete anchoring in space these landmarks provide, there is something slightly unreal, oneiric about the New York that Akerman draws us towards. As the edges of these buildings and monuments are softened and blurred by the intervening coastal mist, it is almost as if the thick atmospheres of memory and feeling that adhere to and envelope them have become momentarily visible.

These images depict the Statue of Liberty and the New York shoreline as trans-historical symbol, captured in all of their suggestive iconicity. These are the same images that, over the years, would have come suddenly into sight across the water to greet countless generations of other incomers as they completed seaborne voyages of migration in search of a better life. As her camera moves steadily towards shore, rocked by the waves, Akerman reenacts these earlier instances of anonymous arrival. In retracing trajectories of inter-continental migration, this reenactment shares something with the extended example that subtends the montage of *D'Est*; but in recreating a specific viewing perspective previously held by someone else, this reenactment simultaneously foreshadows the closing sequence of *Sud*. Akerman adopts this recreated position of viewing and asks us to share it, exposing herself and us to the memories and feelings (exhaustion, regret, longing, hope, fear, relief...) that still cling to this space. Through the mise-en-scène of its opening, *Histoires d'Amérique* reenacts countless previous arrivals from centuries of American migration, layering other moments where this iconic point of ingress granting access to a promised city of hopes and dreams had moved similarly into view, beheld by other eyes. In such a way, the New York we watch slide into visibility on screen is posited as a site that, then as now, has offered a point of influx, a terrain of immigration, a land of disembarkation. Whilst very different from the mythology of beauty and danger that first drew Akerman to the landscapes of the Deep South, this other American mythology — similarly sustained through cultural representation — is equally potent.

Within Akerman's life and filmmaking, New York of course also has a further significance. New York is a prominent part of what we might think of as the filmmaker's own mythology, her own American story, that is also inscribed in the temporal layers of these opening images. This is, after all, the city that housed Mangolte, Mekas, Snow and Warhol, the city of the Anthology Film Archives, the city that provided the backdrop to many of the filmmaker's early works and first experiences of being away from Belgium. New York stands in Akerman's life and work as a home-away-from-home, as the adopted city of new, generative encounters, both personal and artistic. Commentators have rightly drawn attention to how the opening of *Histoires d'Amérique* reverses the closing shots of departure from New York seen in one of those films Akerman had made in her first American sojourn: 1976's decidedly better-known *News From Home* (see particularly Margulies 1996: 195). The opening sequence to *Histoires d'Amérique* immerses us in the point at which multiple pasts intersect, both the individual and the collective: through these layered images, Akerman simultaneously reenacts her own earlier arrival in this city and that of the countless others who, in other times and other circumstances, made the journey before her.

From within the multiple, variegated histories of migration that are evoked through the film's introductory reenactments, it is the experiences of East-European Jewish arrivals that directly concern Akerman in *Histoires d'Amérique*; it is through consideration of this diasporic cultural identity in its specificity that the possibility of inscribing a personal trajectory within a collective history, initially promised by the reenactive images of the film's opening, is questioned. As the film's prologue develops, dusk gives way to night and the blue-tinged images of the Upper Bay described above give way to more proximate images of the illuminated Manhattan shorefront. The towering city viewed from this closer, tilted perspective feels more solid, weightier than the city glimpsed previously through the haze. The scale of the buildings is amplified by their closeness; dwarfed by the sheer size of this imposing landmass, the waterborne movement of the camera suddenly feels more exposed, more precarious, conveying a sense of vulnerability. Against these nocturnal images, a chorus of whispered but urgent voices speaking in Yiddish swells, overlaid so as to form an indistinguishable body of sound. It is as if, in reenacting earlier arrivals, Akerman has awoken the multiple ghosts of Jewish history that haunt this shoreline. The accompanying sounds of Bruch's plaintive *Kol Nidrei*, played on cello by Sonia Wieder-Atherton, emphasise a sensation of hearing voices from a different time and place.

The voice of Akerman herself gradually detaches itself from amongst the mass of these accumulated voices. She speaks in hesitant English, amplifying the polyglossic contrasts already present in her film's title. Recounting a story marked by the rhythms and tonal qualities of fable, she evokes a cultural identity transmitted across time, space and generational divides:

> A rabbi always passed through a village to get to the forest, and there, at the foot of a tree — and it was always the same one — he began to pray and God heard him. His son too always passed through the same village to get to the forest, but he could not remember where the tree was, so he prayed at the foot of any old tree and God heard him. His grandson did not know where the tree was, nor the forest, so he went to pray in the village, and God heard him. His great-grandson did not know where the tree was, nor the forest, not even the village, but he still knew the words of the prayer, so he prayed in his house and God heard him. His great-grandson [sic] did not know where the tree, nor the forest, nor the village were, not even the words of the prayer, but he still knew the story, so he told it to his children and God heard him.

As Schmid suggests, '[t]he Jewish legend laments the loss of origins and the gradual transformation of rite into tale, of religious practice into family anecdote'. At the same time, however, the story asserts that 'transmission — keeping the story alive — not only allows diasporic Jews to remain in touch with their past but also with their God' (2010: 86–87). Akerman's spoken text narrates a story of loss, but one that nevertheless holds out the possibility of cultural resilience, of enduring connection in the face of spatial dispersal and the passage of time, and of the infinite power of the Jewish God.

Whilst entertaining the redemptive possibility of inter-generational transmission of memory and knowledge on a collective level, Akerman nevertheless denies herself this residual glimmer of hope. The prospect of resilient connection across generational divides that the story of the rabbi appeared to offer is immediately shaken by the personal addition that, after a short pause, Akerman brings to the tale: 'My own story is full of missing links, full of blanks, and I do not even have a child'. Whilst the story of the rabbi's mnemonic lineage foregrounded resilient cultural survival, Akerman explicitly presents herself as last and lost scion, as the recipient of incomplete transmissions from the past who finds herself similarly unable to transmit to the future. Through Akerman's addendum, collective identities of continuity and transmission give way to a personal identity of severance and interruption — to the same uprooted and disoriented 'histoire pleine de trous' that defined so much of her life.

Faced with this perforated story, *Histoires d'Amérique* resumes the difficult labour of *ressassement*, doggedly experimenting with modes of representation that might allow Akerman to work through these feelings of uprootedness and disorientation. Throughout the remainder of her film, Akerman retrieves memories that once belonged to those who came before her and whose journeys of arrival she had reenacted, reinventing them, reappropriating them, filtering them through fiction, as a means of bringing them back to life in the present, as a means of reconnecting, recathecting her own story with a wider collective history. Seeking an alternate kind of connection across history, she conjures the insistent, whispered voices that seemed to emerge spontaneously from the darkness of the New York harbour, channelling them into physical form and asking them to fill the gaps in her own autobiography with their ghostly bodies. As in those ambiguous moments from *D'Est* where the modern bodies Akerman filmed in the haunted landscapes of Eastern Europe seemed to provide the site at which memories of historical atrocity were drawn forth to be reenacted anew at the supposed end of history, so in *Histoires d'Amérique* do the ghostly bodies that Akerman summons from the spectral geographies of New York repeat something from a much earlier time in the present. Through the repetitions they perform, these figures drag with them generations of resuscitated diasporic experience that Akerman seeks to make her own.

The New York that Akerman depicts, once the shoreward journey begun in her film's prologue has concluded, unfurls as a curiously desolate landscape of vacant lots, abandoned and overgrown spaces, shadowy passageways. This is, as Bérénice Reynaud suggests, a decidedly phantom city (2004: 201). Into the darkness of the New York night there materialise a succession of unknown figures who often enter the frame silently from its wings before disappearing just as discreetly. They talk, sing, joke and deliver accounts of their experiences directly to camera, to their audience — to Akerman and to us. As they appear before us, we are left with the distinct impression of watching bodies from the past as they occupy a present time that is clearly not theirs. As the first of these figures describes arriving in America having fled nineteenth-century pogroms in Poland, enduring gnawing hunger and biting cold, a police car with flashing lights drives slowly past her, illuminating one side of her face in an artificial glow. Further tales of experiences accrued from centuries of migrant experience are accompanied by other modern vehicles, by thoroughly late-twentieth-century graffiti painted on nearby walls. *Histoires d'Amérique* assembles bodies from across histories of Jewish migration and brings them, anachronistically, into 1988.

Many of these figures announce themselves explicitly as ghosts. A young girl raped in an eastern pogrom confesses to feeling neither dead nor alive but in some spectral in-between state. As two elderly men quibble elsewhere in the film: 'Both of us are ghosts. | But from where? | I certainly do not know and I don't want to go back there!' The accounts delivered by such ghostly figures bear witness to the violence and traumas of history. Through them is woven a continuous thread of ethnic persecution — of pogroms, rampant antisemitism and the ever-present shadow of mass extermination. We encounter the man who is tormented by the thought of his parents' sudden death, scandalised by their nakedness and by the lack of anyone to say Kaddish, the prayer of mourning, for their souls. There is the man who meticulously plans his own suicide to coincide with the date of his parents' violent death, so incapacitated is he by the insistency of their memory. Cumulatively there emerges a presentation of Jewish cultural identity as a transgenerational history of suffering and loss: 'My great-grandparents were Jewish and they died in a pogrom. My grandparents were Jewish and they starved to death. My parents were Jewish and they died at Auschwitz. And I am a Jew, and for the moment I am doing very well, thank you!'

Both in direct accounts of genocidal violence and in the nostalgia for a distant homeland and for those left behind that is discernible in many of these tales, *Histoires d'Amérique* recognises the painful impossibility of making the past return identical and intact, of reversing often catastrophic loss; but the film also forces a shift in focus away from what has been irreparably lost to what remains despite the odds. These varied accounts represent, as Adam Roberts rightly suggests, the 'verbal survivals of European Jewish culture, cast up by diaspora on these shores, preserving certain forms of life in the shtetls and cities of the lost old world' (2019: 203). Importantly, the accounts delivered by these ghostly figures offer 'anecdotal proof that something has persisted, something that defines has survived, despite loss and trauma and death' (ibid.). For the most part these accounts are concerned with the ordinariness of everyday experience, albeit an everyday from a very different historical moment. Together they offer an oral history of the East-European Jewish diaspora in America which returns again and again to the poles of food, family and philosophy that were highlighted by the film's English subtitle. There are tales of borscht, chicken soup and veal cutlets; tales of wayward partners, parental hopes and expectations, of children who wish only to throw off the weight of ethnic origins

FIG. 1.6. and 1.7. *Histoires d'Amérique: Food, Family and Philosophy* (1988), Chantal Akerman © Mallia Films/Paradise Films/La Sept/La Bibliothèque publique d'information/Le Centre Pompidou/RTBF.

and become young Americans; tales of happiness, disappointment and responsibility. What strikes us more than anything as we watch the film is the sense of everyday humour that emerges from these stories. The film subjects us to a constant barrage of often deliberately clichéd jokes, anecdotes and quips that, as Akerman suggests in her *Autoportrait en cinéaste*, provide a means of laughing through the pain and of 'taming' the unbearable (2004: 166) — a form of humour that, without denying loss, holds out the possibility of forging other relationships with the past, ones that go some way to drowning out histories of suffering.

As Margulies writes, spoken in a weighty, recitative tone that functions as part of a deliberate strategy of theatrical distanciation, the stories voiced in *Histoires d'Amérique* betray their own nature as quotation, always pointing towards their pre-existence, towards their sources beyond the performers' mouths (1996: 195; see also

47–48). Listening to these stories, our impression is one of witnessing something borrowed from another time that is repeated in the present. The accounts of migrant experience heard in *Histoires d'Amérique* are indeed quotations, albeit ones filtered and distorted through Akerman's fictionalising imagination. Akerman has described how she and her friend Eric de Kuyper had long planned to adapt Isaac Bashevis Singer's Yiddish historical novels *The Manor* (1967) and *The Estate* (1969) for screen (2004: 46–48). This adaptation project was never completed, but the ambition of drawing upon Singer's depiction of the East-European Jewish diaspora in New York was nevertheless realised in *Histoires d'Amérique*. Supplementing Singer's texts with extracts from the archives of the self-help columns of the long-running American Yiddish language newspaper *The Jewish Forward*, Akerman distilled these quoted sources, borrowing the lived experiences they held.

Akerman's original sources included fictive and factual material; but as she reinvents them, the historical experiences of real-life New Yorkers from the past become indistinguishable from the fictional experiences of Singer's Jacoby family. The promise of renewed connection and cathexis offered by these remade memories is fragile, ephemeral, artificial even. The memories that Akerman borrows from other lives, translating from Yiddish to English, transplanting from past to present, transforming through fiction, can never fully be hers. The repetitive structure of the tales these figures tell, and of the film more broadly, again suggests endless, cyclical returns rather than the prospect of durable resolution or escape. The figures that populate Akerman's film bring with them a mass of questions, doubts, anxieties and traumas that, by the film's conclusion, remain unanswered, unassuaged. But, as Janet Bergstrom suggests, *Histoires d'Amérique* may well be the closest the filmmaker ever came to making her definitive 'film of rememoration' (2003: 98). Within the space of her *vérité imaginaire*, borrowed memories provide Akerman with a means of reinventing her own autobiography, of forging a partial connection between her life in the present and the past lives from which she had felt so painfully cut off. The figures that appear on our screen throughout *Histoires d'Amérique* reenact the fundamental gesture of telling one's story that had been elided from Akerman's own personal history. They replicate the orality that characterised the story of the rabbi and his descendants heard at the opening to the film, foregrounding instances of resilient verbal survival. They speak endlessly, volubly, seemingly compulsively, giving accounts of themselves and of their lives, describing their pleasures and pains, hopes and transgressions in equal measure. Assembled in this way, these reinvented memories offer a plausible account both of centuries of shared migrant experience, and of what the family history of Akerman, daughter of displaced Polish Jews, *might have been like*.

As they repeat their stories, the ghostly figures of *Histoires d'Amérique* respond to the first half of the personal addendum that Akerman grafted onto the fable of the rabbi, granting her a way of temporarily filling in the blanks and missing links in her story. The second half of this addendum is, however, left unaddressed, with the words *I don't even have a child* allowed to hang over Akerman's film. The anxiety that frequently attaches to childlessness in Akerman's work is perhaps best illustrated in *Les Rendez-vous d'Anna* in a conversation between Aurore Clément's protagonist and a friend of her mother: 'Quand les parents sont morts, et qu'on n'a pas d'enfant, qu'est-ce qu'il reste? Rien. Sinon, il reste les enfants' ['When the parents are dead and you don't have any children, what's left? Nothing. Otherwise, the children are left']. Whilst *Histoires d'Amérique* seeks continually to remedy the stalled transmission of memory and knowledge from earlier generations towards Akerman, it does not address this particular *Rien* and the anxieties attached to it surrounding onwards transmission and continued cultural survival into the future.

Commentators have highlighted the sometimes uneasy coexistence of Jewishness and queerness found in Akerman's work. *Histoires d'Amérique* indeed reflects how, as Lebow suggests, Akerman can simultaneously seek to reclaim a position as recipient for the transmission of Jewish tradition, restoring its continuity, whilst also knowingly presenting herself as a point of rupture within this same tradition through her childless status (2008: 125). That the uneasiness of this coexistence is not resolved by the conclusion to *Histoires d'Amérique* is reflective of what Albertine Fox identifies as a 'queer dynamic of slippage' at play in Akerman's work, as it explores the continually shifting intersection of competing facets of her identity (2019: 6). *Histoires d'Amérique* sees Akerman once again foreground a tension which she deliberately refrains from attempting to diffuse.

The ambivalent slipperiness of queer identities sustained by this refusal to resolve and disarm is explored more directly in my final case study — Akerman's television commission *Portrait d'une jeune fille de la fin des années 60 à Bruxelles*. Here the unresolved ambivalences of identity again go hand in hand with haunting forms of temporal indeterminacy. The spatialised forms of haunting encountered in this episode are very different from the unsettling reverberations of genocide and racist violence that we have seen previously; but as it evokes the discoveries and disappointments of youth, this work displays a similar preoccupation with the ghostly recurrence of experiences that refuse to be fully experienced as past. The autobiographical 'ghosts' encountered in this work, though more ambiguously marked than those of New York, also drag with them feelings from an earlier moment — both pleasurable and painful — as they stage their disruptive reappearance in the present.

My 68: *Portrait d'une jeune fille de la fin des années 60 à Bruxelles*

D'Est and *Histoires d'Amérique* attempted to stage surrogate forms of homecoming, respectively to an ancestral homeland that the filmmaker herself never knew and to an adopted home-away-from-home in which she temporarily settled. Both films announced simultaneously the impossibility of definitive return to a lost origin (*nóstos*) and the unquenchable yearning (*álgos*) to do so. *Portrait d'une jeune fille de la fin de années 60 à Bruxelles* (henceforth *Portrait d'une jeune fille*), first broadcast in the autumn of 1994 on the Franco-German television network ARTE, takes us to Akerman's actual home city — to the streets and enclosed spaces of the Belgian capital. Considered in isolation, the autobiographical inquiry Akerman develops in Brussels would appear to stretch stable categorisation as reenactment. But this work nevertheless replicates effects seen above. Approaching *Portrait d'une jeune fille* as the final link in the definitional chain I have traced through preceding case studies alerts us to points of similarity with clearer instances of reenactment and helps us to rethink exactly what it is doing.

As *Portrait d'une jeune fille* scrutinises urban landscapes still enveloped in the feelings, memories and associations of an earlier time — here, that of adolescence — Akerman again deliberately revives a lingering affective charge, channelling it into the present across bodies, exposing herself to it. In allowing herself once again to be haunted by ghostly bodies captured in repetition, Akerman explores anew how her identity is subject to the affective pressure of experiences that came before, experiences that are resuscitated but never entirely put to rest. Within these experiences, the intimate traumas of growing up queer coexist with inchoate but equally powerful sensations of joy, lust, love, desire, excitement, ecstasy. *Portrait d'une jeune fille* sees Akerman once again reinvent her autobiography inside the space of an imaginary truth, recreating those vital feelings and discoveries that shaped her life, investigating the influence they continued to exert.

As resumed aporetically in a contemporary interview, the titular *jeune fille* both is and isn't Akerman herself: 'Mon film n'est pas autobiographique mais les émotions qu'on y trouvera m'appartiennent...' [My film isn't autobiographical, but the emotions found there belong to me...] (Akerman quoted in Honorez 1993). *Portrait d'une jeune fille* presents a day in the life of fifteen-year-old Michèle (played by Circé Lethem, daughter of Belgian experimental filmmaker Roland Lethem, in her first major screen role) as she navigates the pavements, cafés, cinemas, shops and apartments of a Brussels which an opening intertitle situates in April 1968. Michèle dominates the screen for the duration of *Portrait d'une jeune fille*; she is held for the most part in a shallow depth of field, largely either in lateral tracking shots or in frontal and rear close-up, in a way that allows Akerman to foreground her emotional responses to the events of the day. Michèle steals money from her sedately bourgeois father before determining never to return to school, marking the definitive abandonment of her studies with the jubilant act of tearing up her school record card and scattering the pieces to the wind. Having apparently turned her back on scholarly conformity, Michèle wanders the streets whilst nevertheless returning regularly to the school gates to keep appointments with her best friend Danielle. In a cinema she meets Paul, a twenty-year-old French army deserter with whom she discusses love, sex and the ubiquity of human suffering at length, before breaking into an apartment and losing her virginity. In the film's finale, Michèle and Danielle attend an erotically charged party where the two dance and flirt, before Michèle effectively gifts Paul to her friend, walking off into the night, alone and in tears.

Portrait d'une jeune fille is the third episode of the anthology television series *Tous les garçons et les filles de leur âge* [*All the Boys and Girls of Their Age*] (1994). This influential series comprised episodes from nine directors commissioned to offer autobiographically inspired reflections on the period of their own adolescence, within a timespan ranging from the early 1960s to the beginning of the 1990s. Akerman's contribution to the series sits alongside episodes from André Téchiné,

Claire Denis, Olivier Assayas, Laurence Ferreira Barbosa, Patricia Mazuy, Émilie Deleuze, Cédric Kahn and Olivier Dahan. Constraints for the series commission included the use of contemporary music and the inclusion of a party scene. The title chosen for the series clearly borrows from the eponymous opening track of Françoise Hardy's 1962 debut album, foregrounding love, longing, loneliness and the various pains and anxieties of youth as the prevailing thematic concerns that would come to define the series' various instalments. This musical evocation combined with the remit of the series more broadly and the content of certain other contributions would initially seem to place Akerman's episode firmly under the sign of adolescent nostalgia.

A yet more conspicuous form of nostalgia is seemingly announced by the positioning of Akerman's episode in 1968. This particular year, and the waves of political contestation that it brought, of course represents a very specific site of cultural-historical nostalgia, particularly for the European and American left, with virulent debates having continued in the decades since the *événements* over how far the movement's promises have been fulfilled or betrayed. 1968 and the nostalgia which often clings to it has provided conspicuously fertile terrain for various forms of reenactment in the domain of visual art. We see this, for instance, in *Farbtest II, Die Rote Fahne [Colour Test II, The Red Flag]*, Felix Gmelin's 2002 remake of Gerd Conradt's 1968 footage of students running through the streets of West Berlin waving a red flag. Gmelin's father had been one of the original film's flagbearers and this remake participates in a broader reflection threaded throughout the artist's work on how revolutionary dreams can find themselves dashed or co-opted. Mark Tribe's *The Port Huron Project* (2006–08) staged in-situ reenactments of protest speeches from the New Left movements of the Vietnam era, in a series that has been criticised for fetishising historical junctures as a way of avoiding addressing the challenges of the present, and for thus lapsing into a immobilising form of 'New-Left-wing melancholy' (Sarlin 2009; Schneider 2011: 179–86). Viewed from such a perspective, the positioning of *Portrait d'une jeune fille* in the *April* of 1968, in the 'beforeness' of the *avant-mai*, might appear to indicate a desire to return to an anticipatory moment when the radical potential of this contestatory movement was still intact, before the varied political disappointments, revisionist reframings and conservative counterrevolutions seen in subsequent decades.

Certainly at first glance, *Portrait d'une jeune fille* would appear to corroborate this reading, taking pains to reconstruct a credible version of this specific historical moment, to restore this lost past to the present along with the vanished optimism it still allowed. The consistency of what we see and hear with this clearly marked temporal frame, a matter of weeks before the international social and political upheaval of the following month, is repeatedly foregrounded. *Portrait d'une jeune fille* contains frequent contextual markers that corroborate the accuracy of Akerman's temporal reconstruction, the veracity of her historical mimesis. As Michèle and Paul break into an empty apartment and sleep together, for instance, it is Leonard Cohen's 1967 song 'Suzanne', stolen from a record shop earlier in the episode, that provides the musical soundtrack. Walking together in the streets of Brussels,

Michèle describes her recent experiences of an anti-Vietnam War protest and the feverish exhilaration of losing oneself in a moment of collective fervour. Entering a Brussels bookshop, Michèle quotes memorised lines from Søren Kierkegaard on the inevitability of human suffering and professes a love for Sartrean notions of incommunicability.

Elsewhere, the instances of sexual initiation, generational conflict and rejection of bourgeois respectability and comfort depicted in *Portrait d'une jeune fille* inevitably lead us to associations with a broader socio-historical context, providing further corroborating markers. The respectful *vouvoiement* that marks Paul and Michèle's early conversations also feels decidedly of another era. From their verbose dialogues there frequently emerges an impression of ambient cultural inertia and suffocation, of existence having stalled, of the impossibility of resolution and decision. The pair express pity for the unquestioning conformity they diagnose in the lives that surround them and confess to a utopian longing for a wave of transformation that, they feel, seems destined to erupt at any moment, bringing with it the promise of absolute freedom and equality in social, sexual and economic terms:

> — Tu sens pas toi que quelque chose va arriver?
> — Ça peut pas rester comme ça.
> — Non, faut que ça pète, faut que ça pète.
> — On étouffe.
> — Quand ça aura pété, tout sera différent. On sera plus obligé de se laisser tripoter ni de se marier ni de bien s'habiller.
> — Ni d'aller à l'armée.
> — Et il y aura plus d'injustice sur la terre.
> — Ni de pauvres ni de riches.
>
> [— Don't you feel like something's gonna happen?
> — It can't stay as it is.
> — No, it has to blow up, has to blow up.
> — We're suffocating.
> — When things have blown up, it'll all be different. We won't have to let ourselves be groped or get married or dress nicely anymore.
> — Or join the army.
> — And there'll be no more injustice in the world.
> — And no rich and no poor.]

So far, so 1968. Viewed in these terms, *Portrait d'une jeune fille* offers a convincing reconstruction of the revolutionary atmospheres of a particular moment before the watershed of May and of the (untainted) hopes this moment then sustained. In recreating this specific point in time, *Portrait d'une jeune fille* would appear motivated by a desire to resist historical loss, to restore possibility to the past and to return to an April 1968 in which the conviction that *quelque chose va arriver* remained a potential waiting to be explosively activated.

I want to argue, however, that something else is going on; that *Portrait d'une jeune fille* is not primarily concerned with reversing this specific form of loss and with restoring possibility to a vanished historical moment — that ultimately it is not a film *about* May 68 and its contested afterlives. As soon as we entertain this possibility, we begin to notice elements that draw the film into proximity with

Fig. 1.8. and 1.9. *Portrait d'une jeune fille de la fin des années 60 à Bruxelles* (1993), Chantal Akerman © IMA/La Sept-Arte/SFP Productions/Sony Music Entertainment France SA.

the autobiographical reenactments seen elsewhere in this chapter. These elements, initially registering as fleeting *errors* in the reconstruction of a past historical moment, lead us to see in *Portrait d'une jeune fille* a decidedly more complex work than is perhaps immediately apparent. These errors entail points of temporal dissonance, discordant instances of anachronistic inconsistency, which seem to fight against time, to interrupt its smooth running, blurring the stability of its coordinates and the direction of its flow. These elements of temporal ambiguity gradually unsettle what might otherwise seem to be a relatively straightforward example of autobiographically inspired narrative fiction of a kind found elsewhere in the other episodes of *Tous les garçons et les filles de leur âge*, turning the work into something much stranger, much ghostlier.

As Paul and Michèle walk and talk through the streets of Brussels, the cars that drive past them seem, for instance, not of the late-1960s but of the early-1990s.

As the pair cross a busy section of road, it is modern advertising billboards which provide the urban backdrop. Elsewhere, when Michèle surreptitiously slips an otherwise era-appropriate vinyl copy of Leonard Cohen's *Songs of Leonard Cohen* (1967) into her satchel, Paul holds in his hands not another vinyl record but a thoroughly modern CD, with the display cases in the background of the record shop filled with further examples of such apparently anachronistic formats. As Michèle runs past a sales assistant to use the bathroom at the rear of an electrical goods shop, she enters into a space filled with row upon row of colour televisions, with an incongruous computer placed prominently on the cash desk.

The anachronistic elements we encounter throughout *Portrait d'une jeune fille* initially appear to represent momentary failures of historical authenticity which stage the irruption of a very different temporal moment into a reconstructed 1968 — what Elizabeth Freeman would call the '*punctum* of the present' (2010: 72). And yet, the more we become attuned to these points of anachronism, the more we begin to realise that the temporal slippage we witness is, in fact, moving in the other direction. What we observe in *Portrait d'une jeune fille* is not the sudden appearance of the cars, CDs and computers of 1993 into 1968, but rather the protracted, almost ghostly re-emergence of bodies from an earlier moment into the present. In sequences filmed in Brussels shopping streets that clearly belong to the early-1990s, modern bystanders can be seen to stop and watch as Paul and Michèle walk amongst them, looking and even pointing towards the actors and the camera that captures them. Recalling Jean-Luc Godard's *A bout de souffle* [*Breathless*] (1962) right down to the visibly bemused onlookers and Jean Seberg's breton jumper, these are, in certain ways, also the ghosts of film history. On the one hand, we can see in the filmed reactions of Brussels bystanders Akerman's rejection of a certain kind of representational verisimilitude, as she refuses to sustain the illusion of a self-contained filmic reality, choosing instead to foreground and proclaim its artifice, the material circumstances of its production. But at the same time, as we watch *Portrait d'une jeune fille* it is also as if the bystanders who stop in their tracks to stare in surprise at these revenant figures for whom it is seemingly still the 1960s are reacting to their temporal incongruity, their belated reappearance in a later time that is not their own to inhabit. *Portrait d'une jeune fille* is not an attempt to definitively regain a lost moment of past reality and to restore it in sameness to the present. It seeks instead to revive and amplify the feelings, discoveries and influences this past moment once housed and to explore the disorienting, haunting persistence of affect across time.

Within this persistence, there is a queerness to the feelings these revenant bodies bring back with them. Scholarly responses to *Portrait d'une jeune fille* — a film in which Michèle's sexual relationship with Paul coexists with her perhaps more intense, though unconfessed, erotic longing for her friend Danielle — have identified in it an illustration of the extent to which characters in Akerman's films eschew any ready assimilation into stable sexual identities, and of how her filmmaking more broadly resists alignment with specific identity politics (a resistance also reflected in the filmmaker's well-known rejection of certain distribution and exhibition

FIG. 1.10. *Portrait d'une jeune fille de la fin des années 60 à Bruxelles* (1993), Chantal Akerman © IMA/La Sept-Arte/SFP Productions/Sony Music Entertainment France SA.

circuits for her work). Patricia White exemplifies this view when she suggests that *Portrait d'une jeune fille* delivers a compelling study of 'girlhood self-recognition', but not one that can be adequately or uncomplicatedly described as a coming-out narrative (2008: 411). Refusing the cathartic resolution or definitive closure that might be expected from more conventional exemplars of the teenage coming-out genre, the self-recognition of *Portrait d'une jeune fille* remains instead ongoing and open-ended, sustaining sexual identities that appear mobile and 'nomadic' (Schmid 2010: 141; see also Mayne 2003: 150). As she investigates a form of autobiographical haunting, leading bodies from the past to reemerge in the present, Akerman revives the sensations — both pleasurable and painful — of a moment of queer awakening.

The mix of pleasures and pains that Akerman draws across time in *Portrait d'une jeune fille* is well illustrated in the dance sequence from the party scene that occurs towards the episode's conclusion. From the outset of this extended, single-shot scene, Akerman's camera places us at the centre of a rapidly moving circle-dance as teenagers cycle round arm-in-arm to the rhythms of Trini Lopez's 'La Bamba' (1963). The camera moves to track the lateral movements of Michèle, her gaze fixed resiliently, lustfully even, on Danielle at the centre of the circle. Michèle has to choose her dance partner and the camera moves in on her searching face as she seeks out her friend; Akerman withholds the reverse shot meaning that Michèle's smiling gaze feels as if it is cast directly towards the spectator. Michèle looks outwards beyond a cinematic fourth wall, thrusting the spectator into the position of gazed-at love-object, asking them to become complicit in this projected desire. She twice choses Danielle as her dance partner, looking into her friend's eyes and smiling bashfully towards her, apparently uninterested by the other bodies in the room. These are images of pure excitement and happiness. As the assembled party divides into couples for slower, more intimate dancing, the camera closes in once more on Michèle's face, capturing her now pained expression and the intensity of her stare as her eyes follow Danielle dancing with a boy outside the frame; her eyes dart occasionally up and down, as if tracing the contours of a desired body that the spectator now cannot see. In this instance, instead of eliciting complicity, the absence of a reverse point-of-view shot (which here would have revealed the dancing couple watched so intensely by Michèle) now constructs a 'point-of-view of exclusion' as the camera lingers on the protagonist standing alone at the centre of the room (White 2008: 418). The duration and arrangement of Akerman's shot confronts us with the intensity of Michèle's desire and the heady mix of love, lust, excitement, happiness, jealousy and loneliness that sustain it.

It is from this perspective that, I would suggest, we are to interpret the setting of *Portrait d'une jeune fille* in the *April* of 1968. This is a positioning in time that inevitably announces its *beforeness*, directing our attention expectantly forwards to something that promises to be just around the corner, but that never fully arrives. In the context of this expectant beforeness, it is of course far from incidental that 1968 also saw Akerman's first experience of filmmaking with the incendiary *Saute ma ville* [*Blow up My Town*], a work that put Michèle's exhortation *faut que ça pète* into practice. The symbolic historical moment of 1968, marked by expectancy and anticipation, intersects with a personal history through which Akerman evokes the pleasures and pains of a moment of queer self-discovery that is marked as emergent, one to which definitive, cathartic resolution is also withheld. *Portrait d'une jeune fille* revives a prior moment of incipient self-recognition, not to restore possibility to that moment but to reignite the mixed feelings that this moment supported. The feelings here resuscitated are sometimes ones of optimistic joy, such as those sparked by a snatched opportunity for fleeting contact with an unconfessed love. But, as perhaps best illustrated by closing images of Michèle walking tearfully into the post-party night, alone, they are also ones of lonely suffering. As she makes bodies from the past reappear in the present, Akerman seeks to keep these feelings alive without working through or exorcising them, without letting them fully solidify. *Portrait d'une jeune fille* offers an affectively charged portrait of an identity at a moment of becoming — neither entirely past nor present, before nor after, in nor out (Mayne 2003: 150).

Akerman's work is concerned with how the experiences of the past continue to make themselves felt long after they are ostensibly over; with how we find ourselves continually called back through memory to certain moments of transition and self-discovery, where new versions of ourselves come partially into focus; with how certain spaces seem to retain the reverberations of these feelings within them in atmospheres of memory and affect. *Portrait d'une jeune fille* compels us to think about the pull, the pressure, that the foundational experiences of the past that we never fully leave behind — in all of their pleasures and in all of their pains — continue to exert on the present. It confronts us with how, looking backwards from the present, we endlessly reimagine those same past experiences, ultimately with how we can be haunted by earlier versions of ourselves. This autobiographical recollection, of the discoveries and discomforts of queer adolescence in the Belgian capital at the end of the 1960s, explores how we ceaselessly return to moments of awakening and self-recognition — how these moments become the magnetic poles around which memory develops and repeats, how these moments condition the ongoing construction of selves.

What we see in *Portrait d'une jeune fille* is not readily identifiable as an instance of reenactment in the same way that, say, the profoundly unsettling closing sequence of *Sud* decidedly is. And yet, as it returns to and repeats something from an earlier time, exploring the memories that linger in certain spaces, awakening and amplifying past feelings in the present whilst refusing to lay them to rest, questioning what the continuing significance of these feelings might be for Akerman's life and identity, *Portrait d'une jeune fille* nevertheless fits within the definitional chain I have traced through this chapter. By concluding the series of dialogues I have drawn out over preceding pages between four very different films with a piece that, by itself, appears much more ambiguously defined, I am also encouraging an opening outwards from my chosen examples of reenactment to the rest of Akerman's art and to further potential points of resonance in what might at first glance appear entirely unconnected films. Seeking these points of resonance helps us to begin to see the extent to which the varied instances of reenactment I have identified in this chapter exist as part of a much broader logic of repetition and return that permeates Akerman's work. This is a logic that questions the relation of the past to the present and hence to the uncertain futures that appear on the horizon; it directs our attention to that which crosses these temporal divisions and to the shifting pleasures and pains that are aroused by such crossings.

As I move into my next chapter, I operate another opening outwards — one that, in moving away from Akerman, foregrounds the influence she continues to exert over other artists. I turn first to Vincent Dieutre, whose filmmaking has been profoundly shaped by Akerman and who engages in sustained dialogue with her work. As we will see, Dieutre's autobiographical uses of reenactment both knowingly replicate effects seen above and move in very different directions. My analysis of Dieutre thinks further about the *queerness* of reenactment, showing how Dieutre mobilises this queerness more explicitly than Akerman as a disruptive force to unsettle and bend categories of time, being and knowledge. Dieutre's work, like Akerman's, displays what Carla Freccero presents as a queer openness to haunting that seeks to do justice to the ways in which we find ourselves 'impelled by demands that confound the temporalities we call past, present and future' (2011: 22). Through his own reenactments, Dieutre will mourn for very different losses from those explored above and will do so with very different results.

Notes to Chapter 1

1. <http://www.thebyrdfoundation.org/> [accessed 3 March 2021].
2. From *Blessing the Boats: New and Selected Poems 1988–2000* (Rochester, NY: BOA Editions, 2000).

CHAPTER 2

❖

Vincent Dieutre — Queerness

Introduction — The Queerness of the Copy

The filmmaking practice of French director Vincent Dieutre is one that often explicitly acknowledges its influences. This is particularly apparent in relation to Akerman, without whose decisive influence the work of Dieutre would today be fundamentally different. Writing in a text contributed to *Chantal Akerman: Autoportrait en cinéaste* where he describes his stunned reaction at watching *Sud* at its Cannes festival premiere, Dieutre presents her as an artist who, on numerous occasions, has led him to reassess the meaning of cinema and his relationship to it (2004: 211). A particularly clear acknowledgement of Akerman's importance to Dieutre is found in Fleur Albert's 2013 documentary study *Vincent Dieutre, la chambre et le monde* [*Vincent Dieutre: The Room and The World*]. Amongst images of Dieutre at work and interviews where he attempts to schematise the guiding motivations and aspirations of his filmmaking practice, one sequence stands out in particular for the unambiguous illustration it gives of the extent to which the filmmaker consciously positions his own work in proximity to Akerman.

We accompany Dieutre as he journeys to Brussels and makes a deliberate pilgrimage to number 23 Quai du Commerce in the north of the city — perhaps still the most famous address in the cinematic history of the Belgian capital. The filmmaker appears visibly disappointed to find no mention of any Dielman family on the entranceway's intercom, but he seems interested to see that one of the building's apartments is for sale, apparently delighted at the prospect that it could be the same apartment that, in Akerman's breakthrough film, once housed the titular Jeanne. Filmed by Albert, Dieutre enthusiastically recounts watching *Jeanne Dielman, 23 Quai du Commerce, 1080 Bruxelles* (1975) as a teenager at the film's release in France, presenting it as the first of many encounters with the work of a filmmaker who would forever change his conception of what it is possible to do with cinema.

The influence of Akerman is felt throughout Dieutre's cinema; as is illustrated particularly clearly in the sequence described above, this is an influence that Dieutre often proudly foregrounds. To view many of Dieutre's films is indeed to be reliably confronted with a series of more or less explicit quotations from the work of Akerman. Watching a film such as 2003's *Mon voyage d'hiver* [*My Winter's Journey*], an autobiographical travelogue of Dieutre's own eastwards journey across snow-clad landscapes, for instance, we encounter static images of apartment interiors and exterior tracking shots that, in their framing and composition, directly recall what we saw of Akerman's *D'Est* in the previous chapter, as well as lateral pans amongst rows of squat, grey houses that recall the German industrial towns of *Les Rendez-vous d'Anna*. Elsewhere, the closing sequence of Dieutre's 2001 short *Bonne Nouvelle*, an almost ethnographic study of the titular Paris neighbourhood, concludes with a circular pan of the rooftops of the French capital that cannot but recall the 360–degree survey of the Brussels skyline found at the ending of Akerman's *Les Années 80* [*The Eighties*] (1983). In the varied films Dieutre has made over the past three decades, the influence of Akerman often coexists with that taken from a great number of other artists; but it remains always discernible. The many such deliberate nods and evocations that fill Dieutre's work consistently register as profoundly devoted, even reverent gestures of tribute and homage to a filmmaker who fundamentally shaped his own art.

A film by Akerman that is frequently evoked in Dieutre's work is one that he first viewed shortly after the initiatory encounter with the inhabitant of 23 Quai du Commerce, described above. Writing elsewhere in his contribution to Akerman's *Autoportrait en cinéaste*, Dieutre acknowledges the impact of her 1976 film *News From Home* on his life and work: 'News From Home m'avait, à seize ans, fait entrer en cinéma' [*News From Home* had, at the age of sixteen, brought me into cinema] (ibid.). The influence of *News From Home*'s distinctive layering of directorial voice and urban imagery is felt in much of Dieutre's work, no more abundantly so than in his 2001 short *Entering Indifference*, a film I read as a self-conscious remake of Akerman's original. The images of Dieutre's film are unmistakably similar to those produced twenty-five years earlier by Akerman: *Entering Indifference* contains the same seemingly random succession of pavements, crossroads, alleyways, subway carriages and anonymous interiors; the same continual alternation between steady, lateral pans of roads and building façades and extended, static takes of an urban environment in which a reverse shot is durably withheld. As was also the case in *News From Home*, these urban landscapes are overlaid throughout the film with the disembodied voice of the filmmaker. Through the careful replication of such elements, Dieutre's copy announces its similarity to Akerman's original.

Throughout *Entering Indifference*, this sense of similarity is nevertheless tempered by multiple points of difference: as Dieutre remakes Akerman's film, he also reinvents and reframes it on his own terms, carrying the filmic inheritance he has taken from his predecessor's work in other directions. The urban landscapes that Dieutre's camera scrutinises are, for instance, no longer of New York but of Chicago. The aesthetic of Dieutre's film seems markedly more impure, almost febrile, as blurry echoes of advertising logos and fragments of television programmes irrupt into the carefully framed urban imagery, contaminating the depiction of these wintery mid-western cityscapes. This footage is at moments digitally manipulated, with city-centre traffic appearing blurred and distorted, visibly ghosted, as one temporal moment bleeds into another. In perhaps the most pronounced shift, instead of reading letters penned by a maternal hand far across the Atlantic Ocean, Dieutre reads his own letters addressed to an unnamed and absent male lover. In the 'News *to* Home' of *Entering Indifference* as elsewhere in Dieutre's filmmaking, the central relationship through which all else is filtered and interrogated, the gateway between public and private lives, is no longer the mother-daughter dyad that conditioned so much of Akerman's work, but rather that of the gay couple. The confessional voice-overs recounting sex, desire and hard drug use in saunas, gay bars and budget hotel rooms that accompany Dieutre's urban images displace the mundane but undeniably intimate quality of Nelly Akerman's original missives. *Entering Indifference* replaces the prosaic refrain of money, shoes, family gatherings and business problems that rhythmed the letters of *News from Home* with a stylised, literary tone of autobiographical expression through which the filmmaker seeks echoes of his own feelings of alienation and emotional disconnection in the freezing American landscapes that surround him.

In constructing a deliberately imperfect remake of Akerman's *News From Home*, Dieutre's *Entering Indifference* confronts us with what, following Rebecca Schneider, we might think of as the *queerness of the copy* — a strange, often uncanny quality of being almost the same but not quite as something that has come before. As varied acts of repetition scramble the coordinates allowing us to say with certainty when and where (or even *who*) we are, this is a queerness that, as I have suggested, is found in so many examples of reenactment. It is a queerness that — as ambiguous dialogues are sustained between originals and their copies around stakes of authenticity, authority, power and desire — has often been brought out with particular force in a great deal of contemporary reenactment art. We will find this queerness in the varied instances of autobiographical reenactment considered in this chapter, instances in which Dieutre creates further imperfect copies of earlier originals and, as above, uses these queer copies to explore aspects of his own autobiography, endlessly reinventing himself and his experiences as he does so. In its refusal of definitive, fixed decidability, the queerness of Dieutre's copies shares something with what we saw in Akerman toward the end of the previous chapter; but in Dieutre's work, this queerness is decidedly more conspicuous, more consistently foregrounded as a disruptive political force.

It is indeed in the shifting, irresolvable tension between original and copy, sameness and difference sustained by Dieutre's autobiographical reenactments that other forms of queering are amplified in his filmmaking. As they announce both what draws them into proximity with the originals they replicate but also what separates them, the reenactments I identify in what follows encourage forms of temporal bending and seepage where dialogues and exchanges are thrown open between past and present. Through the unruly mobility of identification, affect and desire, they repeatedly unsettle the solidity and boundedness of identity, forcing the borders marking one life as fully distinct from another life to become porous, offering a hybrid, composite mode of autobiographical expression. In assembling disparate, conflictual elements, they make truth and fiction, reality and imagination, the authentic and the forgery commingle and merge. They allow Dieutre to investigate the felt realities of queer lived experience, questioning how these realities might be represented and communicated. As Didier Roth-Bettoni writes in a survey of representations of homosexuality in contemporary French film, framing Dieutre alongside the work of other experimental queer filmmakers such as Alain Guiraudie or the duo Pierre Trividic and Patrick Mario Bernard: 'ce qui distingue ces œuvres d'autres plus grand public, c'est leur radicalité, leur étrangeté unique: que celle-ci soit thématique et/ou formelle' [what distinguishes these works from other, more mainstream ones is their radicalness, their unique strangeness, whether this be thematic and/or formal] (2007: 615). This is a radical strangeness, both formal and thematic, that, as we will repeatedly see, is particularly apparent in the queer copies that Dieutre builds through reenactment in this chapter.

In the case studies considered over the following sections, Dieutre's use of reenactment will assume a variety of forms, sometimes very different from those uses seen in the previous chapter. I begin by analysing a film (*Leçons de ténèbres* [*Tenebrae Lessons*]) in which Dieutre uses his own body and its intimate contacts with the bodies of others to restage canonical paintings. These imperfect artistic copies allow Dieutre to access the emotional intensity of past art in the present, whilst consciously positioning himself in relation to queer histories and histories of queer representation. Identifying in this engagement with earlier images a broader tendency in Dieutre's filmmaking, I move on to consider a pairing of works — *EA2 (Deuxième exercice d'admiration: Jean Eustache)* [*EA2 (Second Exercise in Admiration: Jean Eustache)*] and *EA4 Viaggio nella dopo-storia (Quatrième exercice d'admiration: Roberto Rossellini)* [*EA4 Journey into Post-History (Fourth Exercise in Admiration: Roberto Rossellini)*] — in which he reenacts sequences from films by other directors whom he admires, reworking his own autobiography through fictions borrowed from the history of cinema. Through the tension these reenactments sustain between sameness and difference, copy and original, his life and the lives of others, Dieutre begins to work through his own feelings and, in particular, to mourn the loss of a relationship — a process in which the final case study also participates.

I close this chapter by considering a film (*Jaurès*) in which Dieutre mobilises a form of autobiographical reenactment that is seemingly far removed from his various visual cultural remakes — one that alerts us once again to the decisive influence that Akerman continues to exert over his work. Whilst, in this extended case study, experience is no longer filtered through pre-existing artworks, it is still subject to the same tensions of fact and fiction, sameness and difference, real and unreal, the authentic and the forgery, in a way that leads us to again see in it an exploration of the copy's strange queerness. Through the affectively charged reenactment that propels this final queer copy, Dieutre poses a number of deeply political questions: in particular, he asks us to reflect on what counts as a valid form of autobiographical proof, experimenting with alternate forms of evidence for experiences that do not always leave a visible trace behind, before asking us to join him as he imagines a transformative, sometimes ethically uncomfortable, politics of empathy that might connect separate lives across categories of difference.

As they imperfectly revive something from the past in the present, often seeking a way of dealing with varied experiences of loss, Dieutre's queer copies again shuttle between reenactment's competing pleasures and pains. But from within the ambiguous space of undecidability thrown open by these copies where something created in the present can be simultaneously the same as and radically different from what came before, Dieutre sometimes attains a greater degree of working-through, even of partial release, than was possible in Akerman's ever-renewed cycles of melancholic *ressassement*. In such a way, as he explores through reenactment his relationship with what appears to have been lost, Dieutre gains access to perhaps slightly more durable (if still precarious and ambivalent) pleasures than those seen in the previous chapter. Through the queerness of the copies that it builds, Dieutre's use of reenactment does not seek to fully regain the past or to restore a lost original unaltered to the present, but rather strives to tease out often disorienting encounters across time that can elicit powerful affective responses, in him and in us.

Feeling Baroque: *Leçons de ténèbres*

A form of cultural production that explicitly announces itself as non-original, as deliberately derivative and imitative, that loudly confesses its borrowings as well as the various 'mistakes' and 'faults' that these borrowings introduce, directs a potent challenge to notions of artistic value anchored in standards of uniqueness, novelty or purity. To suggest, through repetition, that a work of art can come into being again or in duplicate, appearing sometimes very differently with each iteration, or that the meaning of an artwork is not fixed and finished but rather subject to belated modification and to ongoing conversation with other later creators is to challenge understandings of art as the singular, unique, unrepeatable product of creative genius. Within a system of marketisation that depends upon unambiguous and verifiable attribution, to reproduce and lay claim to the work of another artist is to introduce the threat of the forgery, the hoax, the problematic authentication. To revisit works from the past in the present in this way is to unleash the threat of what Schneider refers to as the 'imposter status' of the copy, the double, the mimetic, the second, the surrogate, the feminine, or the queer — a status viewed as predatory, corrupting, perverting, that throws ingrained cultural anxieties around ideality and originality into overdrive (2011: 30).

These challenges have been deployed extensively by a wide range of contemporary artists who, through modes of parody, pastiche, de- and reconstruction or radical recontextualisation, have chosen to recreate works from earlier points in histories of visual culture, with such strategies appearing particularly prominently within queer and feminist practices. Certain of these artistic reenactments seek to interrogate the dominant codes of visual representation, as is the case, for instance, in the drag film remakes of artists such as Ming Wong and Brice Dellsperger, or in the unsettling of patriarchal authority staged in the photographic copies of artists such as Sherie Levine. Elsewhere, artists such as Trajal Harrell, Wu Tsang and duo Pauline Boudry and Renate Lorenz have used forms of reenactment to break down heteronormative historical narratives and categorisations, making space for those who might have been forcibly excluded or defined against their will; to imagine counterfactual histories that stage impossible encounters and redeem missed opportunities; to excavate (even rescue) lost or illegible moments of historical queerness and make them available for recognition to the present; to forge a queer kind of filiation and lineage across time and generations; or to explore how the queer art of *then* might still speak to the needs and desires of *now*. The complex space of inquiry and experimentation that is accessed by such uses of reenactment is one in which the case study I consider in this section actively participates.

Dieutre's 1999 film *Leçons de ténèbres* remains one of his best-known works. This is in no small part due to the prominence afforded by its inclusion in *Cinema and Sensation: French Film and the Art of Transgression* (2007), Martine Beugnet's influential post-phenomenological study of haptic modes of film spectatorship. A still taken from one of the film's sequences of artistic reenactment that I go on to analyse indeed features on the front cover of Beugnet's text. *Leçons de ténèbres* offers a travelogue of the filmmaker's journey across the nocturnal landscapes of Europe, from Utrecht in the Netherlands to the Italian cities of Naples and Rome. Dieutre appears on screen throughout the film, wandering through these three cities at night, drinking in bars and clubs and cruising in darkened parks. He is accompanied for much of this journey by his on-screen partner, Tadeusz, who, he suggests, is increasingly suffering from the symptoms of the AIDS virus and whose fragile state of health is a source of tension and anxiety within the couple. As it describes the couple's successive states of closeness and estrangement, the second-person address of Dieutre's repeated voice-overs draws us within the autobiographical account he delivers, asking us to share in the conflicted emotions he narrates. Here as elsewhere in Dieutre's work, this couple provides the privileged context for interrogating the changing realities of affective experience; but as will also be the case in the other case studies explored in this chapter, under the distorting pressure of autobiographical fictions that allow Dieutre to continually refashion himself and his interactions with others, we are left permanently unsure of exactly how directly the couple depicted on screen in *Leçons de ténèbres* might correspond to an off-screen relationship between two real men.

The ambiguous distortions of fiction cohabit with other of the film's recurrent elements of instability and conflict. *Leçons de ténèbres* provides a particularly clear illustration of the taste for formal impurity and hybridity that is found throughout so much of Dieutre's filmmaking. Writing in his 2003 article 'Abécédaire pour un tiers-cinéma' [A-Z For a Third-Cinema] — a text that can be read both as a manifesto for his own creative practice and as a call to arms for other artists to join him in the self-consciously fragile and minor counter-cinema he seeks to offer — Dieutre advocates an approach to filmmaking that assembles radically disparate elements, refusing to smooth out their contrasts but using them to create striking new effects: 'jeu de matière, de frottements, d'impureté, d'installation des possibles' [interplay of materials, of frictions, of impurities, of the introduction of possibilities] (2003: 81). Within the decidedly heterogeneous montage of *Leçons de ténèbres*, depictions of Dieutre alone or with his on-screen partner alternate with instances of reenactment, with filmed interviews, with images of canonical paintings and sculptures, with explorations of interior and exterior space. Dieutre deliberately amplifies the contrasts between the different film formats he combines or between the cinematic and non-cinematic forms that jostle for space in his film, and allows visual and sonic elements to fight against each other, to enter into overt contradiction, maximising the generative frictions created by often jarring juxtapositions.

The journey Dieutre traces from Utrecht to Naples to Rome is one that is undertaken in the hope of affective renewal and in anticipation of the restoration of loss — a loss that is foregrounded right from the film's title. 'Leçons de ténèbres' is a genre of French baroque music composed around the biblical Book of Lamentations. Extracts from the *Tenebrae* arrangements of prominent baroque composers such as François Couperin are indeed heard at points throughout Dieutre's film. As an epigraphic intertitle informs us at the film's opening, these musical compositions were traditionally performed during liturgical services held to mark Catholic Holy Week. The distinguishing characteristic of these services was the gradual extinguishing of the flames of a candelabra, culminating in sustained and total darkness. This is a darkness that is matched in Dieutre's film by that which clings to the nocturnal cityscapes the filmmaker traverses. Throughout *Leçons de ténèbres*, this ceremonial extinguishing of the light is used to allegorise an increasing sense of affective disconnection from reality — an interruption of emotional connectivity that Dieutre presents in an introductory voice-over:

> Les années 90 commencèrent plutôt mal. Revenu à la vie, tu n'as fait que tester les autres, les choses. Comme eux, tu as appris à jouer. Cela te semble à présent une longue nuit de veille, d'attente. Aucun combat n'arrive plus à te retenir. Émotion, sensation: tout a sombré dans l'équivalence. Il est temps de rétablir quelques certitudes, de t'assurer une nouvelle fois de ce que tu es, et de qui tu aimes vraiment. Tu le sais, ce ne sera pas un voyage comme les autres.
>
> [The nineties started pretty badly. Brought back to life, all you did was test others and things. Like them, you learnt to play along. Now it feels like a long night of sleepless vigil, of expectancy. No cause manages to grab you anymore. Emotion and feeling, all has plunged into equivalence. It's time to re-establish a few certitudes, to check again what you are and who you really love. You know this won't be any old journey.]

Leçons de ténèbres stages, as Beugnet suggests, 'a voyage of mourning, where the link between desire, sensation and affect seems to have been severed' (2007: 123). Life has, Dieutre here hints, lost all meaning for him. Nothing around him, no contact or exchange claims his attention and desire, and he withdraws into the undifferentiated obscurity of the night. Within these drained affective landscapes, only art seems to retain the capacity to pierce through the surrounding darkness, to elicit feeling and lead Dieutre back to the restored certitudes and intensities that are so desperately sought. As Jules O'Dwyer convincingly argues, in making art-historical commentary on the varied works to which he turns and which he assembles within his film overlap with explorations of his own autobiography, what Dieutre here proposes is a form of '*self*-curation' (2018: 55). It is through this self-curation, an ambiguous merging of art and experience, that Dieutre attempts to reclaim his own depleted capacity to feel.

The three urban locations chosen for the chapters of Dieutre's itinerary in *Leçons de ténèbres* are significant in a very specific way. Utrecht, Naples and Rome all house important collections of baroque art — most notably paintings by Michelangelo Merisi da Caravaggio, but also significant works by other baroque figures such as Guido Reni and Stefano Maderno or members of the later *Utrecht Caravaggisti* such as Dirck van Baburen and Gerrit van Honthorst, many of which appear, whole or in fragments, within the montage of Dieutre's film. The specific qualities that draw Dieutre towards this art in *Leçons de ténèbre* are expounded in interviews with queer theorist Leo Bersani that are inserted at intervals throughout the film. Bersani's discussions in these sequences echo arguments developed in his book *Caravaggio's Secrets*, co-published with Ulysse Dutoit the year before the release of *Leçons de ténèbres*. In his on-screen appearances, Bersani returns to certain elements of his earlier reading of Caravaggio's painting and the powerful homoeroticism that characterises it; but as Dieutre integrates the works of other artists into the montage of his film, Bersani's reflections are also framed as a more broadly applicable interpretive key to the art of the Baroque. Caravaggio's images are, Bersani's interviews and writings suggest, defined by an ambiguous cohabitation of sensuality and death. Knowledge of impending (and often painful) death is inscribed within the various bodies that populate Caravaggio's visual universe; but this morbidity is simultaneously to be understood as contributing to these bodies' sensual appeal (Bersani and Dutoit 1998: 35). Throughout *Leçons de ténèbres*, the art of Caravaggio and of the Baroque more broadly is presented as a repository of sometimes overwhelmingly intense affects, where pleasurable sensations rub up against equally potent painful sensations. It is in this affective intensity that the Baroque is approached as a potential remedy to the emotional drainage Dieutre diagnoses within himself.

So much of *Leçons de ténèbres* seems oriented towards the possibility of drawing out the affective charge of these artworks, of accessing it in the present. Throughout the film, Dieutre continually tests the border between such canonical images and the modern world that surrounds him, encouraging forms of seepage between levels of reality and representation. As baroque paintings are held on screen at certain points, the sounds of roaring street traffic or grunts from pornography irrupt into the frame, unsettling the definitiveness of these images' temporal anchoring. This seepage also occurs in the opposite direction. In extended pans and static shots that, in their composition and through the combination of image and voice, belie the continuing influence of the Akerman of *News From Home* whilst also pointing to the parallel influence of filmmakers such as Marguerite Duras (see particularly O'Dwyer 2018: 58), Dieutre scrutinises the material textures of the urban spaces he traverses in the limpidity of 35mm. In his presentation of these spaces, Dieutre creates an interplay of light and darkness that deliberately quotes the painterly *chiaroscuro* for which Caravaggio in particular is so known. Bringing this painterly technique into filmic form, Dieutre creates oppositions between illumination and shadow, exposure and concealment, visibility and invisibility, that offer an evocative visual backdrop to his detailed voice-over descriptions of handjobs and anal fisting taking place in the dark corners and saunas of the cities he visits.

FIG. 2.1. *Leçons de ténèbres* (1999), Vincent Dieutre © Les Films de la Croisade.

In framing twentieth-century city spaces through visual idioms borrowed from the artworks of the sixteenth and seventeenth centuries, teasing out a tension between the painterly and the cinematic, *Leçons de ténèbres* shares concerns with the work of a large number of other contemporary artists who, like Dieutre, have chosen to revisit and reimagine the art of the Baroque. Surveying the work of artists such as Ken Aptekar, David Reed, Ana Mendieta, Andres Serrano, Liet Heringa, Maarten van Kalsbeek and Carrie Mae Weems in domains as varied as painting, sculpture, photography, collage, land art, installation art or process art, cultural theorist Mieke Bal has identified a late-twentieth-century mode of art-historical recycling that she describes not as 'neo-baroque' but rather as '(contemporary) baroque' — a designation explored in her 1999 book *Quoting Caravaggio: Contemporary Art, Preposterous History* as well as in subsequent texts. Emphasising a persistent, even emphatic transgression of the boundary between pleasure and nonpleasure (1999: 20), Bal's engagement with Caravaggio in such writing is wholly compatible with that offered by Bersani. But, more than the specific qualities found in this painter's work, what interests Bal is how the art of the Baroque and its creative reuse at the hands of later artists can help us to think differently about questions of artistic temporality and influence — questions that are central to *Leçons de ténèbres* and to the forms of reenactment it contains, as I will go on to show.

The Baroque stands in Bal's analysis less as an identifiable style or periodisation, and more as a perspective, a way of reasoning, an epistemology: she approaches the Baroque as 'historiography', as a tool that urges us to interrogate the possible relationships that might exist between different temporal moments (1999: 16; 2011: 184). This function of Baroque as historiography is one that, Bal suggests, is already inscribed in the works of the Old Masters themselves, as reflected in art historian Irving Lavin's famous statement that classicising drapery — that most iconic of baroque elements — was a device used to create 'the almost hallucinatory relationship between past and present that is the hallmark of the period' (Lavin 1995: 5; Bal 1999: 3). This 'hallucinatory' relationship becomes yet more pronounced and yet more complex as it is explored in works of the '(contemporary) baroque' that attempt to open active dialogues with their art historical predecessors. For Bal, as contemporary artists quote the work of much earlier artists, the key question conditioning the interactions of present art and past art that they trigger is: 'Who illuminates — helps us understand — whom?' (1999: 3). Surveying contemporary uses of the Baroque, Bal questions whether ancient art must always (or only) be seen as *source*, exerting a foundational influence on everything that follows in its wake; or whether contemporary revisitations might also offer 'a key, a seduction' to continually reappraise and reenvision works that chronologically predate them, to transform them through the act of quotation (ibid.). Bal is interested particularly in how, as they flatten hierarchies of authenticity and authority and multiply the directions of flows of influence, such reciprocal forms of dialogue unsettle linear conceptions of history, opening it to the queerness of back-and-forth movement and exchange.

Dieutre's quotation of the Baroque in *Leçons de ténèbres* is most visible in the film's numerous instances of reenactment. These reenactments are significantly more literal and direct than many of the baroque quotations found in the contemporary artworks assembled by Bal, ranging as these do from Mendieta's earthworks to the congealed resin sculptures of Heringa/Van Kalsbeek. But as he seeks to access

FIG. 2.2. *Leçons de ténèbres* (1999), Vincent Dieutre © Les Films de la Croisade.

the affective intensity of past art in the present, Dieutre establishes encounters and contacts across (art) history that are just as hallucinatory as those hinted at above. In sequences encountered throughout *Leçons de ténèbres*, Dieutre appears in images that consciously replicate the visual textures and tonal qualities of baroque painting. Dieutre is initially alone in these scenes, but as the film develops he is shown locked in loving embrace with other bodies. These sequences do not seek to reproduce specific, identifiable artworks, but rather to capture something of the *feel* of baroque imagery, and the visual techniques that sustain its powerful affective charge. In this regard, they contrast with certain of the artistic reenactments from Varda we will see in Chapter 4. The super-8 format used in Dieutre's reenactments grants a grainy sensuality to these images that contrasts with the clarity of the film stock used elsewhere to record the exterior spaces of Utrecht, Naples and Rome. These images attempt to communicate the warmth of oil paint through the visual resources of film. The bodies that appear on screen are held within a tension between shadow and light that once again deliberately quotes painterly chiaroscuro. Dieutre's reenactments reproduce the shallow depth of field and closeness of cropping that characterises so much of the painting of Caravaggio in particular, allowing the screen to be entirely filled with the materiality of entwined bodies, their folds of skin and caressing touches.

Dieutre's copies foreground their imperfections, inconsistencies and the artificiality of their illusions at various points. We glimpse, for instance, the hard, shining edge of a spotlight within the frame or the silhouette of an assistant who directs the spotlight's beam over the surface of Dieutre's skin. In one instance, Dieutre experiments with the shadows cast over his partner's body by his moving hand before being audibly advised by the cameraman on how best to attain the precise chiaroscuro effect that he seeks. Elsewhere, it is decidedly modern clothing that is stripped off by fumbling hands. Dieutre's baroque copies openly announce themselves as forgeries, as imperfect fakes, but simultaneously explore the intense *realness* of the feelings that, through reenactment, they revive from past art in the present. One of Dieutre's reenactments is accompanied by a muffled, static-fuddled Italian voice-over text of a kind we might expect to hear in a gallery audio-guide or an introductory art history documentary. As Dieutre and his partner appear, this informational soundtrack asks a question, pauses, then provides us with the answer: 'Attenzione, quello che sta per apparire è un quadro di Caravaggio? ... Esatto! Questa decollazione del Battista è stata dipinta dal pittore caravaggesco nel 1610' [Is the image that is about to appear a painting by Caravaggio? ... Correct! This beheading of John the Baptist was painted by Caravaggio in 1610]. The reenactments that appear in *Leçons de ténèbres*, filled as they are with the disruptive presence of twentieth-century objects or recording technologies and marked by a constant drive to deconstruct their own mimesis, are clearly *not* by the same Caravaggio who died almost 400 years earlier; but through the strange seepage they foster between painted bodies and live bodies, between the images of then and the experiences of now, they grant access to an authenticity of feeling that seems to flow across time, authorship and between modes of representation.

As Dieutre imperfectly recreates artworks from the baroque past, he simultaneously opens dialogues with other, much more recent artists, with his references shifting from the painterly to the filmic. Whilst very different from sensually grainy, chiaroscuro-bathed scenes where what is reconstructed is often an impression of *baroqueness* rather than specific artworks, the more readily identifiable, *tableaux vivants*-like reproductions of Derek Jarman's *Caravaggio* (1986) offer a vital point of reference for Dieutre's reenactments. Filled with anachronistic typewriters, calculators, motorbikes and electric lights, Jarman's biographical study anticipates the elements of temporal incongruity described above. *Leçons de ténèbres* knowingly announces a debt to Jarman more broadly. The imprint of other of Jarman's works is felt in various sites: Dieutre's images of loving embrace recall scenes from *The Angelic Conversation* (1985), for instance, whilst the enumerated male names heard in voice-over as Dieutre circumnavigates Rome's Piazza del Popolo recall the echoing list of friends and lovers lost to AIDS from *Blue* (1993).

It is also via Jarman that the chain of influences Dieutre draws into his film is extended. Writing in early entries from his autobiography *Dancing Ledge* (1984), Jarman evokes the extent to which his own cinematic foray into the Baroque was informed by the work of Pier Paolo Pasolini, most particularly by *La Ricotta* (1962), Pasolini's contribution to the 1963 *Ro.Go.Pa.G.* omnibus, and the striking artistic reenactments it contains. Pasolini's recreations of deposition scenes by Rosso Fiorentino (1521) and Jacopo da Pontormo (1528) are similarly buffeted by points of anachronism and by a drive towards deconstruction. Acknowledging the Italian writer and director's influence — one we will see again and that has been addressed particularly explicitly in other films (see Cuthbertson 2022) — Dieutre integrates an extract from the Pasolini poem heard in *La Ricotta* directly into the soundtrack of *Leçons de ténèbres*. This poem's famous opening, *Io sono una forza del passato* [*I am a force from the past*], could well stand as an effective statement of intent for Dieutre's art historical engagement. As he seeks to call upon the force of past art in the present, Dieutre traces an intergenerational and intermedial tradition of queer image-making that extends from Caravaggio to Pasolini to Jarman to... *Dieutre*, within which he positions his own filmmaking.

It is through the authenticity of revived feeling — the affective *forza del passato* found in baroque artworks — that reenactment offers the antidote to Dieutre's dwindling affective resources, a means of negotiating the loss that drives his nocturnal journey. Certainly by the time this journey reaches its Roman conclusion, such instances of tender sensuality, increasingly filled with smiles of joy and the refrains of Italian pop music, seem to announce a happy reconnection with the intensity of affect through intimate encounter with another living and loving body. Dieutre's voyage of mourning is here apparently complete, with the severed link between desire, sensation and affect successfully repaired. But as Dieutre revives the complex affects he finds in the art of the Baroque, it is not only pleasures that return. In the closing sequence of *Leçons de ténèbres*, Dieutre stages a very different baroque reenactment. Replicating the posture of Maderno's *Martyrdom of Saint Cecilia* (1600), glimpsed earlier in the film, Dieutre appears on screen lying unconscious, a tourniquet around his arm. His return journey towards feeling is here rerouted back towards darkness, towards what Beugnet presents as the ultimate desensitisation: 'the death-like sleep induced by hard drugs' (2007: 123). The sensual pleasure that Dieutre had accessed from the art of the past and reinjected into his own lived experience is here swamped by the obliterating death that, as Bersani and Dutoit presaged, also hangs over these artworks. The affective complexity of the Baroque would seem to have caught up with Dieutre.

But as Dieutre forges a kind of historiography of feeling through artistic reenactment, this is an affective complexity that is actively and knowingly pursued. Like the varied artists surveyed by Bal, Dieutre rethinks the relationship between past and present art, scrutinising concerns that are both of now and of then, asking what the Baroque might mean for us today in a radically different historical moment. Crucially, the contemporary moment into which Dieutre attempts to draw the emotional charge of earlier artworks is one that is indelibly marked by the lengthy shadow cast by the AIDS virus. It is from this perspective that the presence of Jarman as a key interlocutor for the film, always discernible just beneath its surface if never explicitly named, makes itself particularly felt. References to AIDS — to its impact on Tadeusz's health and relationship with Dieutre, to the transformed modes of intimacy it imposes, to the behavioural and cultural shifts it has forced — are woven throughout *Leçons de ténèbres*, with Dieutre framing what Bersani and Dutoit present as the 'compatibility of death with sensuality' (1998: 35) that so defined the work of Caravaggio in distinctly modern terms. This is a framing in which Dieutre's reenactments also participate.

Amongst the numerous anachronisms that fill Dieutre's reenactments, one stands out particularly forcefully: in a sequence that once again recreates the tonal and textural qualities of artworks produced centuries earlier, Dieutre appears on screen struggling with a condom wrapper, eventually ripping into it with his teeth. This out-of-time condom recalls other quasi-prophylactic barriers referenced in the film. Speaking in an early voice-over, Dieutre describes an impression of being cut off from the world and insulated from sensation: 'cette fine couche infranchissable qui aseptise tout, rend tout interchangeable: ce même empêchement que tu ressens quand soir après soir tu enrobes le sexe de Tadeusz d'un préservatif luisant' [this fine, impassable layer that sterilises everything, makes everything interchangeable — the same obstacle that you feel when, night after night, you wrap Tadeusz' penis in a glistening condom]. Dieutre's baroque reenactments explore the possibility of reconnecting with feeling; but they simultaneously mourn for a moment from queer history that, it is suggested, has been lost; for the forms of intimacy that seemed available in the past but that appear denied in a present that exists with knowledge of the virus. *Leçons de ténèbres* stages a highly political form of queer mourning of a kind that was described by Douglas Crimp in his 1989 article 'Mourning and Militancy'. For Crimp: 'Alongside the dismal toll of death [from AIDS], what many of us have lost is a culture of sexual possibility' (1989: 11). Like Crimp, Dieutre's film mourns for the vanished sexual possibilities of the past, for the lost pleasures of uninhibited and unprotected sex that are now either proscribed or forcibly shielded by latex (ibid.). Through the dialogue it throws open between the art of then and the art of now, *Leçons de ténèbres* foregrounds both what brings these distant historical moments into proximity but also what ultimately, poignantly, separates them.

Exercising Admiration

As illustrated particularly clearly by Jarman's unequivocal descriptions of 'the most homosexual of painters' (1983: 22), the paintings of Caravaggio are, of course, not the most refractory works from art history to queer readings and queer reappropriations. In this section I analyse two films in which Dieutre creates further copies of pre-existing artworks — ones that, in contrast to Caravaggio's art, have not standardly been seen to invite queer readings. The originals that Dieutre here copies are no longer works of sixteenth and seventeenth-century painting, but of twentieth-century cinema. These are works in which, in a different way from the tribute paid by *Entering Indifference* to Akerman's *News From Home*, Dieutre positions himself in relation to the films that have influenced his own filmmaking practice and his life, seeking to settle the personal and artistic debts that he feels he owes to them. The two examples I explore in this section are part of a distinct sub-thread within Dieutre's filmography, one to which he applies a particular label: *Exercices d'admiration* [*Exercises in Admiration*]. Whilst, as I have suggested, Dieutre's filmmaking as a whole often proudly acknowledges the inspiration it has taken from the work of other artists, the (to-date) five instalments of his *Exercices d'admiration* offer particularly pointed engagements with what he presents as the 'images qui m'ont nourri, et me nourrissent encore' [images that have nourished me and that nourish me still].[1]

If the label of *Exercices d'admiration* clearly recalls Emil Cioran's 1986 text of the same name, Dieutre himself attributes it instead to his reading of Jean-François Lyotard's *Moralités postmodernes* [*Postmodern Moralities*] (1993) and to the emphasis on postmodern modes of cultural citation that he finds in this text (Sauvage 2018). We indeed find a pronounced citational quality to the expressions of admiration Dieutre has devoted to Naomi Kawase in *EA1 Les Accords d'Alba (Exercice d'admiration 1: Naomi Kawase)* [*EA1 The Alba Agreement (Exercise in Admiration 1: Naomi Kawase)*] (2004), Jean Cocteau in *EA3 (Troisième exercice d'admiration: Jean Cocteau)* [*EA3 (Third Exercise in Admiration: Jean Cocteau)*] (2010) and Alain Cavalier in *EA5 Frère Alain (Cinquième exercice d'admiration: Alain Cavalier)* [*EA5 Brother Alain (Fifth Exercise in Admiration: Alain Cavalier)*] (2017), with Dieutre consciously replicating certain aspects of the style and tone of these filmmakers. But it is the more sustained dynamics of citation and replication found in the homage Dieutre pays to the work of Jean Eustache and Roberto Rossellini in *EA2 (Deuxième exercice d'admiration: Jean Eustache)* (2007) and *EA4 Viaggio nella dopo-storia (Quatrième Exercice d'Admiration: Roberto Rossellini)* (2015) that interest me here. In these two *exercices*, Dieutre seeks to express the admiration he feels for the work of Eustache and Rossellini through extensive strategies of reenactment, directly restaging sequences from their films with his own body and the bodies of others.

The filmic reenactments encountered in Dieutre's treatment of Eustache and Rossellini are autobiographical in multiple ways: on the one hand, as he himself reenacts sequences from earlier films, Dieutre revisits the ways in which they have 'nourished' him and his work, experiencing anew the impact that they once had, exposing himself to their decisive and continuing influence; on the other, as he copies these films, he reappropriates them, once again accessing the affective charge they contain and using it to frame aspects of his own contemporary experience. What O'Dwyer presented as Dieutre's work of 'self-curation' here continues. In the transformations that are produced by the act of copying a prior original, these filmic reenactments reveal the extent to which Dieutre conceives of admiration not as a passive stance, but as an active, explicitly creative mode of artistic engagement. Through this creative engagement, often very familiar artworks are reimagined and reinscribed with new meaning, as a dialogue is once again thrown open between the art of the past and the art of the present that is used to support often disorienting forms of autobiographical self-staging. Through the tension between sameness and difference, original and copy that these filmic reenactments produce, autobiographical identity is unmade and remade, merged with other identities, in a way which teases out ambiguous forms of passage across time and between fact and fiction, art and reality, self and other. In picking apart these multiple forms of passage, I consider first Dieutre's engagement with Eustache, before turning to his treatment of Rossellini.

Dieutre appears for much of the duration of EA2 (Deuxième exercice d'admiration: Jean Eustache) (henceforth EA2) alongside the actor Françoise Lebrun. Lebrun is a frequent collaborator of Dieutre: she contributed, for instance, to Fleur Albert's documentary study Vincent Dieutre, la chambre et le monde that we saw earlier, having also appeared in Dieutre's Fragments sur la grâce [Fragments on Grace] (2006). She is, however, probably best known to film history for her career-defining performance as Veronika in Eustache's La Maman et la putain [The Mother and the Whore] (1973), where she famously played one point in a conflictual love triangle with Bernadette Lafont's Marie and Jean-Pierre Léaud's Alexandre. Lebrun's tearful monologue to Marie and Alexandre from this film's conclusion, with its ideologically ambiguous questioning of sexual morality that careens between defending total sexual freedom ('tu peux sucer n'importe qui, te faire baiser par n'importe qui, tu n'es pas une pute' [you can suck off whoever you want, get fucked by whoever you want, you're not a whore]) on the one hand, and claiming that the only valid form of desire is that which is oriented towards heteronormative reproduction ('l'amour n'est valable que si on a envie de faire un enfant ensemble' [love is only valid if you want to have a child together]) on the other, is still notorious for its excoriating violence. It is this monologue that Dieutre chooses to reenact in EA2, himself assuming the role originally played by Lebrun.

Care is taken in EA2 to directly replicate aspects of Eustache's film. Dieutre's delivery in his sequences of reenactment convincingly reproduces the distinctive cadences and rhythms with which Lebrun originally spoke the same lines. The film is recorded in black and white with contrasts heavily amplified to recall the unadorned starkness of La Maman et la putain. As Dieutre delivers the lines of his

FIG. 2.3. *EA2 (Deuxième exercice d'admiration: Jean Eustache)* (2007),
Vincent Dieutre © Bonne Nouvelle Production.

FIG. 2.4. *EA2 (Deuxième exercice d'admiration: Jean Eustache)* (2007),
Vincent Dieutre © Bonne Nouvelle Production.

borrowed monologue, his face is framed similarly to Lebrun's, captured in close-up against a blank background. In such a way, Dieutre's *EA2* announces the ways in which it is the *same* as Eustache's earlier film. And yet, this is a *sameness* that, as *EA2* develops, is continually deconstructed. In 'behind-the-scenes' footage, Dieutre instructs an assistant to move the camera so as to achieve the specific interplay of shadow and light that he remembers from Eustache's film. Elsewhere, he appears on screen struggling to memorise his lines, repeatedly stumbling over his words. Sitting next to him, Lebrun corrects his mistakes and directs him on how the lines should be delivered, on how she herself had once delivered them three and a half decades earlier. In showing himself as he revises his lines, correcting his articulation and the emphases of his speech, Dieutre foregrounds a desire to accurately, authentically replicate the infamous closing monologue; but in laying bare this faltering search for accuracy and authenticity as well as the repetitive hard labour that it entails, *EA2* openly presents itself as a copy, as an act of imperfect imitation, in which the search for sameness is always unsettled by disruptive points of difference.

In an echo of the intruding spotlight glimpsed in *Leçons de ténèbres*, the behind-the-scenes sequences of *EA2* repeatedly reveal the camera and microphones with which Dieutre's reenacted monologue is recorded. We see the clap that signals the beginning of takes and hear the cameraman asking Dieutre to speak louder. At one point, Dieutre interrupts his reproduced monologue mid-flow upon hearing the buzz of a mobile phone, embarrassedly confessing that it is probably his own. In exposing these imperfections, revealing the technologies and context of its own construction, *EA2* does not bemoan its failure to fully and convincingly regain a prior original; rather, Dieutre's copy encourages us to see in the *admiration* that propels it a deliberate, active mode of artistic engagement. This is a mode of engagement that finds in the transition from original to copy not a process of loss or corruption, but one of transformative creation through which new meanings, effects, confrontations and ambiguities are produced.

In the shift from Eustache's original to Dieutre's copy, many of these transformations emerge automatically from the uncanniness we encounter in witnessing lines that are so inextricably associated with one actor be delivered by someone else. This is an uncanniness that snaps us out of a sense of familiarity with these famous words, alerting us to the changes these words inevitably undergo as they are repeated in a different time and from a different mouth. Veronika's suggestion from *La Maman et la putain* that 'un couple qui n'a pas envie d'élever un enfant n'est pas un couple, c'est une merde, c'est n'importe quoi, c'est une poussière' [a couple that doesn't want to raise a child isn't a couple, it's a piece of shit, it's rubbish, it's dust] assumes, for instance, a particularly curious, provocative charge when delivered from the lips of a gay man, evoking a kind of reactionary natalism wholly at odds with the rest of Dieutre's art. Elsewhere, the transformations introduced by repetition are more active, as Dieutre deliberately modifies certain of the lines he delivers. Veronika's 'cinq ans de vie sexuelle, c'est très peu' [five years of having sex, it's not much] thus becomes Dieutre's 'trente ans de vie sexuelle, c'est long' [thirty years of having sex, it's a lot]. The insistence that 'il n'y a que des cons, il n'y a que des sexes' [there's just cunts, there's just cocks] is replaced in Dieutre's delivery with 'il n'y a que des culs, il n'y a que des sexes' [there's just asses, there's just cocks], whilst 'la fille' [the girl] who fucks and is fucked in Veronika's tearful account becomes 'le mec' [the guy] who does the same. As it evoked Eustache's own relationships, including his then recent separation from Lebrun, *La Maman et la putain* was already a heavily autobiographical film; as he modifies the lines from the past that he repeats in the present, Dieutre seemingly reappropriates this autobiographical charge and reorients it towards his own lived experience, directing this lacerating, confessional account of sexual weariness not to the Marie and

Alexandre that once sat beside Veronika in 1973 but to the Françoise that sits beside him and whom he addresses by name in 2007.

And yet, through the tension that is sustained in *EA2* between sameness and difference, this is an autobiographical reappropriation that is never fully complete: through this tension, the account that we hear is never entirely Veronika's, never entirely Dieutre's, but is instead *both* at the same time, held in a strange form of back-and-forth dialogue between the two. As Lebrun indeed suggests to Dieutre in one of the behind-the-scenes sequences from *EA2*, interrogating the nature of the film they are making: 'on joue entre cet état d'il y a trente ans et ce qui se passe maintenant' [we're playing between this state from thirty years ago and what's happening now]. It is precisely in this *betweenness* that the autobiographical investigation developed in *EA2* is located. As he reenacts the closing monologue from *La Maman et la putain*, Dieutre stages a version of himself through fiction, through words penned by Eustache in the past and that he modifies in the present, constructing an autobiographical identity that both is and isn't him, that merges ambiguously across time, gender and sexuality with an identity articulated through sobs and tears in 1973. As this identity is delivered back to the same person whose earlier articulation of it has gone down in the annals of film history, the temporalities of Dieutre's copy become a disorienting, knotty tangle. Reflecting on the motivations that lie behind his distinctive engagement with the history of cinema and with one of its most emotionally devastating scenes, Dieutre describes his first encounter with Eustache's *La Maman et la putain* as a 'choc irrémédiable' [irreversible impact].[2] Throughout his *exercice d'admiration*, reenactment allows Dieutre to revive this 'choc', to reimagine it, to examine the ways in which it has shaped him and his work and to invent a means of expressing how it continues to do so, to question where and why he still recognises himself within it.

As it throws open a yet larger space of indeterminate *betweenness*, *EA4 Viaggio nella dopo-storia (Quatrième Exercice d'Admiration: Roberto Rossellini)* (henceforth *EA4*) contains even more pronounced autobiographical ambiguities than those encountered in Dieutre's imperfect copy of *La Maman et la putain*. This later *exercice d'admiration* copies scenes from Rossellini's *Viaggio in Italia [Journey to Italy]* (1954), another work that, like Eustache's film, carries strong autobiographical overtones shaped by a male filmmaker's relationship with his female lead. Rossellini's film narrates the troubled journey of married couple Katherine (Ingrid Bergman, then married to Rossellini) and Alex (George Sanders) to the Italian city of Naples as they seek to sell an inherited villa. The trip precipitates a crisis in the couple's relationship: alone together for the first time since their marriage, latent tensions, resentments, regrets, incompatibilities and jealousies arise between them, with any affection they may once have had gradually evaporating. The pair decide to divorce before reconnecting and redeclaring their love for each other at the film's conclusion. Through the admiration that he declares for Rossellini's film, Dieutre performs another autobiographical reappropriation. In the extensive reenactments that he stages of *Viaggio in Italia* in modern-day Naples, Dieutre assumes the role originally played by Bergman whilst that of her on-screen husband is assigned to actor and singer Simon Versnel, someone with whom Dieutre has a real–life relationship. In an uncertain interplay between reality and fiction, *EA4* leaves us always uncertain as to exactly where to draw the border separating the extra-filmic relationship between two real men, the 2015 filmic representation of this relationship, and the iconic relationship between a male character and a female character that Sanders and Bergman brought to the screen in 1954 and that Dieutre here admiringly revives.

In a comparable way to the preceding exercise in admiration, *EA4* sees Dieutre work to continually deconstruct his own reenactments. This deconstruction is again pursued in part through behind–the–scenes sequences that expose the labour of copying as well as the deliberations and challenges that inform it. In these sequences, Dieutre lays bare the research that underpins his project, showing the YouTube videos and Google searches that allow him to reacquaint himself with Rossellini's film and with the images from it that have lodged in his memory. Dieutre's voice-overs in such sequences recount his attempts to persuade his on-screen partner to participate in the film, as well as email exchanges with Isabella Rossellini seeking her opinion (and implicitly her approval) of this homage to the work of her parents. Many of these behind–the–scenes sequences reveal *EA4* as a film that is particularly concerned with its own status as copy, as repetition, and with the potentially disruptive charge this status assumes. This is most evidently the case for instances in which Dieutre appears on screen in interviews with the intellectual property lawyer Emmanuel Pierrat to discuss the legal framework within which his expression of admiration operates, its uncertain classification — adaptation? remake? nod? citation? counterfeit? pastiche? détournement? tribute? — and the extent to which it might offer the possibility of an act of artistic resistance within cultural industries where a concern for what constitutes the unique 'essence' of an artwork is, they imply, driven predominately by a desire to protect royalties. Tracing the legal limits of admiration, such interviews establish the delicate juridical tightrope Dieutre treads in *EA4*: barred from too closely replicating those elements deemed to constitute the originality of the source material at risk of entering into the domain of the forgery; but similarly prevented by the strictures of *droits moraux* [moral rights] from overly altering the integrity of the original work — concerns which have perhaps assumed a more pressing charge in Dieutre's work since the expression of admiration he devoted to Jean Cocteau was restricted from distribution after clearance was withheld by the rightsholders.

Elsewhere in these behind–the–scenes sequences, Dieutre's voice-overs acknowledge how far, even as he seeks to faithfully replicate the relationship of Alex and Katherine, the Neapolitan context that surrounds it has been entirely transformed. He describes a city in which municipal waste management problems have left rubbish littering the streets, where football has become the state religion, where Camorra violence has been allowed to proliferate, where the Europeanism that so defined the work of Rossellini has been shaken by the rise of populisms, where sex and coupling have become online and digital. Amongst these transformations, Dieutre emphasises in particular what he presents as a key symptom of the titular

FIG. 2.5. *EA4 Viaggio nella dopo-storia (Quatrième exercice d'admiration: Roberto Rossellini)* (2015), Vincent Dieutre © La Huit/Ciné+.

dopo-storia [post-history] he borrows from the same Pasolini poem heard in *Leçons de ténèbres* and that serves as *EA4*'s sonic epigraph: a sensation of being unmoored from the past; the severance of a connection to history that, through relics and archaeological remains, had once seemed so palpable for Katherine and Alex.

As Dieutre's behind-the-scenes sequences explore the legal limits of admiration and the transformed realities of twenty-first-century Naples, the relationship between original and copy is firmly framed in terms of a shifting tension between sameness and difference — a tension that is also continually teased out by the film's reenactments. Dieutre's sepia-toned, English-language reenactments follow the development of the plot of *Viaggio in Italia* closely. In the marked similarity of certain sequences of reenactment to Rossellini's original film, we are left with an impression of watching a repetition of the same relationship once brought to the screen by Bergman and Sanders. Images of Dieutre and his on-screen partner sunning themselves against the backdrop of Mount Vesuvius, for instance, are particularly striking for their resemblance to the corresponding, instantly recognisable, sequence from *Viaggio in Italia*. But as they follow the events of Rossellini's film, Dieutre's reenactments also update them, introducing references to iPads and the Amazon website, to saunas and HIV-positive friends, foregrounding the very different tensions at the heart of a very different couple.

These changes initially register as instances in which Dieutre attempts to express something particular about his own relationship with the man who appears beside him on screen; but as *EA4* returns continually to the same locations and situations of Rossellini's film, the exact truth-status of what we are told of this modern relationship remains permanently uncertain, with this autobiographical account appearing always indeterminately drawn towards the fictions of an earlier film. As

Dieutre stages a version of his own relationship through a relationship revived from film history, it is never clear what is real and what is not, never entirely apparent what the corrosive conflicts and emotional clashes we watch on screen might tell us about an extra-filmic reality. Right from its opening images, *EA4* announces itself as a strange instance of layering: at the film's beginning, the two men appear shirtless with the introductory credits of *Viaggio in Italia* projected onto their naked torsos. As emblemised by this striking image, Dieutre's film encourages continual slippage between layers of autobiographical truth and autobiographical fiction in which an imagined relationship played out by actors in the past merges with the relationship of two real men who act out versions of themselves in the present.

This ambiguous merging becomes particularly pronounced in certain instances. In a key sequence from *Viaggio in Italia*, Bergman's Katherine drives angrily through the streets of Naples en route to the city's famous National Archaeological Museum, cursing her husband's arrogance. Throughout this sequence, Rossellini's camera shifts between the interior of the car and images of the city outside that are framed to suggest Katherine's subjective point of view on the nuns, priests, shoeshines and soldiers she passes. In Dieutre's reenactment of this sequence, the external footage that appears on screen alternates between images of modern Naples and images borrowed from Rossellini's film, in a strange cohabitation of past and present, major and minor art. Adopting an alien point of view as if it were his own, seeing with borrowed eyes, Dieutre here again constructs a subjectivity, an autobiographical identity that merges ambiguously with that of a fictional character — not entirely him, not entirely her, not entirely then, not entirely now, but somewhere in between.

Importantly, it is the ambiguity of this merging that allows Dieutre to carve out a space of autobiographical possibility at the heart of *EA4*. At the film's conclusion, the closing sequences of Rossellini's *Viaggio in Italia* are projected onto the topless bodies of Dieutre and Versnel. Here it is possible to detect yet another nod to the influence of Pasolini, with Dieutre's bodily screens recalling Fabio Mauri's *Intellettuale* [*Intellectual*] (1975), a mixed-media performance in which Pasolini's *Il Vangelo secondo Matteo* [*The Gospel According to Saint Matthew*] (1964) was projected directly onto the filmmaker's own chest. Dieutre's installation-like sequence might equally be seen to recall the closing images of corporeal projection seen in *Illibatezza* [*Chastity*] (1963), Rossellini's own contribution to the *Ro.Go.Pa.G.* compendium. Facing each other, Dieutre and Versnel perform reworked lines of dialogue from the scenes of *Viaggio in Italia* that are simultaneously playing onto their bodies, reading from the scripts they hold in their hands. The projected images of Rossellini's film show the sudden reconciliation of Katherine and Alex amidst the chaos of Naples's San Gennaro procession and their declaration of renewed love for each other. Within Dieutre's montage, Rossellini's original images of this religious procession are intercut with decidedly more modern footage and sounds of seething crowds at Napoli football matches. As Katherine and Alex embrace, Dieutre and Versnel do the same at exactly the same moment. In reenacting Rossellini's film, reviving its affective charge in both its pains and its pleasures, Dieutre reimagines

FIG. 2.6. and 2.7. *EA4 Viaggio nella dopo-storia (Quatrième exercice d'admiration: Roberto Rossellini)* (2015), Vincent Dieutre © La Huit/Ciné+.

his own relationship within the space of borrowed fictions, scripting it differently, imagining new realities for it. As *EA4* replicates the ending of Rossellini's film, updating it, foregrounding the simultaneity of two instances of sudden embrace, it holds out the same hope of reconciliation, the same optimism for new beginnings. By merging Dieutre's real relationship with a fictional relationship, bringing the art of the past into contact with the art of the present across the surface of Dieutre's exposed skin, reenactment here once again functions as a potential strategy of autobiographical mourning, a tool for the negotiation of personal loss. This *exercice d'admiration* allows Dieutre to revisit a film that, he suggests, once changed his life; in so doing, he also reimagines that life. In Dieutre's creative take on admiration, *exercising* in many ways resembles a form of *exorcising*.

The name Simon and the relationship(s) that it suggests appears in various sites in Dieutre's work. It features extensively, for instance, in Dieutre's 2010 experimental text project *(07/09)X2*, written collaboratively with artistic programmer Gilles Collard, and is also at the heart of the film examined in the next section. Under the pressure of the pronounced fictionalising impulse that pervades Dieutre's work, the extent (if any) to which occurrences of this name designate the same individual, or indeed whether the man seen on screen in *EA4* is exclusively or entirely 'Simon' is, however, never wholly certain.[3] What interests Dieutre in each of these instances is reviving the intensity of certain feelings (whatever their precise provenance or reality) as well as what these revived feelings might help us to think and feel differently about. I turn now to an earlier account of a relationship with a man Dieutre calls 'Simon'. In this longer case study, the relationship is negotiated in very different ways from what we saw above in Dieutre's imperfect remake of Rossellini. In contrast to *EA2*, *EA4* and *Leçons de ténèbres*, the use of reenactment in this final example does not entail remaking pre-existing images from visual culture. But as Dieutre imperfectly reenacts autobiographical experience, reimagining it, this film still confronts us with what I have identified so far in this chapter as the strange queerness of the copy — a queerness that again draws us within shifting tensions between sameness and difference, truth and fiction, veracity and falsity and that opens another strange form of dialogue between the images of the past and the images of the present, between notionally separate identities and experiences.

Reconstructing Politics: *Jaurès*

The opening images of *Jaurès* (2012) show the flickering LED lights of a mixing console. The camera moves outwards slightly to reveal the dimly lit space of a cramped mixing studio, filled with microphones, editing equipment and monitors. Describing *Jaurès* in an accompanying text, Dieutre presents this studio as 'le ventre du film, le lieu de remémoration d'un amour' [the belly of the film, the site of rememoration of a love affair] (Dieutre 2014). As it brings us within a space that is marked as one of editing and manipulation, where filmic illusions are produced, *Jaurès* immediately announces that the form of rememoration to which Dieutre's love story with a man called 'Simon' is to be subject will again be an often ambiguous one. Dieutre appears on screen within this studio, sitting alongside his friend and frequent collaborator Eva Truffaut. As the film develops, she will question him on the three years he spent with this Simon in an apartment in the eponymous Jaurès district of north-eastern Paris, with the process of working-through sustained by this sentimental rememoration becoming collaborative, conversational and interrogative.

Jaurès explores a model of autobiographical filmmaking as talking cure. Through this dynamic of question and answer, a confessional account gradually emerges of an emotionally complex relationship, one that differs significantly from that presented through the lens of Rossellini in *EA4*, even if we encounter certain echoes between the descriptions offered in the two films. On the one hand, Dieutre describes a sexually intense relationship that granted a transformative but ephemeral form of happiness through the repeated contact of two mutually dependent bodies: 'à chaque fois un peu mieux, un peu plus parfait. Peut-être une forme de bonheur, je ne sais pas, qui restera toujours liée à ce moment-là, de Jaurès, de Simon' [each time a little better, a little more perfect. Perhaps a form of happiness, I don't know, that will always remain linked to that moment, of Jaurès, of Simon]. On the other hand, he describes a precarious situation in which he was given no certainty or stability, one in which he felt cut off and excluded from aspects of his partner's life — never introduced to his adult children, never given a key to the apartment, thrust into a position that Truffaut resumes at one point in their conversations as that of a 'clandestin dans une vie amoureuse' [stowaway in his love life]. Overall, Dieutre's words grant insight into what he presents as the most important relationship of his life, one grounded in mutual admiration, one that offered an enriching exchange between differing political and artistic values, an emotionally charged dialogue that led Dieutre to continually revise his ideas surrounding responsibility, love and attachment.

It is in an attempt to revisit the affective intensity of this period of his life that Dieutre shows Truffaut footage recorded during and immediately after his time with Simon, projecting these collated images onto the screen suspended at the darkened studio's centre. In such a way, Dieutre invites Truffaut to 'cherch[er] avec moi une vérité dans l'"après-coup" des images' [look with me to find truth in the 'afterwardsness' of the images] (ibid.). Throughout the film, Truffaut and Dieutre scrutinise these images for traces of past feeling, for belated understanding of a now vanished moment. But from within the studio, the site of editing, as they apprehend these images in what the filmmaker refers to as the *après-coup*, their *afterwardsness*, a past reality is continually reconfigured in the present in a way that increasingly unsettles the autobiographical *vérité* that *Jaurès* claims to seek, as we will see.

Whilst we hear what is presented as his voice, Simon never appears on screen in *Jaurès*. This is an absence that is pre-emptively announced by the first images that appear on the studio's projection screen, images that are pointedly *not* of Simon. Dieutre directs a perfunctory 'Vas-y' [Go ahead] to a studio technician hovering nearby and the screen flickers into animation. The camera zooms in on this projected footage and these images in turn fill our screen. This footage depicts a bedroom captured in the gentle light of early morning. The sounds of church bells and crickets accompany this tranquil scene. Dieutre himself appears in these images, sitting naked on the edge of the bed next to an unnamed man. This man reaches out to caress Dieutre's back affectionately before turning over and pulling the bed sheets back over himself. Dieutre stands and walks across the frame, his penis semi-erect. From within the space of the studio, Dieutre observes this filmic trace of himself and describes what he sees to Truffaut. He explains what these images contain and, more poignantly, what is missing from them:

FIG. 2.8. and 2.9. *Jaurès* (2012), Vincent Dieutre © La Huit/Cinaps TV.

C'est dans le midi. C'était pendant le festival. Évidemment ce n'est pas Simon à côté, c'est quelqu'un d'autre, un mec que j'avais rencontré. C'est à partir de ce moment-là que je me suis rendu compte que Simon me manquait vraiment. Il manquait. Oui, c'est ça, quelqu'un manquait.

[That's down South. It was during the festival. Obviously, it's not Simon next to me, it's someone else, a guy I'd met. It was from then on that I realised that I really missed Simon. He was missing. Yes, that's it, someone was missing.]

From the beginning of *Jaurès*, Simon is framed in terms of twin forms of loss: he is absent both from Dieutre's life in the present and from the images that appear on the studio's projection screen. This double absence will persist throughout the film as Dieutre and Truffaut continue to scrutinise the other images that appear on the screen before them.

Dieutre explains how Simon had never wanted to be filmed and how, in an attempt to preserve an indexical trace of the relationship, he had begun recording out of the window of Simon's apartment (Dieutre 2014). As this assembled footage of the Jaurès neighbourhood outside appears on the studio projection screen, Dieutre narrates to Truffaut what it shows. This footage captures the streets and pavements below the apartment, anonymous vehicles and passers-by, the overhead metro line, the comings and goings above and below the Voûte Lafayette, flocks of pigeons, all as they appeared at different times of day and at different points in the year. Most of all, this footage shows the various groups of Afghan asylum seekers who sought shelter by the nearby Canal Saint-Martin in front of Simon's apartment during the period of the relationship. Dieutre's images reveal the daily routines of these unnamed men, their struggles for survival, their improvised camps, their frequent encounters with police and charity workers. As it indexes daily life in the Jaurès neighbourhood, this footage captures the small transformations that mark the passage of time, the slowly shifting textures and rhythms of the city.

Describing *Jaurès*, Dieutre foregrounds the *archival* nature of the outwards-facing footage he had iteratively assembled from Simon's apartment window. For Dieutre, the gradual development of this inventory of urban details brings *Jaurès* into proximity with archival projects such as those offered by Georges Perec, most notably in his *Tentative d'épuisement d'un lieu parisien* [*An Attempt at Exhausting a Place in Paris*] (1975): 'C'est devenu un geste à la Perec, l'épuisement d'un point de vue sur un lieu donné' [It became a Perec-style gesture — exhausting a viewpoint on a given site] (Dieutre 2014). In their respective attempts at exhaustiveness, in their sensitivity to rhythms of repetition and change, in their attentiveness to small, overlooked details and to minor shifts in light and weather, there are certainly similarities between Dieutre's depiction of the Jaurès neighbourhood and Perec's enumerative study of the Place Saint Sulpice, over on the other bank of the Seine. And yet, what separates these two Parisian archives is the extent to which Dieutre's is permanently haunted by what it is prevented from showing. As we watch this visual record of the world outside, we hear the sounds of daily life taking place inside the apartment: morning showers, the bleep of a microwave, the blare of a radio, shared breakfasts, Simon endlessly practising the same piece of piano music. We even occasionally glimpse the very faint reflection of a human form wrapped in a patterned dressing gown (Dieutre? Simon? The same dressing gown seen on Versnel in *EA4*?) in the glass of the window. But as the recording camera faces always outwards, the apartment space and the bodies it contains remain concealed. From the images that appear on the studio projection screen, we certainly see nothing of the physical intimacy that dominates Dieutre's account to Truffaut of his experiences inside the apartment. With Simon out of sight, Dieutre's love story lacks its main protagonist. As Jean-Louis Comolli resumes: 'Règne l'absence du corps de l'aimé. Évoqué, caressé de mots, ce corps manque et ce manque ouvre la possibilité même du film' [The absence of the body of the loved one reigns. Evoked, caressed with words, this body is missing and this lack opens the film's very possibility] (Comolli 2012).[4]

In the negotiation with loss and absence that is staged in *Jaurès*, the *possibilité* that Comolli identifies is fulfilled by a form of autobiographical reenactment. In the scenes filmed inside the darkened mixing studio, there are instances in which

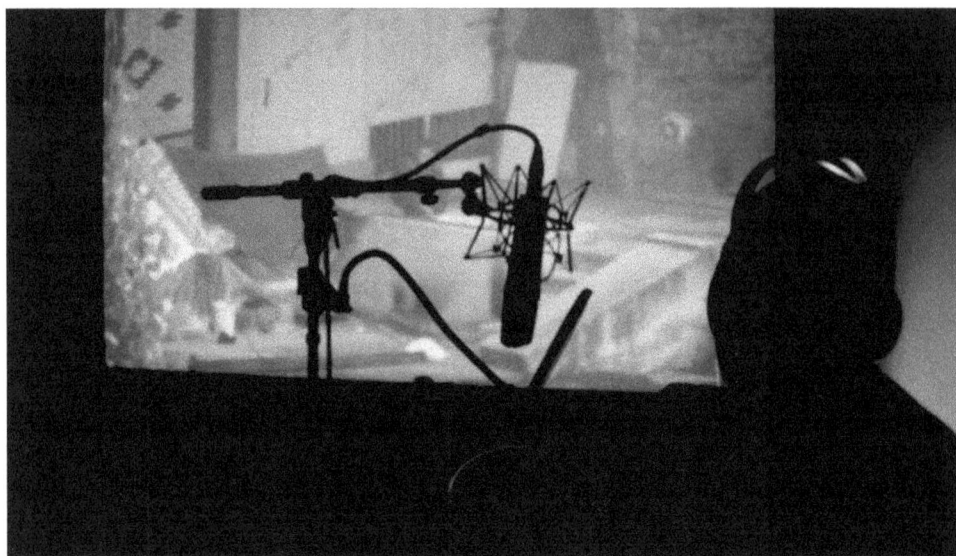

Fig. 2.10. *Jaurès* (2012), Vincent Dieutre © La Huit/Cinaps TV.

the camera moves behind Dieutre as he reviews his outwards-facing footage. The shadowy silhouette of the filmmaker appears outlined against the images of the Jaurès neighbourhood projected onto the screen before him. As the exterior images we watch alongside Dieutre provide a source of illumination in the darkened space of the studio, flooding the room with recorded light, there are points at which Dieutre's suspended projection screen begins to resemble something else. From within the studio space, the screen begins to look distinctly like a *window* — a window that stands in for the one from which Dieutre had previously recorded the world outside Simon's apartment. Dieutre here reconstructs a viewing position and reenacts the gesture of looking out of an apartment window to contemplate the Parisian landscape that he had performed so many times before. As he discusses his time with Simon whilst looking out of this 'window', Dieutre revives the lost moment of this now past relationship and the intense feelings that accompany it. Importantly, this is a form of autobiographical reenactment in which we are also asked to participate.

At certain moments, the camera in the studio moves forward from behind the silhouetted shoulders of Dieutre so that the projected urban images fill our screen. In such instances, *Jaurès* forces us to accept Dieutre's reconstructed point of view as our own. Observing this visual archive of the Jaurès neighbourhood whilst listening to the detailed oral account of the relationship that is delivered to Truffaut and simultaneously hearing the faint sounds of Dieutre's daily life with Simon, we realise that in being made to watch alongside Dieutre, to share his perspective and look out of his filmic 'window', we are simultaneously being asked to occupy a reimagined version of Simon's apartment. In such a way, we are also asked to experience the feelings and memories that this shared position evokes for ourselves.

In the development of this specific mode of spectatorship, the formal influence of

Akerman is once again clearly discernible. This is most obviously the case in relation to Akerman's *Là-bas* [*Down There*] (2006), a work largely composed of footage filmed from the window of a Tel Aviv apartment that sustains similarly mobile tensions between inside and outside, visibility and invisibility, introspection and projection, physical and mental space, directorial and spectatorial perspectives (Bruno 2016: 155; Schmid 2020: 120). To the extent that the viewing position reconstructed in *Jaurès* revives feelings from an earlier moment, asking us to 'remember' them as if they were our own, Dieutre's film simultaneously recalls the closing reenactment from Akerman's *Sud*, seen in the previous chapter. In its spatialised, participative sharing of memories and feelings linked to the breakup of a relationship as well as in its concern for the border separating public and private lives, *Jaurès* also shares something with works such as Sophie Calle's mixed-media installation *Douleur exquise* [*Exquisite Pain*] (1984–2003). In ways that overlap partially with these very different influences, as Dieutre recreates an imagined version of the apartment from within the darkened studio space, we are made, through mise-en-scène and framing, to participate actively, affectively, in his process of autobiographical rememoration.

Dieutre's use of autobiographical reenactment in *Jaurès* represents a very particular negotiation with absence and loss. Dieutre does not attempt to retrieve his experiences with Simon as they really were, to expose them to visual scrutiny. Rather, he reconstructs a site of experience through imagination and, so doing, revives feelings from the past that we are asked to share. There is an explicitly cathartic force to this process, something that is emphasised in the conclusions that Dieutre offers to Truffaut towards the end of the film. He confesses that, however his relationship with Simon finally ended, he does not regret a second of the years he spent with him in this apartment at Jaurès. This was, he suggests, a relationship that, more than any other, led him to fundamentally re-evaluate both who he was and the links that bound him to others. Some of the memories and feelings associated with this period are positive, others are inevitably more negative, but his time with Simon would always be part of his life that mattered to him. Reenactment allows him to reconnect with this fact and share it with us.

As Dieutre suggests in the film's closing line of dialogue, in vocabulary that reinforces the transformative quality he ascribes to the relationship and to the time he shared with Simon:

> Même si je vois plus Simon, même si je le reverrai peut-être plus jamais [...] je sais que ce moment-là a eu lieu et que, un tout petit peu, le monde a été transformé. Pas grand-chose, mais tout a un petit peu bougé.

> [Even if I don't see Simon anymore, even if may never see him again [...] I know that that moment happened and that the world was transformed just a little bit. It's not much but everything moved just a little.]

Whilst the suggestion that he may never see a man called Simon again might have been unsettled by the subsequent *EA4*, these words remain vital for our understanding of *Jaurès*. Insofar as they allow him to proudly assert that *ce moment-là a eu lieu*, Dieutre's autobiographical reenactment also assumes a certain proof value.

Truffaut and Dieutre are listed in the credits of *Jaurès* as *Les Témoins* — the *Witnesses* — and the film continually questions how it might be possible to bear witness to something that we do not see. In reviving the feelings of the past and in leading us to 'remember' them as if they were our own, *Jaurès* explores a use of affect as evidence and asks us to bear witness alongside Dieutre to invisible experiences as a means of proving that they indeed took place. In inviting the spectator within its own 'archive of feelings' (Cvetkovich 2003) and offering itself as a queer kind of evidence, *Jaurès* outlines a possible model of what José Esteban Muñoz (1996) described as alternate evidential modes able to grant access to minoritarian identities and experiences that have often been locked out of official histories or whose experiences do not always fit into discrete archives of visual proof. In mobilising a distinctive form of autobiographical reenactment, *Jaurès* invites us to participate in the development of alternate forms of proof, an affectively charged means of bearing witness to things that do not always leave a visible trace behind.

This queering of proof and evidence is sustained throughout *Jaurès*, as Dieutre leads us to question exactly what *counts* as a valid evidential form as well as the specific kinds of knowledge that these forms can sustain. Speaking in an interview from Fleur Albert's documentary *Vincent Dieutre, la chambre et le monde*, Dieutre suggests that all of his films encourage what he presents as a pervasive 'questionnement du régime de la croyance' [questioning of regimes of belief]. He argues that, by introducing elements of doubt into his work, he subjects spectatorial belief to a form of deliberate 'flottement' [wavering], creating a continual interplay between the imaginary and the real. Writing in his 'Abécédaire' manifesto, he suggests that this is done in an attempt to elicit more critical, questioning modes of spectatorship through which we continually interrogate the truths presented to us (2003: 78). Such sceptical forms of spectatorship are indeed solicited throughout *Jaurès*, as Dieutre again animates a tension between truth and fiction, sameness and difference, that unsettles the film's status as proof and that leads us to question exactly what we are witnessing on screen, deliberately leaving us uncertain.

Throughout *Jaurès*, we encounter a number of authenticating strategies that attest to the truthfulness, the accuracy, of Dieutre's autobiographical reconstruction — its status as valid, reliable proof. In its durational, observational qualities, filmed spontaneously from a window with a handheld camera, much of the footage that appears on the studio projection screen offers an impression of veracity and immediacy, of reportage-like objectivity, for instance. Elements such as overheard snippets of *France Inter* radio news broadcasts emanating from within the space of the apartment also serve as points of contextual corroboration for Dieutre's recreated moment of experience. In the film's perhaps most pronounced authenticating strategy, immediately before the scrolling end credits the screen is filled with the text of an official, dated statement from France's then immigration minister, Eric Besson. The reproduced text, bearing the marks of governmental authority, describes the police eviction in July 2010 of the camps of Afghan refugees that are observed so extensively throughout the film. In integrating this text within *Jaurès*, Dieutre seemingly seeks to ground his autobiographical account in the authenticity of an official, documental form of proof, anchoring it concretely in real space and time.

And yet, throughout *Jaurès* these authenticating strategies continually enter into conflict with elements of overt fiction that introduce forms of doubt into the images we watch. In the background of much of *Jaurès*, we hear the same piece of music being repeatedly, and falteringly, played. This piece is 'A Chloris' (1913) by the Franco-Venezuelan composer Reynaldo Hahn. Dieutre explains to Truffaut early in the film that he had asked Simon to learn to play this composition for him, even modifying the original lyrics, substituting Simon's name for the titular nymph of Greek myth, personalising the song to the couple's relationship: 'S'il est vrai, *Simon*, que tu m'aimes | Et j'entends que tu m'aimes bien | Je ne crois pas que les rois eux-mêmes | Aient un bonheur pareil au mien' [If it is true, *Simon*, that you love me | And I wish you to love me well | I do not believe that the kings themselves | Have happiness to equal mine]. There is a touching quality to this hesitant musical refrain each time that it emerges, as Simon struggles to fulfil Dieutre's request, but nevertheless still perseveres as a gift to his partner. Whilst, towards the beginning of the film, this music certainly does seem to be emanating from the concealed space of the apartment, as *Jaurès* progresses we begin to detect slight tonal inconsistencies in the sound. At points this music seems to have been superimposed, inserted as a means of increasing our emotional investment in certain passages of the autobiographical account Dieutre delivers. At the very end of the film, Dieutre and Truffaut sing the reworked version of the song in its entirety, against a full, unbroken piano accompaniment, in an unexpected theatrical flourish. Tellingly, on the film's closing credits, the piano-playing that we hear is attributed not to Simon, but to a professional musician.

In certain instances, the footage that appears on the studio's projection screen seems to have been manipulated as a means of further amplifying the affective charge of Dieutre's account. In one such instance, Dieutre describes to Truffaut a particularly poignant moment of intimacy with Simon. He recounts how, one night, he awoke from sleep. In the darkness, he watched Simon as he slept and listened to his breathing. Dieutre tells us that, overwhelmed by the contented peacefulness of his sleeping partner, he began to quietly cry. Against this description, one of the young Afghan refugees appears on screen, dancing on the banks of the canal. This footage is slowed down, accentuating the emotional intensity of the specific moment that Dieutre describes. Elsewhere, Dieutre's filmic manipulations are more pronounced. At intervals throughout the film, a series of elements chosen seemingly at random from the neighbourhood outside the apartment — cars, trees, pigeons, street signs, abandoned mattresses, clothing, metro carriages, rain drops — are digitally animated, offering a partially enhanced version of the recorded past. Occasional details are digitally 'coloured in', creating an almost cartoon-like effect that plays ambiguously on the encounter between the ostentatiously fictive and the supposedly real. There is a moment where a digitally rendered car suddenly disappears from the screen as these elements of augmentation trouble the filmic record, intervening directly in a past reality. Towards the beginning of *Jaurès*, these elements are subtle, possible to overlook; but as the film develops, these elements multiply and demand more and more of our attention.

FIG. 2.11. *Jaurès* (2012), Vincent Dieutre © La Huit/Cinaps TV.

These digital enhancements proliferate and progressively contaminate filmic reality until they finally invade the protected zone of the mixing studio, the site of the film's process of rememoration, with a red lamp facing the studio's mixing console suddenly animated. As these animated elements cross from remembered past to remembering present, Dieutre fundamentally unsettles the border between temporal frames, between layers of representation, between concrete and mental space, between autobiographical truth and fiction. Unsettling these borders, Dieutre frames the dynamics of memory as a process of editing and manipulation where the past is continually transformed in the present through creative acts of imagination. So doing, he leads us to interrogate the truth status of autobiography and the position of credulity in which we often find ourselves as soon as someone begins to give an account of themselves and their life through a confessional mode.

As these elements of manipulation and distortion suffuse the film, complicating its possible status as proof, Dieutre simultaneously urges us to question the nature of cinema and the cinematic capture of reality. It is from this perspective that further filmic influences for *Jaurès* become particularly clear. In the arrangement of a male and female figure sitting inside a darkened room watching visible images that stand in for images that remain invisible, there emerges, for instance, a telling reference to Marguerite Duras's *Le Camion* [*The Lorry*]. For much of this 1977 film, we watch similarly configured images of Duras sitting alongside actor Gérard Depardieu inside a room in the filmmaker's house at Neauphle-le-Château. From within the 'chambre noire' [dark room] of this curtained space (Duras 1977: 11), Duras reads to Depardieu the scenario of an unmade, virtual film that recounts the journey of a woman as she hitchhikes with a Communist lorry driver, forging a fleeting relationship that we never see on screen. Sequences in which Depardieu questions Duras on her imaginary film are interspersed with images of the titular lorry as it traverses the industrial landscapes of northern France, images which stand in for human interactions that are described but remain hidden from sight. In evoking this filmic precedent through the distinctive mise-en-scène of *Jaurès*, Dieutre draws our attention to the preoccupations that his work shares with Duras, to the uncertain border that separates the concrete reality of the world outside from the virtual reality of the imagination (see particularly Cooper 2019: 140–46). In such a way, Dieutre's editing studio — his own *chambre noire* — stands as a twenty-first-century Plato's cave, a site for the production of perhaps misleading cinematic illusions. Sequences in which Dieutre appears silhouetted against his projection screen 'window' similarly recall Jean-Luc Godard's *Scénario du film Passion* [*Scenario of The Film 'Passion'*] (1982). Godard's work, like *Jaurès*, foregrounds the labour of cinematic image-making, exploring how cinematic realities are called into being from fantasy and imagination or how an entirely new film might be constructed through the assemblage and manipulation of pre-existing images. In its meta-cinematic dimension, *Jaurès* of course also recalls Alfred Hitchcock's *Rear Window* (1954), a film deeply concerned with the dynamics of viewing and with the possibility that *what you see* is not necessarily *what you get*.

   Jaurès — like the works that have influenced it — deliberately problematises an understanding of film as a window on the world. And yet, within the fundamental queering that *Jaurès* stages of notions of proof, evidence and knowledge, even as it deliberately thrusts us into a stance of doubt, announcing the artificiality, the imperfection, the distortion of its autobiographical account, it still asks us to believe in it, to invest emotionally in it. *Jaurès* maintains that if we do so, embracing the feelings that are resuscitated from the past and that we are made to experience as if they were our own, these feelings can be used as the basis of new modes of political engagement. The autobiographical reenactment of *Jaurès* allows Dieutre to mourn the loss of his relationship in a way that opens to the possibility of a form of release; it also allows him to use the revived experiences of the past as the material with which to construct something new for the future.

   We are indeed led in this direction by the filmic influences identifiable in *Jaurès*, concerned as they all are (albeit in radically different ways) with ways of thinking and representing the political. From so much of Dieutre's account to Truffaut there emerges a concern with the interactions of different forms of politics, their changing status in the early years of the twenty-first century, their conflicts and irreconcilabilities. Dieutre recognises that the presence of Afghan men in the Jaurès neighbourhood represents the human face of a much larger geo-political crisis — one in which, through its military intervention in Afghanistan, France is actively implicated. He recognises the suffering encountered by these men who have fled from warzones and suggests that this lived reality has been made so much worse by the anti-immigration and anti-immigrant policies of Eric Besson — detailed in the government communique quoted at the conclusion to *Jaurès* — or, as referenced elsewhere in the film, of the then Interior Minister Brice Hortefeux. These forms of political repression are implicitly contrasted with the efforts we witness throughout *Jaurès* of individuals who seek to help the refugees, who volunteer their time and resources to improve their lives. Dieutre pays a great deal of attention in his descriptions to the political beliefs and affiliations of Simon, presenting him as an ideologically committed left-wing militant hugely involved in the defence of refugee rights. He describes his frequent disagreements with this man who believed only in the concrete, in the direct, in the pragmatic, who maintained that art was a frivolity that could never change the political structures of the world. Dieutre suggests that in Simon's eyes the Jaurès neighbourhood — named for the assassinated founder of the French Socialist Party — was still a solidly working-class district and that his partner had not noticed the transformations brought by successive waves of gentrification at what he presents as the Parisian epicentre of 'Bobo-land'. It is in the context of this concern for these shifting and intersecting political cultures that Dieutre's use of reenactment allows him to experiment with the possibility of a different (deliberately provocative) mode of political engagement.

One of the most challenging aspects of *Jaurès* lies in its depiction of the Afghan refugees. These men are a near constant presence throughout *Jaurès*, dominating the footage filmed from the apartment window as well as much of Dieutre's descriptions to Truffaut. The assembled video footage reveals an enduring fascination for them, for their rituals and interactions, and Dieutre's responses grow increasingly affectionate towards these unknown figures. As this affection leads Dieutre to draw parallels between his own life and theirs, a degree of discomfort potentially creeps in. Describing his film, Dieutre suggests that he was originally guided by a desire to: 'Voir comment deux réalités parallèles, ma réalité affective dans l'appartement et celle des réfugiés en bas, pouvaient entrer en résonance, en empathie' [See how two parallel realities, my affective reality in the apartment and the reality of the refugees down below, could enter into resonance, into empathy] (Dieutre 2014). Expanding on these resonances, he explains how the refugees were forced to leave their makeshift camps every morning, just as he was forced to leave Simon's apartment only to return in the evening. He underlines how, in a striking coincidence, the refugees were cleared from their Jaurès encampments at exactly the same time that his relationship ended. In his descriptions, Dieutre increasingly emphasises a parallel between his own relational precarity — what Truffaut presented as a stance of amorous clandestinity in the life of Simon — with the refugees' socio-political precarity.

This is a form of identification that Dieutre claims to reject at one point in his conversation with Truffaut, clearly aware of the ethical difficulty arising from these parallels: 'Évidemment je vais pas comparer ma situation à la leur, c'est la vie qui nous a rapprochés, puisque moi j'étais en haut dans l'appartement, puis eux ils étaient en bas' [Obviously I'm not going to compare my situation with theirs, it's life that brought us closer since I was up in the apartment and they were down below]. But throughout *Jaurès*, this is precisely what Dieutre does: despite his occasional claims to the contrary, he continually draws provocative connections between his own experiences inside Simon's apartment and those of unknown, unnamed men who remain permanently out in the cold. If the subtle space of resonance Akerman opened between distinct experiences of vulnerability in *Sud* had steered clear of the slippery terrain of equivalence, Dieutre here seems to trample right through it.

Jaurès reflects risks identified by art theorist Hal Foster in what he presents as an 'ethnographic turn' in the visual arts of the closing decades of the twentieth century. In his 1996 text *The Return of the Real*, Foster examines the 'ethnographic envy' he saw consuming a great number of contemporary artists and critics (1996: 181). Identifying a new development in the 'cultural politics of alterity', he explores the ethnographic or anthropological zeal that drove contemporary art production to engage increasingly with various forms of social othering. He criticises many of these interactions, often seeing in the presentation of the other offered in these artworks merely the projection of the self of the artist. For Foster, artists working in these ways often use the other as blank canvas upon which to project the aesthetic and political values they sought in their own work: 'In this case an ideal practice might be projected onto the field of the other, which is then asked to reflect it as if it were not only authentically indigenous but innovatively political' (183). Within the context of the extended institutional critique underpinning much of this artistic production, Foster alerts us to 'shifts in the siting of art' through which the complex realities of people's real lives, their pain and suffering, can become merely the subject and site for someone else's art (184).

Foster nevertheless goes on to concede that, although problematic, over-identification is surely better in such instances than total dis-identification, with the 'fantasmatic fear and loathing' of alterity that this dis-identification inevitably entails (203). Conscious of such risks and of their painful human cost, *Jaurès* proclaims a *responsibility* to identify. Dieutre describes to Truffaut how one of the young refugees had once propositioned Simon in exchange for money, explaining how Simon had been distraught at the desperation and stark battle for survival that lay behind this sexual offer. He explains how it was through Simon's reactions on such occasions that he came to more fully understand the dangerous lived realities of these men and to reconsider what it meant to feel compassion for them:

> Pas du tout au sens d'une espèce d'apitoiement sur telle ou telle situation ou d'indignation polie devant telle ou telle chose, mais vraiment le fait de complètement participer de la souffrance de l'autre, la prendre physiquement presque.

> [Not at all in the sense of a kind of pity towards such-and-such a situation, or polite indignation when faced with such-and-such a thing, but really the fact of participating completely in the suffering of the other, taking it almost physically.]

Jaurès encourages us to see in this kind of heightened emotional response the basis for a transformative politics of empathy. As he draws parallels between his own experiences of relational uncertainty and the Afghan refugees' experiences of destitution, Dieutre explores the extent to which, as Judith Butler suggests, we all exist, in a sense, in a shared state of vulnerable precariousness, held in networks of social definition and dependent upon forces that we do not control. The structures to which we are exposed have, of course, developed to maximise precariousness for some and minimise precariousness for others (Butler 2009: 2–3), as Dieutre indeed acknowledges in his protestations to Truffaut. But, Butler suggests, if we were to recognise what these different experiences of precarity have in common, to recognise what of the other could also be found in ourselves, this would be to offer the possibility of a more radically democratic, empathetic, egalitarian politics (32). *Jaurès* moves a stage further than both Butler and Foster, asking us to entertain the possibility of a politics that fully embraces the risk of over–identification, however provocative or uncomfortable this may be, encouraging an affectively charged, almost physical identification with the lives of others. This is a progressive politics for which Dieutre's autobiographical reenactment offers a strange kind of proof of concept. Just as reenactment led us to experience the feelings of an other as if they were our own, to 'remember' them for ourselves, so Dieutre attempts to do the same for these unknown refugees as part of a politics of identification across categories of difference that rethinks the links of responsibility and dependency binding individuals together.

Writing in an entry from his 'Abécédaire', Dieutre presents the challenge of defining the relationship between the individual and the collective as one of the most pressing political questions that confronts us today, identifying in the mode of experimental filmmaking he seeks to undertake an attempt to 'donner une forme filmique à ce questionnement' (2003: 83) [give a filmic form to this questioning]. In *Jaurès*, the 'forme filmique' through which Dieutre interrogates the implication and responsibilities of the individual in the collective is accessed through reenactment. Dieutre explores how the intimate feelings he revives from the past can both allow us to share in the lived realities of the time he spent with a man he once loved inside a Parisian apartment, and simultaneously provide a platform for rethinking much larger realities in the world outside. As Dieutre suggests to Truffaut towards the conclusion of *Jaurès*, reflecting upon what he learnt from his time with Simon:

> J'ai l'impression qu'aujourd'hui, justement, cette notion d'attachement, d'amour, on a beaucoup de mal à en définir la nature, comme on a beaucoup de mal aussi à définir le rapport qu'on a avec la politique ou même tout simplement avec la justice.

> [I get the impression that people today have great difficulty in defining the nature of this particular notion of attachment, of love, in the same way that they also struggle to define the relationship they have with politics or even just with the justice system.]

Jaurès explores a mode of autobiographical filmmaking in which feeling and politics are wholly intertwined. He asks us to believe in the authenticity of the past feelings that, through autobiographical reenactment, he revives in the present, even if these feelings are marked ambiguously as fictions that have been transformed through imagination, even if believing in them can confront us with ethical challenges. He asks us to accept that the feelings of the individual can be used to reimagine the collective, and that the intensity of affect can be used as the basis of new political cultures. That such possibilities are brought into focus by a work of cinema has the added benefit of standing as an implicit rebuttal of the scepticism of Dieutre's former partner around the political utility of art.

In this second chapter, the precise 'forme filmique' assumed by reenactment has varied hugely, often entailing strategies far removed from those identified in my reading of Akerman. Throughout my analysis, I have framed Dieutre's autobiographical reenactments in terms of what I have identified as the queerness of the copy, exploring how they each announce themselves as strangely almost the same, but not quite, as the various originals they replicate, whether these originals be earlier experiences or earlier artworks. In this shifting interplay of sameness and difference, Dieutre's queer copies generate new, often disorienting pleasures that flow across time. These pleasures often hold out the promise of forging alternate modes of being in and of the world, of communicating with those from the past and the present with whom we find ourselves identifying. The labour of mourning performed by Dieutre's autobiographical reenactments opens at points to the possibility of release in a way that was denied by the cycles of *ressassement* within which Akerman was held. This prospect of release, of catharsis, is pursued yet further in the next chapter. In the work of Boris Lehman, reenactment's possible therapeutic function is foregrounded yet more explicitly. As above, I initially frame Lehman's work in relation to the influence of Akerman; but I will also show how his autobiographical uses of reenactment respond to certain questions that, as we have seen, are powerfully asked by Dieutre.

Notes to Chapter 2

1. Quoted in <http://www.film-documentaire.fr/4DACTION/w_fiche_film/51125_1> [accessed 8 March 2021].
2. Quoted in <http://www.film-documentaire.fr/4DACTION/w_fiche_film/25793_1> [accessed 8 March 2021].
3. Dieutre has admitted, for instance, to having modified the identity and biography of the 'Simon' referred to in the next case study (see Dieutre 2014; see also Sauvage 2018).
4. In the abridged version of Comolli's text that appears in the Jaurès DVD liner notes, the word 'possibilité' is replaced with 'promesse' [promise].

CHAPTER 3

❖

Boris Lehman — Archives

Introduction — Provocations and Catharsis

There exist various links between Belgian filmmaker Boris Lehman and the film-makers considered in the two previous chapters. My analysis of Dieutre referenced at various points his 2003 article 'Abécédaire pour un tiers-cinéma', an alphabetised manifesto text that, in criticising both the rampant commercialism of mainstream film production and the conventionalised mannerism of European art-house cinema, traced the uncertain contours of an alternate 'third cinema' at the edges of contemporary film. Lehman is identified in this text as one of the fellow *tiers-cinéastes* contributing to the kind of cinematic renewal that Dieutre advocates. Lehman's work indeed amply fulfils many of the aspirations detailed by Dieutre in his manifesto and in subsequent writing: as will be well illustrated by the films explored in this chapter, Lehman proposes a model of experimental cinema that remains always 'absolument différent, forcément indépendant, balbutiant, auroral [...] bricolé, autoproduit, réactif, à vif' [absolutely different, unfailingly independent, incipient, emergent [...] thrown together, self-produced, responsive, raw] (Dieutre 2005).

Just as Dieutre's filmmaking would not be what it is today without the foundational influence of the director of *News From Home*, so too do tight links, aesthetic but also personal, bind Lehman to Akerman. Lehman and Akerman shared a background and upbringing: both were born to Polish families who had been subjected to antisemitic persecution before settling in Brussels. Both grew up within similar diasporic communities in the Belgian capital, with parents active in the city's clothing trade. The two filmmakers knew each other well and collaborated on a number of occasions, with Lehman having worked as on-set photographer for the production of *Jeanne Dielman, 23 Quai du Commerce, 1080 Bruxelles*, for instance. In a testament to the relationship that existed between the two filmmakers, Lehman (like Dieutre) contributed a text to Akerman's *Autoportrait en cinéaste* in 2004. Whilst the majority of the other texts written by filmmakers and film scholars for the critical dossier attached to Akerman's photo-textual self-portrait offered analyses of individual films, Lehman's stands out for its poetic evocation both of the guiding preoccupations of Akerman's work as a whole, and, perhaps more prominently, of his friendship with her. Lehman's deeply personal text, entitled 'Ma nuit avec toi' [My Night With You], is accompanied by a touching photograph of the two filmmakers sitting side by side on a park bench, smiling, seemingly comfortable in each other's company.

Lehman's contribution to *Autoportrait en cinéaste* references a large number of the films that Akerman made during her life, whilst also gesturing towards the two filmmakers' common acquaintances, experiences that they shared in a friendship that spanned several decades, reminiscences of the streets of the Belgian capital that they had both explored, and the scandals unleashed at home by the release of Akerman's early incendiary films. Lehman's fragmentary words simultaneously recall the traumatic reverberations of histories of mass destruction that, as we saw, were such an insistently haunting presence in Akerman's life and work: 'musique des noms | des langues mortes dans la synagogue | musique des morts et des mot ressassés | ressuscités en mélopées' [music of names | of dead tongues in the synagogue | music of the dead and of words endlessly repeated | resuscitated as dirge] (2004: 190). These reverberations also exert a palpable pressure upon Lehman's filmmaking, with so much of his work deeply preoccupied with the memories, texts, sites and rituals that bolster contemporary Jewish identities, and with how these have been transformed in the wake of the Holocaust.

Lehman and Akerman both occupy what we might think of as a shared post-Holocaust cultural space and sensibility, marked by experiences of loss and severance from the past, by the violent truncation of knowledge and tradition, and by the permanent threat of forgetting, erasure and extermination. And yet, Lehman often addresses the thematic concerns he shares with his friend and collaborator in a way that, in many regards, actually bears a closer resemblance to effects identified in the previous chapter in my analysis of Dieutre. I demonstrated in particular how Dieutre's *Jaurès* unsettled the forms of knowledge sustained by visual archives of proof and proposed instead a queer mode of evidence that asked us to bear witness alongside the filmmaker to bodies, lives and experiences that do not always leave a visible trace behind. Throughout this current chapter, I identify in Lehman's filmmaking a similarly intense but more extensive preoccupation with notions of evidence and more specifically with the archive as a figure of memory and as site of (self-)knowledge. As was the case in Dieutre's *Jaurès*, this archival preoccupation is explicitly political: in the case-studies I examine over the following sections, Lehman interrogates the ways in which, through their various manifestations and mobilisations, archives control access to the experiences and identities of the past and shape our understanding of them. Lehman shares with Dieutre a concern with the obstacles that stand in the way of witnessing and testimony along with a staunch desire to overcome them through the development of alternate practices of archiving; but in his work this desire is pursued through very different means and with very different results.

Lehman's autobiographical filmmaking is propelled by an all-encompassing archival compulsion. In its avowed aspiration to exhaustiveness, this compulsion replicates something of the desires that led Dieutre to place his camera at a Parisian apartment window: to preserve a trace of every transient detail of the time and space that surrounded him. But the archive that Lehman builds is on a significantly larger scale. In his life and in his work (as far as the two can, in his case, possibly be separated) Lehman is a consummate collector, a hoarder, the archivist of his own existence. Over the course of multiple decades, Lehman has actively accumulated an endless stream of objects, images, encounters and experiences that he has painstakingly recorded in a dizzying number of films. The materials he has thus assembled are the disparate components of an enormous *archive of self*, an autobiographical repository built to durably house and preserve a record of every possible detail of who he is and of the place he occupies in the world. Every film that Lehman makes, every new interaction he arranges, every item he amasses and refuses to throw away, is a new entry to this straining personal inventory.

In the case studies I explore, Lehman's uses of autobiographical reenactment are to be understood in relation to this immense archive of self — as yet more entries to be indexed and included within it. But autobiographical reenactment is also to be understood in his work as a practice of archiving in and of itself, one that grants access to very particular engagements with memory, knowledge and identity. The instances I analyse — found successively in *A la recherche du lieu de ma naissance* [*In Search of my Birthplace*], *Histoire de mes cheveux: de la brièveté de la vie* [*History of my Hair: On the Shortness of Life*], and *Funérailles (de l'art de mourir)* [*Funeral (On the Art of Dying)*] — are all markedly different. What connects them, however, is their recourse to embodied techniques of self-investigation and self-representation, through which Lehman seeks a fleshy kind of understanding of past realities (and sometimes even of realities still to come). Indeed, if certain of the recreations of the past that we have seen in previous chapters also generated new possible futures, Lehman amplifies this prospective, speculative focus much further: in the examples that follow, autobiographical reenactments intersect with what can only be understood as *pre*-enactment. Whether they look forwards or backwards, in allowing Lehman to experience something from a time other than the present directly for himself or to bear witness as others do so on his behalf, these varied experiments all offer strange modes of autobiographical proof that are sometimes mobilised in opposition to other evidential forms.

As we will see throughout the case studies examined in this chapter, the distinctive engagements with memory, knowledge and identity that are sustained by Lehman's autobiographical use of (p)reenactment hold out the possibility of potentially therapeutic, cathartic negotiations with experiences of loss. Such negotiations notably hold out the possibility of moving beyond the *musique des morts et des mot ressassés* that Lehman identified in Akerman's work, but also allow him to negotiate other losses. From this perspective, it is far from incidental that one of Lehman's initiatory experiences of filmmaking was in the seventeen years he spent from the mid-1960s onwards volunteering in a day centre for mentally ill patients, working with film as an explicitly therapeutic tool of self-expression. Recalling this formative time at Brussels's (strikingly named) Club Antonin Artaud, Lehman writes: 'Nous ne voulions pas faire de "beaux films" mais permettre à des non-professionnels, à des marginaux d'exprimer leur souffrance, leur problèmes à l'aide d'une caméra' [We didn't want to make "beautiful films" but rather to allow non-professionals, those on the margins, to express their suffering and their problems with a film camera] (1985: 26). Even as he turns his gaze upon himself and upon his own problems and suffering, making films that are often unquestionably *beaux*, such therapeutic objectives remain. This therapeutic function operates throughout Lehman's work; but it is encountered with particular force in the examples explored in this chapter, as we will see.

   This possibility of salutary closure and release is often supported by a willingness to address the preoccupations Lehman shares with Akerman in a much more direct manner. As we saw in a film such as *D'Est*, Akerman's filmmaking apprehended sites of suffering through evocation, always maintaining a distance, always reluctant to move too close to the gaping hole at the heart of her life and art. In contrast to his compatriot, Lehman often chooses to approach the myriad pains of history head-on, plunging into its holes, displaying a much greater willingness to grapple with the fraught politics of identity directly; to expose the frictions of the personal and the historico-political; to level accusations at the agents of historical atrocity; to carry journeys left incomplete in Akerman's work to their frequently painful end-points; to lay claim to the modern iconography of Jewishness in its full extent, from the minora to the death camp. Lehman's filmmaking often entails a much greater degree of deliberate and active provocation than was the case in Akerman's work, and across this chapter we will encounter some of the most bewildering, occasionally challenging images considered anywhere in this book, as Lehman uses reenactment to push the extremes of self-knowledge. I open the main body of this chapter by reflecting further on the recurrent questions, intentions, habits and anxieties that propel what I present as the archive of self at the heart of Lehman's life and work, and on how these condition the specific uses of (p)reenactment that I will go on to analyse.

In Lehman's Terms: Archives of Self

Imagine trying to navigate a room piled so high with teetering stacks of film cannisters that you are forced to squeeze through gingerly, conscious that everything might at any minute come tumbling down, trapping you underneath this colossal mass of images. This is a scenario that is not left to the imagination in a number of the films Lehman has made; it also encapsulates something of his work more broadly. What strikes us immediately when we first encounter the work of Lehman is inevitably the sheer prodigiousness of his creative output: over five decades, Lehman has produced almost 500 films, in a variety of genres, lengths, styles and formats, with this cinematic catalogue flanked by the collection of some 300,000 photographs that he has also accumulated consistently across his life. Within his already capacious filmography, certain episodes of Lehman's work also stand out for their own conspicuous size. From 1983 onwards, Lehman devoted himself to his monumental *Babel* project — a continually replanned and reconfigured sequence of autobiographical films that exists in its finalised form with a combined running time of over thirty hours and that came to consume over thirty years of the filmmaker's

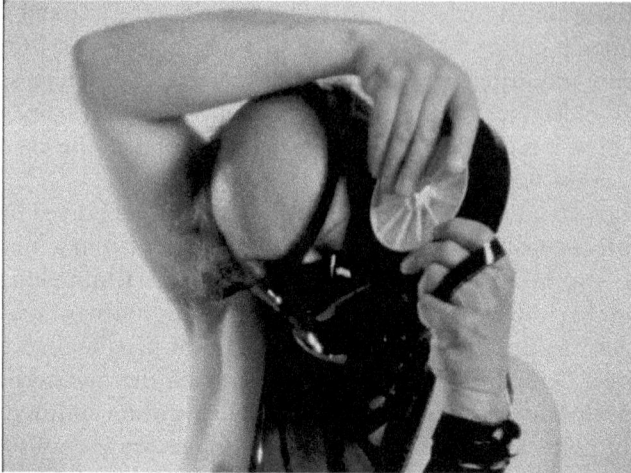

FIG. 3.1. *Mes entretiens filmés* (1995–2012), Boris Lehman © Boris Lehman/Dovfilm.

life. With its echoes of the foolhardy excesses of unattainable, hubristic ambition, the title chosen for this project exemplifies the irony and self-satire characteristic of so much of Lehman's work and the authorial stance he adopts within it.

The *Babel* project's telling title points towards Lehman's own recognition of the extremity, the madness even, of the motivating force that lies behind his work: a desire to devote a life entirely to film, to live that life through film, to capture its every moment in images, to the point that the border dividing art from existence becomes uncertain. So much of Lehman's work betrays a tactile, bodily, sometimes almost festishistic engagement with the matter of film production. Such engagements reveal an enduring fascination with analogue film in its diaphanous fragility, in the seemingly magical role Lehman attributes to it as a medium for preserving his lived experience. In an episode of his compendium film *Mes entretiens filmés* [*My Conversations on Film*] (1995–2012), Lehman binds his body with unravelled reels of film, staging himself as a kind of living totem to the power of cinema. As his facial features are squashed and contorted, as folds of his reddened flesh poke out between gaps, as his genitals are entangled in celluloid, these images assume an almost S&M quality, hinting at a sensual, perhaps even sexual attachment to film, whilst literalising the tight intertwinement of life and art that defines his work. As Lehman himself resumes in a text on his website, underlining this inextricable imbrication: 'Une façon de voir, une façon de vivre. Filmer, vivre, filmer' [A way of seeing, a way living. Film, live, film].[1]

Lehman's autobiographical practice is oriented towards the construction of what I have presented as an ever-expanding archive of self. In its functioning, Lehman's autobiographical archive recalls Jacques Derrida's account of what, through his reading of the life and work of Freud, he termed *archive fever*. Lehman's archive of self replicates certain of the drives symptomatic of the archival pathology Derrida diagnoses: on the one hand, a compulsion to accumulate and collect — a state of being, as Derrida's French rendering would have it, perpetually *en mal d'archive*

FIG. 3.2. *Mes sept lieux* (2013), Boris Lehman © Boris Lehman/Dovfilm
(with: Les Films du Centaure/CBA/Sophimages).

[in need of archives]; on the other hand, and stemming from a conception of psychoanalysis as an essentially archival practice, an exploratory turn to the psyche, to self-knowledge, to memory, to the troubled secrets and uncertainties that populate the border between public and private, or more pointedly that inhabit the particular space of intimacy that exists between oneself and oneself (Derrida 1996: 90–91). Such symptoms manifest themselves clearly in the life and work of a filmmaker who identifies as both the compulsive hoarder of images and things and as the indefatigable self-analyst who obsessively explores the depths of his own being in search of the various coordinates that might tell him who Boris Lehman really is and where he fits in the world.

As a participant appearing in Lehman's *Funérailles (de l'art de mourir)*, the final case study considered in this chapter, laments: 'Vous n'imaginez pas ce que c'est que les archives d'un cinéaste qui a près de 500 films au compteur et qui ne jette rien!' [You have no idea what the archives of a filmmaker who has clocked up nearly 500 films and who never throws anything away are like!]. We are granted insight into the all-consuming extensiveness of Lehman's own brand of archive fever in numerous films. In *Choses qui me rattachent aux êtres* [*Things That Connect Me To Beings*] (2008), Lehman rummages through the crammed storage spaces of his Brussels apartment, presenting a succession of objects to the camera: he names the individual who originally gave each of these things to him in an enumerative self-portrait that is guided by the notion that, as he suggests, 'Je suis la somme de tout ce que les autres m'ont donné' [I am the sum of all that others have given me]. The listing of these disparate *choses* reflects a desire to apprehend and investigate an identity conceived of as mobile and dispersed, as something endlessly updated through new encounters and exchanges, situated at the centre of networks of human attachment and connection. In *Mes sept lieux* [*My Seven Places*] (2013), Lehman's camera surveys the various living spaces that the filmmaker occupies, enumerating the overwhelming superabundance of the personal effects that these overstuffed spaces contain: books, boxes, magazines, trinkets, clothes, the varied detritus accumulated across a lifetime. He presents himself in this film in the guise of *le collectionneur* [the collector] — 'celui qui ne jette jamais rien, qui garde tout comme des reliques, et des fragments de son propre corps' [he who never throws anything away, who holds onto everything like relics and fragments of his own body]. Unable to separate himself from the items he hoards, Lehman appears as a Belgian version of Ilya Kabakov's garbage man. As he adds ever more exhibits to the museum of his life, Lehman dedicates a cluttered shrine to his memories, and invites us inside.

The habits of material hoarding and collecting exposed in these works are replicated in Lehman's filmmaking practice more broadly. Through a vertiginous number of attempts, Lehman has sought to exhaustively capture the myriad traces of his passage through life — the spaces he visits and inhabits, the individuals and groups he meets, his relationships, his experiences, his thoughts, his successes and failures, the physiognomy of his beloved Brussels as it changes around him. As he films, he arranges, stages and orchestrates, corralling reality into a deeply personal mise-en-scène: everybody here (Lehman included) is playing a version of themselves, a role filtered through fiction. Through recording every aspect of his existence, living his life through the lens of his camera, Lehman's reality becomes inseparable from its representation. The enormous filmic archive he creates is a perpetual work-in-progress: Lehman seeks always to expand, consolidate and update, returning repeatedly to the same people and places time after time. Nothing he records is ever abandoned or thrown away: film projects stop and restart, often after lengthy, eventful intervals; sequences are reworked or reinserted into other projects; images are stored for future use, sometimes revived many years later where they are brought into conversation with much more recent images. Everything Lehman films becomes new entries into an already brimming archive of self, catalogued and arranged through complex logics of correspondence and cross-referencing that only he fully masters. As this moving-image archive extends to hundreds of hours or to multiple kilometres of film stock carefully coiled into battered cannisters, it generates yet more objects that Lehman cannot bring himself to dispose of.

Lehman himself acknowledges (and indeed frequently bemoans) the excessiveness of his autobiographical archive and the mass of artefacts it houses. As he resumes neatly in *Histoire de ma vie racontée par mes photographies* [*Story of My Life Told by My Photographs*] (2001), struggling to move in a room where every surface is covered but convinced that the secrets to his identity past and present must be buried somewhere amongst the chaos: 'Je suis un homme encombré' [I am a cluttered man]. Alongside this awareness of the growing unwieldiness of the personal traces he accumulates, their tendency to fill any given repository and test any rigid organising logic or classificatory system, Lehman's practice of self-archiving is beset with two persistent anxieties that encourage the archival proliferation we have seen. The first concerns the nature of the self-knowledge his autobiographical archive might support and is announced clearly in the opening sequence of *Histoires de mes cheveux: de la brièveté de la vie*, the second of this chapter's main case studies. Lehman appears on screen sitting on a park bench in the Ixelles district of Brussels, his voice-over instantly establishing the formidable challenge of this and other of his films: 'Donner une image conforme de moi' [Provide an image true to myself]. The camera zooms in on Lehman's reddened eye and the furrowed wrinkles that surround it, capturing its own reflection on the surface of the filmmaker's iris. Here, as elsewhere in his work, Lehman questions the scrutinising gaze that he casts over himself, interrogating the exactitude, the conformity of the autobiographical impression he creates. As he continues to build his monumental archive of self through objects and films, Lehman is pursued by the awareness that it might never capture and condense his identity in its entirety, providing a reliable or stable route to knowing and understanding himself — the awareness that, even as this archive expands to impossible proportions, something will always be left out.

This awareness never leads to resignation in Lehman's filmmaking: the difficulties of self-knowledge are instead enthusiastically embraced as incentives to new, often bizarre gestures of artistic experimentation. We see this particularly clearly in *Tentatives de se décrire* [*Attempts at Describing Oneself*] (2005), a film whose pluralised title reflects the wide variety of autobiographical experiments that Lehman will here undertake, whilst also pre-emptively announcing these multiple experiments as merely provisional, potentially thwarted trials that may not ultimately be able to deliver the definitive or exact answers that are sought. As Lehman suggests towards his film's opening: 'Je cherche à savoir comment on peut se décrire, comment on peut entrer en sa propre intimité, quels sont aujourd'hui les moyens de vision, d'investigation de soi' [I'm trying to find out how one can describe oneself, how one can enter into intimacy with oneself, what means of seeing and investigating oneself exist today]. Attempting to enter within the shifting space of his own intimacy, Lehman mobilises an endless succession of such strategies of self-representation and self-inquiry. He makes inky handprints on paper, takes plaster casts of body parts and traces his outline on a brick wall, apparently seeking an indexical imprint of his presence. He exposes himself to the scrutiny of others, sitting as the model for the members of a life-drawing class or for his friend, the blind photographer Evgen Bavčar. He films segments of his body as they are rubbed and manipulated by a masseuse. He positions himself, naked and prostrate, on top of a photocopier to scan his body before then attempting to piece together the reproduced fragments into a composite self-portrait. In a film that Lehman himself presents as a meandering attempt at an 'archivage de moi-même' [archiving of myself], the self appears as a scattered puzzle that can only ever be solved imperfectly.

Lehman's uncertainty around the adequacy of his varied attempts at defining himself coexists throughout his work with a concern for the durability of the autobiographical archive he creates, its resilience to corruption and to the passing of time. In a number of films, Lehman mourns the loss or damage of images that he has suffered, and he himself concedes in places that the towering stacks and bursting boxes he is obliged to carry with him as he moves from apartment to apartment do not provide the most hermetic or infallible of storage systems. His website features a plea for public support in finding an appropriate venue in which

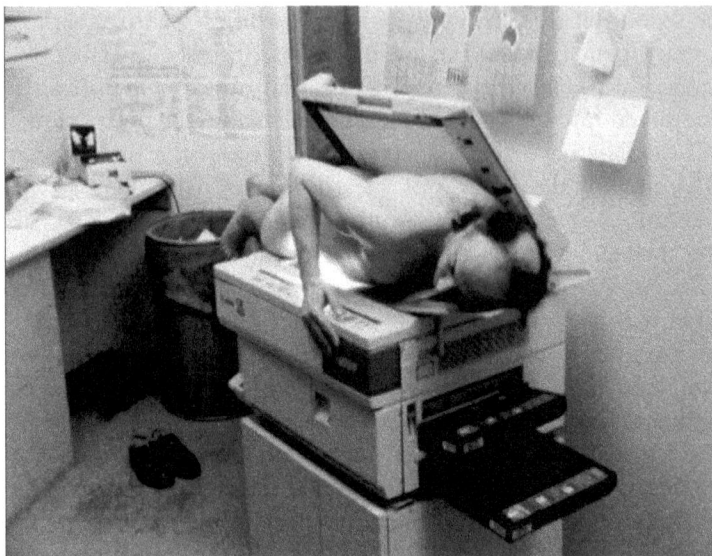

FIG. 3.3. *Tentatives de se décrire* (2005), Boris Lehman
© Boris Lehman/Dovfilm (with: Mainfilm/Cocagne/CBA).

to house his collection of films, emphasising both the urgency of halting further deterioration and the richness of the documentation that will be lost forever if no solution is found.[2] This concern with the loss of archival integrity intersects with Lehman's fears around his own gradual disappearance. Lehman's fate is intimately bound to that of his archive: the more he collects, the greater the chance that some trace of him might persist beyond death; but every threat to the integrity of this archive simultaneously exacerbates the risk of permanent erasure and effacement that torments him. Much as this fear of disappearance stems from Lehman's awareness of the inevitability of ageing, decline and mortality, it is also nourished by the spectre of the catastrophic destruction of the Holocaust. As emblemised by the closing sequences of *Histoire de ma vie racontée par mes photographies*, where Lehman projects his photographs onto the exposed surfaces of his own mortal body before these images are suddenly consumed by flames and chemical decay, the monumentality of his archive of self seeks to protect against the possibility that some obscene combustion might one day permanently delete all trace of him and of his presence on earth.

It is perhaps reflective of the extent to which Lehman conceives of his own body (and the fate that awaits it) as inseparable from the archive he creates that every one of the films referenced above includes sequences in which the filmmaker appears naked before us on screen. This is a naked body that is tested, contorted, prodded, probed, punished, as part of the filmmaker's continual attempts to excavate and preserve something from within himself. This body with its various parts is an essential component of Lehman's practice of self-archiving, an animate site of self-knowledge, with the experiences of a life and the effects of time's passing etched into its changing textures. As he draws us within his archive of self, scrutinising his encounters, his worldly possessions, his precarious living situations, the very materiality of his own flesh, Lehman exposes himself both figuratively and literally before our eyes. Throughout his work, Lehman gives so much of himself, laying bare a whole existence on screen to be considered and consumed, asking in exchange that we accompany him in the often extreme autobiographical experiments that he stages.

Whether they entail enacting a version of experiences from the past or from the future, the experiments analysed in the remaining sections of this chapter generate further entries for Lehman's archive of self to be inventoried alongside countless others; but in condensing the characteristics and gestures outlined above, Lehman's uses of autobiographical (p)reenactment can also themselves be understood as distinctive forms of self-archiving. Functioning as potent *moyens de vision*, *d'investigation de soi*, autobiographical (p)reenactment proposes an improvisational, heuristic tool of self-inquiry that foregrounds the body as a vital (if mutable) site for the production, stockage, retrieval and transmission of knowledge — a tool that offers compelling ways of navigating the anxieties of durability and resemblance that pervade and propel Lehman's autobiographical work. Constructing a subjective mise-en-scène of reality that is both true and false at the same time, autobiographical (p)reenactment allows Lehman to take ultimate control over his existence and its representation. It allows Lehman to patrol his archival jurisdiction, offering him an often oppositional technique of self-definition that can be mobilised whenever (as we will see particularly clearly in my first case study) his sovereignty over his own image is challenged.

In Search of Myself: *A la recherche du lieu de ma naissance*

Although he has spent the overwhelming majority of his life in Brussels, Lehman was not born in the Belgian capital, nor indeed anywhere else in Belgium. The filmmaker was born in the Swiss city of Lausanne on the shores of Lake Léman as his parents fled Nazi persecution across Europe. *A la recherche du lieu de ma naissance* (1990) sees Lehman return, four and a half decades later, to the unfamiliar city of his birth. The film is composed of extended sequences filmed in locations in and around Lausanne — its streets, slopes, interiors, the waters of its lake — and encounters with various residents, all accompanied by Lehman's meditative voice-overs. As he remains hidden behind his recording camera, the images that appear on screen suggest the perspective of the filmmaker seeking to consolidate and expand the knowledge about himself and his origins that he carries with him to Switzerland. This is a self-knowledge that, right from the film's opening voice-over, is tinged with a degree of creeping precarity:

> Moi, Boris Lehman, je suis né à Lausanne le 3 mars 1944. Cette certitude, je l'ai acquise et transmise moi-même, sans jamais vérifier, par les documents officiels: cartes d'identité, passeports, abonnements, diplômes, certificats, Curriculum Vitae, et par mes anniversaires qu'on ne fêtait jamais. Mais qu'est-ce que j'en sais au juste? Qu'est-ce que cela signifie pour moi d'être né à Lausanne, dans un pays neutre, pendant que la guerre sévissait dans toute l'Europe? Pour le savoir,

je suis revenu à Lausanne, chercher en quelque sorte à rassembler les preuves de mon existence.

[I, Boris Lehman, was born in Lausanne on the 3rd March 1944. I myself have acquired and relayed this certitude, without ever checking, though official documents: identity cards, passports, contracts, qualifications, certificates, CV and through my birthdays that we never celebrated. But what exactly do I know? What does it mean for me to have been born in Lausanne, in a neutral country, whilst war was raging across Europe? In order to find out, I have returned to Lausanne to try and assemble the proof of my existence.]

The tone of this opening *Moi, Boris Lehman* — that of contractual engagement and solemn, sworn testimony — combined with the documents Lehman lists, establishes the official, verified nature of his existential certitude. But the question *qu'est-ce que j'en sais au juste?* hangs over the autobiographical inquiry Lehman stages. Throughout his film, Lehman scours his native city in search of other certitudes, other forms of proof of his existence, that might allow him to strengthen his faltering grasp on exactly who he is and where he comes from.

The title of *A la recherche du lieu de ma naissance* of course immediately situates it within a cultural field that pays clear homage to Marcel Proust. And yet, beyond titular overtones, Lehman's autobiographical search resembles less Proust's literary edifice than a number of more recent interventions into the problematics of memory, knowledge and identity. In its form and functioning as well as in the anxieties that adhere to it, what I presented above as Lehman's archive of self exists in close dialogue with the work of varied archival practitioners from other areas of francophone cultural production. In its presentation of selfhood as a dispersed puzzle to be pieced imperfectly back together, so much of Lehman's work recalls, for instance, the photo-textual experimentation of Roland Barthes. Through a shared vocabulary of *tentatives*, *choses* and *lieux*, many of the films surveyed in the previous section openly acknowledge the influence of Georges Perec. Through pieces such as *Recherche et présentation de tout ce qui reste de mon enfance, 1944–1950* [*Research and Presentation of All that Remains of My Childhood, 1944–1950*] (1969), Christian Boltanksi has developed a fictionalising practice of self-archiving that, as it aspires to exhaustiveness, seeks similarly to preserve against the threat of death and apocalyptic destruction (a comparison reinforced by Boltanski's on-screen appearance in *Tentatives de se décrire*). Such similarities alert us to the extent to which Lehman's filmmaking knowingly engages with a much wider archival consciousness. As it has provided the cultural context for a reorientation of autobiographical practice, this consciousness helps us to understand Lehman's search for himself in Lausanne.

In a 2005 analysis of francophone life-writing that highlights the distinctive slant towards the archival discernible in the work of writers such as Perec and Barthes as well as of Patrick Modiano, Michel Leiris, Marguerite Yourcenar, Nathalie Sarraute, Jorge Semprún, Assia Djebar, Annie Ernaux, Pierre Michon and others, Michael Sheringham offered a valuable attempt to map out the causes and ramifications of a continuing cultural fascination with the archive that took root particularly in the second half of the last century. The terms of Sheringham's analysis are, as he indeed recognises, symptomatic of a semantic shift towards the use of the singular, whereby we now commonly speak of *l'archive, the* archive (2005: 47). This singular reminds us, Sheringham suggests, that the archive was originally understood as a concrete place where documents were housed — a reading emphasised by Derrida who identifies its origins in the ancient Greek *arkheîon*, the house of the superior magistrates or *archons* (Derrida 1996: 2). The use of the singular confronts us first and foremost with the archive's physicality, with its three-dimensional spatial reality; but, at the same time, it also generalises, drawing our attention, Sheringham suggests, to what in the archive can be seen as 'generic and archetypal: not only to location, but to a number of gestures, routines and operations' (2005: 47). Indeed, for Sheringham, 'the archive' is increasingly used to designate not necessarily a fixed, physical space but a 'generic space of activity or practice' (ibid.). This shift to a more generalising usage also awakens what Sheringham presents as the archive's 'figurative potential', making it stand as evocative shorthand for something else (ibid.).

Identifying in the writing of those artists named above an evolution of the (auto) biographical towards a confrontation between individual subjects and the products of a quasi-archival practice based in searching, sorting, sifting and other connected gestures, Sheringham offers a tentative definition of what the archive might stand for in such works: 'The archive can be shorthand for a certain kind of encounter between subject and memory, where memory, even one's own, has become other' (ibid.). In texts frequently marked by the multiple traumas of the twentieth century — colonialism, war, occupation, genocide... — where the social and historical nature of individual experience is foregrounded, this otherness so often stems from the uncertain interactions of personal and collective memory and from association with what the social body desires to repress or keep hidden (47–48). Throughout *A la recherche du lieu de ma naissance*, a film which shares many of the sites, tropes and strategies found in the work of archival artists such as those surveyed by Sheringham, Lehman indeed grapples with the archive as a figure of estrangement and concealment where his own memories are extricated from the conflicted mass of history only with difficulty. As he navigates Lausanne, Lehman excavates and assembles an extended series of evidential traces, evaluating the (often hampered) connection with the past and with himself they sustain.

Lehman begins his search for himself with a birth certificate, a form of proof that recurs frequently in archival art and literature, from Modiano's *Dora Bruder* (1997) or *Pour que tu ne te perdes pas dans le quartier* [*So You Don't Get Lost in the Neighbourhood*] (2014) to Perec's *W ou le souvenir d'enfance* [*W, or the Memory of Childhood*] (1975). In the film's opening sequence, Lehman visits the institutional space of Lausanne's registry office, its *État civil*, a site in which the archive is immediately figured in its originary sense as a physical, three-dimensional space of record-keeping. An extended shot of an empty corridor bathed in the artificial glow of neon striplights and filled with the echoing sound of heels on marble floors emphasises an impression of institutional austerity. The record of Lehman's birth is located in a dust-covered ledger before a duplicate certificate is laboriously printed on a typewriter. The document that scrolls slowly in front of the camera attests to the fact that *Lehman,*

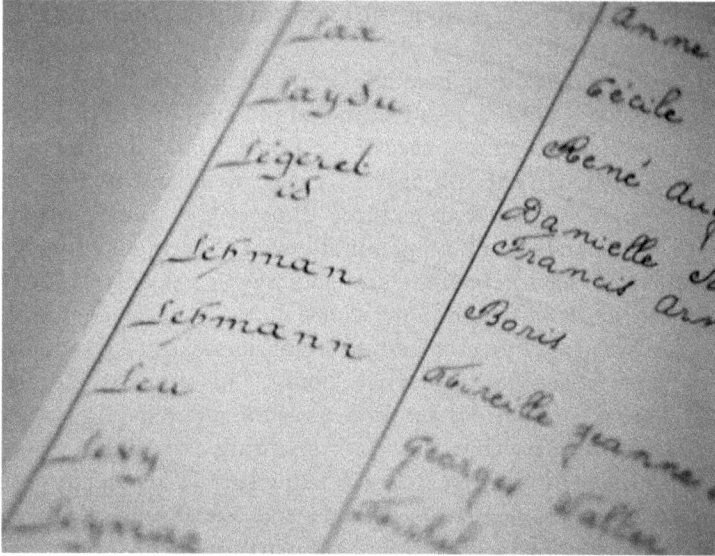

FIG. 3.4. *A la recherche du lieu de ma naissance* (1990), Boris Lehman
© Boris Lehman/Dovfilm (with: Amidon-Paterson/CBA/La Sept/
Ministère de la communauté française de Belgique).

Boris was born in Lausanne at 23:13 on 3 March 1944 to *Lehman, Mksymilian Henryk* and *Berta, née Sznicer*. It bears the marks and seals of state authority and guarantees Lehman a unique identity articulated within a legal framework of recognition. It tells Lehman the time and place of his birth, his name and the identity of those who gave him this name. It contains, in essence, official proof of the existence he sought to verify, all of the information notionally required to say *this is who I am*. And yet, the identity that Lehman extracts from the archives of the Lausanne registry office is no more than inert ink on a page: the question *qu'est-ce que j'en sais au juste?* and the deeper knowledge it demands remains unanswered.

He moves in other sequences to consult less institutionally framed forms of archive than those found within the officialised space of the registry office — ephemera again recognisable from the recurrent topoi of archival art and literature. Lehman searches for a residual connection to the place of his birth, clinging on to the only certainty he retains, his name: 'Mon nom d'abord, il est partout, presque toujours mal orthographié. Le nom que je cherche n'existe pas. Est-il possible que j'aie perdu mon nom? Comment faire pour le retrouver?' [Firstly my name, it's everywhere, almost always spelt wrong. The name I'm looking for doesn't exist. Can it be possible that I've lost my name? How can I find it again?]. The screen is filled with pages of the Lausanne phone book. The tips of Lehman's fingers enter into the frame as he searches unsuccessfully for a record of himself in this text. He finds a *Lehmann* but no more complete entry within which to recognise himself. His montage integrates a further succession of imperfect, unsatisfactory echoes: a *Christian Leemann* on a letterbox; a *Docteur René Lehmann* on a doorway; a *Librairie M. Lehmann* printed on a business card at the entrance to an antiquarian bookseller;

an abundance of references to *Léman* on signs and street names that recall the lake on which Lausanne stands. The few photographs that Lehman unearths — rigidly staged family portraits, holiday snapshots, images of himself as an infant alongside his brothers — offer similarly few answers that might allow him to durably grasp his origins: 'quelques photos dans un album que je ne peux, que je ne veux plus déchiffrer. Est-ce que je me reconnais dans ces images?' [photos in an album that I can't, that I don't want to decipher any more. Do I recognise myself in these images?]. As Lehman's autobiographical search continues through the alien streets of his native city and as the number and variety of traces he assembles grows, the sense of self-estrangement arising from such archival encounters is amplified.

Lehman locates glimmers and fragments but never entirely finds himself nor anything that would grant a reliable route towards deeper self-knowledge. Unable to reconnect with memories of his own past, Lehman's sense of alienation from himself mutates into disorientation and fear:

> Je ne savais pas où j'allais, ou plutôt, j'avais peur d'aller, d'aller quelque part. Peur de découvrir que je n'avais rien à faire ici, que j'allais découvrir un secret qui ne m'était pas destiné, qui ne me concernait pas, qui allait me révéler quelque chose qui me ferait peur, une vérité pas bonne à dire. Peur, oui, de cet inconnu qui était moi, devant moi, ma propre histoire, ma propre naissance.

> [I didn't know where I was going, or rather I was afraid of going, of going somewhere. Afraid of discovering that I had no business being here, that I was going to discover a secret that wasn't meant for me, that didn't concern me, that was going to reveal something to me that would scare me, a truth better left unsaid. Afraid, indeed, of this unknown person who was me, in front of me, my own story, my own birth.]

Confronted with this *inconnu qui était moi*, Lehman is severed from his own history, his own birth, engulfed by the otherness Sheringham found in so many comparable turns to archive. This is a severance that, as emphasised by the images of weathered and overgrown Jewish cemeteries and public monuments to the victims of deportation inserted into the montage of *A la recherche du lieu de ma naissance*, is tightly bound up in much more extensive crises of memory, knowledge and identity, in more pervasive forms of forgetting. In such a way, as Lehman apprehensively glimpses the *vérité pas bonne à dire* that rises to the surface in Lausanne, he is simultaneously led to interrogate broader historical realities. These realities concern, in particular, what the famed neutrality of the country of his birth, referenced in his opening voice-over, might potentially belie. Unearthing difficult truths that have perhaps been deliberately forgotten, Lehman discovers in the archive a site not only of disorienting otherness, but also, it is suggested, of deliberate concealment, manipulation, and distortion, of unreliable, misleading knowledge, of the social control of memory.

This is certainly the impression that is encouraged in scenes where Lehman brings us within another one of Lausanne's institutionalised spaces of national record-keeping: the *Cinémathèque Suisse*. Lehman's camera lingers for a moment on the official emblems etched on the door to the Swiss national film archive before he names the particular archivist he has come here to meet:

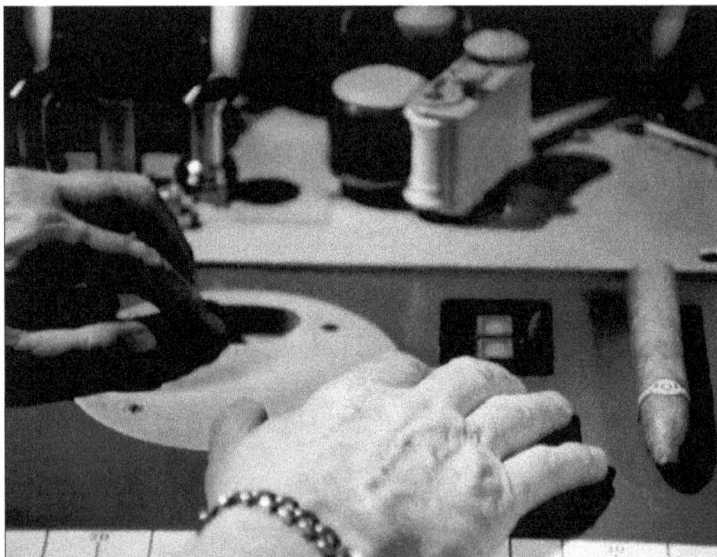

FIG. 3.5. *A la recherche du lieu de ma naissance* (1990), Boris Lehman
© Boris Lehman/Dovfilm (with: Amidon-Paterson/CBA/La Sept/
Ministère de la communauté française de Belgique).

Je ne connaissais qu'une seule personne à Lausanne: Freddy Buache, Conservateur de la Cinémathèque Suisse. Exactement celui qu'il me fallait pour fouiller le passé, mon passé, et pour retrouver peut-être quelques morceaux de moi, enfouis dans les archives et documents d'époque.

[I only knew one person in Lausanne: Freddy Buache, curator of the Swiss Film Archive. Exactly the person I needed in order to go through the past, my past, and maybe find some pieces of myself, buried in period archives and documents.]

Whilst Freddy Buache — a long-time associate of Lehman who appeared in an episode of *Mes entretiens filmés* — is introduced as a relatively benign *archon*, the uncertainty of the archival knowledge to which he symbolically controls access is nevertheless strongly suggested.

In a slightly later sequence, our screen is filled with grainy black-and-white footage showing a wartime bombing attack and an air raid siren. These images show snow-covered rooftops and aeroplanes circling in the sky above. This footage seems looped and distorted: the sound of the siren is reedy and stuttering whilst the aeroplanes move back and forth in the sky as the film is reversed and replayed. The shot changes and we discover that this footage is playing on a screen within a screen. Buache sits alone in a darkened editing suite — a space not dissimilar to that glimpsed in Dieutre's *Jaurès*. He faces away from the camera, watching the archival images as they appear on a small monitor at the centre of the frame. As in Dieutre's studio, our attention is drawn here to the apparatus of filmic production that dominates the space. Buache's hands manipulate the dials and controls of the room's mixing equipment; he plays with the archival footage, reversing and repeating it, slowing it down and speeding it up. On the monitor, the archival footage changes: the new images show trainloads of evacuee children arriving at Basel station. The voice-over of this archival footage, overlaid with Lehman's translated subtitles, emphasises the warm welcome the children receive: 'Viele Kinder werden der helfenden Schweiz stets in Dankbarkeit gedenken/Toute leur vie ces enfants penseront avec gratitude à la Suisse qui les a aidés' [Many/These children will always gratefully remember how Switzerland helped them]. Inside Buache's editing suite, Lehman's camera focuses closely on the film stock as it unfurls and on Buache's hands as they hover, ready to intervene, over the control console. The resilient focus on the technologies of filmic manipulation in this sequence unsettles the stability of the historical knowledge shown to be sustained by archival evidence. Within this institutional space of archiving, knowledge is revealed to be subject to distortion and alteration — potentially transformed by a cut here, a fast-forward there.

These images of archival manipulation are echoed elsewhere in the film in sequences that warn yet more forcefully of the archive's distorting mediation of our access to the events of history. Through such sequences, Lehman suggests that the Cinémathèque's footage of grateful children welcomed with open arms at a Swiss train station might, in fact, hide a different historical reality. Lehman integrates a wide variety of texts and images within his montage that seem chosen in order to evoke repressed, painful truths. We watch an old man as he reads lines from a play that describe a refugee's clash with a Swiss border guard during the war: 'Soyez témoins — les Suisses nous envoient à la mort. L'histoire ne le leur pardonnera pas' [Witness this: the Swiss are sending us to our deaths. History will not forgive them]. Elsewhere, the screen is filled with fragmented segments of the scenes of violence from Charles Gleyre's history painting *Les Romains passant sous le joug des Helvètes* [*Romans Under the Yoke of the Helvetians*] (1858). The front cover of the polemical text *Du bonheur d'être Suisse sous Hitler* [*What Luck to be Swiss under Hitler*] (1968) is shown on screen on more than one occasion. The camera lingers at length over a newspaper article provocatively entitled 'La Croix-Rouge éclaboussée par la croix gammée' [Red Cross stained by Swastika]. Through the inclusion of such sources, Lehman hints that beneath the consensual images of national history there may well lurk concealed images of violence and hypocrisy. As he says in voice-over at one point: 'Je filme parce que tout le monde se tait. La Suisse entière se tait' [I am filming because everyone is keeping silent. The whole of Switzerland is keeping silent].

Lehman later surveys adverts and press clippings published on the day of his birth, further testing the implication of his personal past within a collective past — *le passé, mon passé*. His camera scans over a magazine praising Swiss humanitarian efforts; accounts of foreign airplanes entering illegally into Swiss airspace; updates on fighting on the Italian front; descriptions of the air raids of the London Blitz; adverts for infant flu vaccinations or for Swiss boarding schools. Not only does Lehman not find himself or the *quelques morceaux de moi* he seeks in these documents, but he insists that they distract us from other historical realities. His voice-over enumerates the world events that occurred on that same March day in

1944, the *fait divers* that were reported, the films showing on Swiss cinema screens, before suddenly shifting in tone: '... et dans les camps de la mort, plus de cinq millions de juifs sont déjà exterminés' [... and in the death camps, more than five million Jews have already been wiped out]. The historical accusation that Lehman levels at the country of his birth is the product of scattered, often passing references; but cumulatively the result is lacerating. As Gérard Preszow writes, recalling the images of municipal workers clearing leaves from neat Lausanne paths seen on numerous occasions throughout the film: 'Lehman se montre volontiers acerbe et ironique pour une Suisse qui ne fut pas au-dessus de tout soupçon à l'égard des pourchassés et qui ne supporte toujours pas que les feuilles d'automne tachent les allées d'un parc' [Lehman is deliberately cutting and sarcastic towards a Switzerland that was not above all suspicion when it came to those fleeing persecution and that still cannot bear for autumn leaves to sully the paths in its parks].[3] In his return to the city of his birth, Lehman scrutinises a variety of archival traces in an attempt to obtain irrefutable proof of his own existence. Dissatisfied with the connection with the past these traces sustain, he rejects them as dangerous vectors of both alienation and historical misinformation.

It is in opposition to the varied archival contexts and supports discussed above that Lehman mobilises forms of autobiographical reenactment, using bodily repetition as the basis of an alternate practice of self-archiving. In so doing, Lehman heeds Schneider's call to resist an ingrained cultural habituation to certain assumptions around archives and the kinds of proof they house, a habituation that, she suggests, precludes other possibilities of knowing and remembering (2011: 97–99). Through reenactment, Lehman develops an embodied model of proof-making which embraces the possibility Schneider identifies that a repeated action might itself offer a fleshy kind of *document* of an earlier action (37). In replaying moments of his past across bodies in the present, Lehman's recourse to reenactment in *A la recherche du lieu de ma naissance* corroborates the work of scholars such as Diana Taylor (2003) into how repetitive, embodied practice can function as a platform for the storage and transmission of knowledge and as a tool for navigating the often embattled terrain of cultural memory. Via the live, vital, fleshy connection across time promised by these reenactments, Lehman seeks to wrest control over his own memories, to generate other evidence of his existence and to make knowable the *inconnu qui était moi* that confronts him in Lausanne.

These autobiographical reenactments appear from the film's very opening sequences, alternating with the other forms of evidence described above. In the scene that immediately follows Lehman's visit to the Lausanne registry office, a young boy with black hair gazes over the side of a boat sailing across the surface of Lake Léman. The scene is suffused with a bright natural light that contrasts with the artificial glow that filled the austere, institutional spaces seen in the preceding sequence. The boy, dressed in a sailor suit, looks towards a woman dressed in a bright red bathing costume water-skiing in the boat's wake. He opens a small notebook and we see child-like handwriting and a vintage postcard bearing a depiction of a similar water-skier. The boy drops his notebook over the side of the boat and the real-life water-skier falls into the waters of the lake. Lehman here stages an almost dream-like reinvention of memory. Throughout *A la recherche du lieu de ma naissance*, we encounter a succession of similar dark-haired boys, each of whom offers a fleeting, imagined reenactment of Lehman's past. In contrast to the sailor-suited example seen at the film's opening, these other instances of reenactment appear more concrete, capturing moments of everyday life. The various boys that appear on screen are different ages and appear non-sequentially in different settings and contexts across the film; each of them, however, becomes 'Boris', cumulatively granting Lehman an alternate means of reconnecting with his own origins and identity. Hidden behind his recording camera, the filmmaker is repeatedly brought face-to-face with 'himself'.

We witness 'Boris' learning to swim, playing by the water, suckling his mother's breast, being scolded by his father for spilling his chocolate milk. Points of anachronism in details of clothing and setting consistently foreground the artificial nature of the scenes that we observe, alerting us to the fact that these moments from the past are being performed by bodies that resolutely belong in the present. Lehman displays a pronounced desire to deconstruct his own autobiographical reenactments: in a notable sequence, one of the many dark-haired boys who replay moments of Lehman's past is asked what the purpose or goal of these reenactments might be and seems decidedly unsure of the answer. Elsewhere in the film, a woman struggles with the role of Lehman's pregnant mother: she places a flowery cushion under her dress to suggest the foetal 'Boris' and asks whether the reenactment the filmmaker requests should represent three months, six months or nine months of pregnancy. We hear Lehman chuckling from behind the camera and then hear the friend reprimand him jokingly: 'Boris, tu ne sais pas ce que tu veux!' [Boris, you don't know what you want!]. Through such sequences, the film explores a mode of autobiographical knowledge that is framed in direct opposition to the alienating archival encounters discussed earlier — one that is improvisational and searching, that announces its own dispersal, fragmentation and multiple imperfections, but that, in so doing, holds out the possibility of a radically different form of self-recognition. In the scene described above, Lehman films a cushion, but insofar as this offers a form of affective investment across time, he simultaneously films 'himself' in the belly of his mother. These recreated versions of himself and the memories they hold are still *other*, but this is an otherness that Lehman dictates and shapes as he directs the reenactive movements of a succession of surrogate bodies before him on screen.

A number of these autobiographical reenactments seek in particular to offer a means of reconnecting with a Jewish cultural identity that, as emphasised by the images of cemeteries and deportation memorials seen at points in the film, Lehman frames as a site of loss. The film depicts a wedding ceremony that we take to be a reenactment of the marriage of Lehman's parents. Elsewhere, one of Lehman's reenactive avatars struggles to commit lines from the Torah to memory. In a particularly striking sequence, the film shows an extended, remarkably graphic depiction of the circumcision of a baby boy in a *Brit milah* ceremony. As he bears

FIG. 3.6. *A la recherche du lieu de ma naissance* (1990), Boris Lehman
© Boris Lehman/Dovfilm (with: Amidon-Paterson/CBA/La Sept/
Ministère de la communauté française de Belgique).

witness to this ritual, to the cries of the child and to the blood that pours from its severed foreskin, Lehman casts an unflinching gaze upon 'himself' and reconnects with a cultural identity that is inscribed on his own body through what Derrida referred to as that 'singular and immemorial archive called *circumcision*' (1996: 26). In reenacting such moments of his past, Lehman situates his own personal history in relation to the broader cultural rituals, traditions and identities that, as explored in the work of Akerman, had so often been interrupted by the imperfect transfer of memory in the wake of the Holocaust, seeking to witness them with his own eyes and thus to regain them. Through reenactment, Lehman develops a living connection between cultures past and present that, as it passes across living bodies, stands in contrast to the deathliness of gravestones and memorials.

The images of circumcision described above exemplify the very particular engagement with memory that Lehman pursues through reenactment. In this sequence, the filmmaker restages 'memories' that he himself cannot remember, imagining how they might have been. As he witnesses experiences from his past relived in the present by other bodies, he is able to vicariously feel them for himself anew. This effect is yet more apparent in the film's most striking instance of autobiographical reenactment, one in which Lehman applies techniques described above to his own birth. It is here that Lehman's use of reenactment as a mode of autobiographical proof and as a form of self-witnessing is most clearly (and most strangely) foregrounded. Compared to what we have seen elsewhere in this book, this sequence is closest to Alain Cavalier's reconstruction of his own breech birth; in contrast to Cavalier's use of a watermelon as a bodily surrogate, however, Lehman here emphasises the fleshy *realness* of his recreation.

The sequence begins with a lingering shot of a naked female body semi-immersed in water, the body's pregnant belly jutting just above the surface. The shot changes to show the water of lake Léman churned up by a passing boat. After a sudden cut, we find ourselves watching a woman in labour; the camera moves between the woman's legs and the hands of the midwife firmly draw out a baby. The baby is placed in the woman's arms before the shot changes to show a faded photograph of Lehman's own mother. As with the other autobiographical reenactments witnessed throughout the film, this new-born baby becomes 'Boris'. In an extreme autobiographical gesture, Lehman is able, through reenactment, to record his own entry into the world, to be present at and bear witness to his own birth, to 'remember' it for himself, to validate and provide proof of his existence. As he suggests in voice-over immediately prior to this reenactment: 'C'est maintenant que je vais naître, que je vais assister à ma propre naissance, que je vais pouvoir exister, enfin' [It is now that I shall be born, that I shall attend my own birth, that I shall exist, finally].

There is a sequence in Lehman's later *Histoire de ma vie racontée par mes photographies* where he visits a friend — RTBF producer Carine Bratzlavsky — to present the outline of his new film project. Lehman explains that he has also come to show her the footage he had recorded of her son's birth and circumcision. He loads his reels of film into a viewing console and they watch her labour together. The knowledge that Lehman has on at least one occasion previously recorded the birth of a boy who is identifiably *not* Boris Lehman to a woman who is also demonstrably *not* Lehman's mother directs a potential challenge to the proof-value of the reenacted delivery from *A la recherche du lieu de ma naissance*. And yet, the autobiographical connection offered by this reenactment withstands the charge of falsity. We know that the film's series of boys cannot possibly be Boris Lehman; but this does not prevent them from fulfilling this role, just as it does not prevent Lehman (and us) from believing in it. Both real and unreal, Lehman's autobiographical reenactments wilfully deconstruct oppositions of fact and fiction: these versions of himself are true because Lehman judges and needs them to be so. Lehman's depiction of his own birth, like the other reenactments that fill the film, offers what is consistently sought throughout the filmmaker's work: an *image conforme de moi* where the terms of conformity are set by Lehman alone. Through an impossible autobiographical gesture, Lehman further expands his archive of self, assuming control over the representation of his life from its very beginning. In framing the unruly and unpredictable liveness of a real body where blood, sweat, tears and amniotic fluid mix as an alternative to the dusty austerity of a state archive, *A la recherche du lieu de ma naissance* uses reenactment to construct a different kind of autobiographical evidence, a living, breathing document of self that enables the filmmaker to say with greater certainty *Moi, Boris Lehman...*

Through autobiographical reenactment, Lehman forges a connection with much earlier moments of his life and with much younger versions of himself. There are nevertheless points in *A la recherche du lieu de ma naissance* where this focus on youth enters into tension with a lingering preoccupation with old age. Throughout his film, Lehman frames the human body as a site of autobiographical knowledge and as a method or tool for orchestrating the imperfect encounter between distinct time frames. However, the film's presentation of these bodies is at moments haunted by knowledge of the changes that will inevitably be brought to them by the passing of time — haunted by the knowledge that the living bodies that appear on screen are, through their very vitality, ultimately destined to age, tire and disappear. After all, the reenactive body is, as André Lepecki admits, the most changeable, most precarious of archival supports, one grounded in the absolute certainty of death (2010: 34). Such preoccupations emerge clearly in sequences in which Lehman visits a Lausanne retirement home, drawing our attention to the elderly bodies that this space of repose contains. Through yawning mouths, greying hair, sagging skin, protruding veins, these mortal bodies convey an unavoidable sense of physical weightness and tiredness, of approaching endpoints.

These images are immediately followed by a sequence in which Lehman reenacts a much more recent moment from his own autobiography than seen elsewhere in *A la recherche du lieu de ma naissance*. A gathering of people celebrate Lehman's forty-fourth birthday, serenading yet another version of 'Boris' standing at the centre of the frame — an adult avatar much older than Lehman's multiple young boys. Proximity with the images of aged bodies in a nursing home from the preceding sequence suggests that the future awaiting Lehman will similarly be one of decline and eventual disappearance. The insistence on *origins* that, as we have seen, threads its way throughout Lehman's film is tempered by an underlying anxiety about the unavoidable *destinations* to which we are all drawn. There is a deep sadness to this, one that is much more extensively explored in my next case study, where the threat of disappearance that hangs over Lehman's archive of self becomes yet more oppressively imminent. Penetrating further into points where personal and collective histories meet and into the frictions such histories release, this later film carries the archival possibilities of a living body in reenactment in other directions.

Back to my Roots: *Histoire de mes cheveux: de la brièveté de la vie*

Whilst *A la recherche du lieu de ma naissance* presented multiple on-screen versions of 'Boris', the filmmaker himself remained hidden behind his recording camera for the duration of the film. In contrast to this visual absence, Lehman appears extensively throughout *Histoire de mes cheveux: de la brièveté de la vie* (henceforth *Histoire de mes cheveux*), released twenty years later in 2010. His appearances in front of the camera in this film draw our attention to the effects of ageing visible on the surfaces and volumes of his body. He sometimes appears naked before us, his body betraying the same physical weightness and tiredness evoked in the images of old age in the previous case study. As the film's subtitle, *de la brièveté de la vie*, and the further quotations made from Seneca's *De Brevitate Vitae* announce, *Histoire de mes cheveux* depicts a man faced with the irreversible loss of youth and with the ultimate shortness of life. The film repeatedly foregrounds the sagging of skin, the tensing of posture, above all the thinning and fading of Lehman's titular hair. It is, indeed,

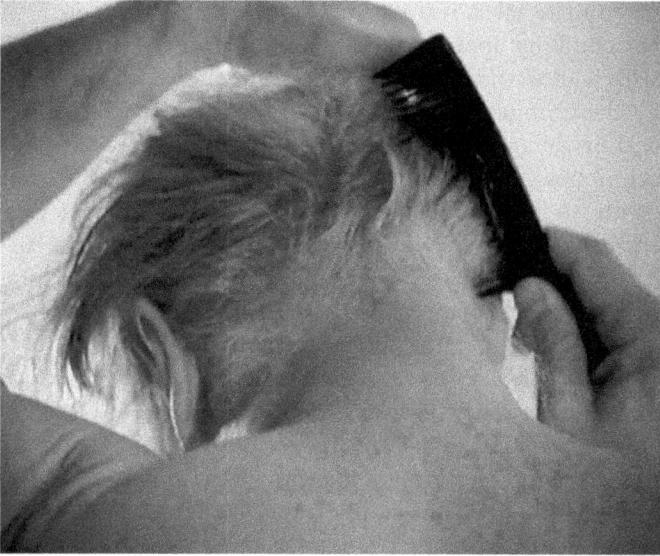

FIG. 3.7. *Histoire de mes cheveux: de la brièveté de la vie* (2010), Boris Lehman
© Boris Lehman/Dovfilm (with: RTBF/Arte/CBA/Good and Bad News).

through a consideration of the effects of ageing visible in hair that *Histoire de mes cheveux* develops a broad mediation on the relentless passing of time and on the physical changes that this passing inevitably brings.

Writing about the film on his website, Lehman resumes the history of his hair (and by extension, of his life) tersely: 'L'histoire de mes cheveux se tient en deux lignes (ou en deux phrases). Ils étaient noirs et longs. Ils sont devenus blancs' [The history of my hair fits into two lines (or into two sentences). It was black and long. It has turned white].[4] He informs us that his now straggly white hair has not been cut for decades. Through sequences of washing, lathering, drying, brushing, the damaged state of this hair and the depletion of his follicles is foregrounded. At various points, Lehman films himself struggling to comb his dry, knotted and tangled locks. These images of combing (and the negotiations of ageing they entail) recall sequences from Varda's *Les Glaneurs et la glaneuse*, similarly concerned as they are with what Mireille Rosello has described as the 'always already defeated fight against time' (2001: 34). Both filmmakers engage with the gendered encoding of their gestures: whilst Varda's images question the cultural definition of female beauty, Lehman's evoke associations of the thinning of male hair with declining virility to then inflect these associations with depictions of self-care that carry a deliberately feminising force. Throughout the film, visual contrasts are drawn between Lehman's damaged and depleted locks along with the increasingly exposed pate that they cover, and the visibly younger, fuller and healthier (as well as predominantly female) heads of hair that also appear on screen.

Lehman's fight against time in such sequences seems 'always already defeated' to a greater extent than Varda's. His hair is presented as being considerably more lifeless: images of combing are accompanied with sounds of ripping and tearing, with the noise of desiccated material as it is wrested from a scalp. The dense, matted clumps produced by his combing appear as unambiguously dead, almost abject matter. In a way that recalls Varda's tidemark dyed hair, Lehman also announces the labour required to halt the changes brought by age. He visits a succession of barbers, who appear perplexed by the questions he asks about possible new hairstyles, transplants and dyeing techniques. Elsewhere, a dermatologist examines his follicles and we are presented with the curious image of a filmmaker watching a video monitor as his scalp is filmed by a microscopic camera. There is humour in these sequences, with Lehman knowingly staging a version of himself that recognises its own ridiculousness, but there is also pathos, as the film depicts a body exposed to the ravages of time and one man's attempts to slow time's passing.

Lehman's decision to frame his reflection on the shortness of life in terms of his hair is telling. The visible hairs that we see on a person's head are largely composed of dead cells, devoid of blood supply, nerves or muscles; at the same time, however, hair is known to continue growing for a period after a person's death. This tension between inert matter and resilient vitality is reflected in the vast array of mourning traditions from around the world that involve hair and its manipulation. In their 2001 book *Death, Memory and Material Culture*, social anthropologists Elizabeth Hallam and Jenny Hockey recall in particular a nineteenth-century European tradition of mortuary jewellery made from the hair of departed loved ones, foregrounding the potency of such human remains as 'facilitators of personal memory' (2001: 136). Quoting the work of cultural historian Marius Kwint, they refer to the almost magical charge of what are presented as strangely animate components of the 'dead margins of the self', situating such hair within an evocative tension between life and death (ibid.; Kwint 1999: 9). For Hallam and Hockey, this recurrent use of hair as an object of memory is made possible by its physical durability, a durability that stands in stark contrast to what are presented as 'the instabilities of the fleshy body' (ibid.). Such tensions and potencies are indeed discernible in Lehman's presentation of his own fading and thinning hair: the dry clumps that he collects from brushes and combs are fondled between finger and thumb in an almost reverential fashion, detrital relics of his own senescence, whilst the remarkable tensile strength of individual strands is elsewhere demonstrated through laboratory testing even as the 'instability' of the filmmaker's mortal flesh is abundantly foregrounded.

Hair is also of course fundamental to cultural identities, with its appearance, distribution and consistency intimately linked to conceptions of ethnicity, class and (as highlighted above) gender, reflecting and informing multiple aspects of our embodied experience. This is a capacity for cultural signification that Lehman acknowledges, as seen, for instance, in a sequence of *Histoire de mes cheveux* where he presents himself as an inheritor to the Old Testament Samson, submitting to a modern 'Delilah' who mimes shearing his locks in defiance of Nazirite law. As these youthful hands work their way slowly through the splayed hair of the prone, vulnerable Lehman, caressing, teasing and curling grey strands around nimble fingers, this scene assumes a deliberately erotic charge. A certain eroticism also hangs over Lehman's depictions of the hairs of others in his film: as he isolates and investigates heads of hair, assembling them through montage, *collecting* them even,

Lehman plays suggestively with the tropes of festishistic partialism. Such possible trichophilic overtones also remind us that hair has long been the coveted object of fetish and fascination and has offered ample subject matter for art: to cite a particularly famous example, the intoxicating smells and textures of apostrophised hair carried Charles Baudelaire far across time and space in 'La Chevelure' [The Head of Hair] (1857) into contact with deeply buried recollections and sensations. Whilst Lehman's stiff, brittle tresses differ markedly from the flowing cascades of curls described by Baudelaire, *Histoire de mes cheveux* nevertheless finds in hair a similarly potent, sensual, mystical significance.

Lehman's presentation of hair in *Histoire de mes cheveux* knowingly engages with the mix of associations with fetish, fascination, memory, time, durability, cultural encoding and the sometimes porous border between life and death, that are described above. Importantly, these associations are explored throughout the film in a way that once again foregrounds a specifically *archival* quality. Referring to traces of cocaine found in the preserved hair of ancient Peruvian mummies, a voice-over heard in an early sequence of the film suggests that:

> Toute notre vie [est] inscrite à l'intérieur du cheveu [...] *le cheveu agit comme une archive, comme un calendrier historique.* Tout ce que nous respirons, tout ce que nous avalons se fixe dans nos cheveux (emphasis mine).

> [Our whole life [is] inscribed within the interior of a hair [...] *hair acts like an archive, like a historical calendar.* Everything that we breathe, everything that we swallow is fixed into our hair.]

This same voice-over goes on to argue that: '[le cheveu] est la mémoire de toute une vie, et finalement c'est toute la mémoire du monde' [[a hair] is the memory of a whole life and after all it's all the world's memory]. The reference contained in this appraisal of hair's capacities as a medium of record-keeping to Alain Resnais's 1956 film *Toute la mémoire du monde* [*All The World's Memory*] (1956) is unmistakable. Resnais's study of the internal workings of the *Bibliothèque nationale de France* famously framed the institutional site of the library as an almost carceral, even concentrationary space, where records are sequestered and inoculated and where knowledge is surveilled and controlled (see particularly Ungar 2012). Viewed in light of the critique of institutions and of officialised channels of knowledge-transmission previously developed in *A la recherche du lieu de ma naissance*, such a conspicuous reference leads us to identify in Lehman's explorations of hair a continuation of his search for alternate archival forms that might provide a more personal, vital, living connection with the past.

In early sequences of *Histoire de mes cheveux*, Lehman closely scrutinises the material qualities of this hair-based archive. A series of scientific diagrams and magnified images of hair follicles are inserted into the film's montage. Elsewhere, a small bundle of Lehman's own hair is examined under the microscope: these enlarged, translucent strands glisten in the light in a way that closely resembles the analogue film stock that, as I have suggested, is so visible in Lehman's work. This is a resemblance that Lehman himself indeed draws out:

> La meilleure analogie que j'ai trouvée, c'est la pellicule de cinéma: elle est

FIG. 3.8. *Histoire de mes cheveux: de la brièveté de la vie* (2010), Boris Lehman © Boris Lehman/Dovfilm (with: RTBF/Arte/CBA/Good and Bad News).

comme un être vivant. Elle s'enroule, se déroule, s'emmêle. On en fait des tresses et des nœuds. Elle est solide et en même temps extrêmement fragile. Il faut en prendre soin.

[The best analogy that I've found is film reel: it's like a living creature. It coils, uncoils and tangles. You make plaits and knots from it. It's strong but at the same time extremely fragile. You have to take care of it.]

Lehman's voice-over contains a playful pun: the French *pellicule* can be simultaneously film stock, skin, but also dandruff. As if to illustrate the analogy he makes, Lehman zooms in on unravelled spools of film suspended in front of a lightbox. Looking closely at this film stock, it is possible to recognise individual frames of previous works from Lehman's filmography. A visual echo is created between these gently fluttering strips of film and the multiple strands of hair of different lengths, colours and consistencies filmed throughout *Histoire de mes cheveux*. Like the traces of experience that Lehman has compulsively captured on film throughout his life, hair is here framed as yet another component of an archive of self.

A turning point occurs early in *Histoire de mes cheveux* during a sequence in which Lehman appears on screen, crawling awkwardly over the knotted roots of a tree before lying face down in the scattered leaves. A child approaches him and inquires as to what on earth he is doing. Lehman's punning response sets in motion the trajectory that will be followed over the remainder of the film: 'Je cherche mes racines' [I'm searching for my roots]. If, in *Histoire de mes cheveux*, life is presented as painfully short, hair is shown to offer a lengthy, unbroken thread that extends backwards across time and space, that allows the filmmaker to explore his own personal history (*la mémoire de toute une vie*) but also to seek his place in a much larger history that dwarfs him (*toute la mémoire du monde*). What begins as a meditation on Lehman's personal experiences of specific bodily loss — of hair, and so of youth, of vitality, of virility — thus extends into an exploration of the other experiences of loss that litter his own extended family history, then to a reflection on the broader historical losses that haunt the European continent. Association with the shorn heads of concentration camps, with those millions of individuals who were shaved and stripped of their own embodied archives, leads Lehman on a journey across the landscapes of Eastern Europe, through Poland, Russia and Ukraine, directly retracing the movements of those condemned bodies who went before him. If hair offers an organic support for the storage of memory, this memory is retrieved and accessed via an alternate archival practice again developed through reenactment.

In the trajectory it follows and in the form of reenactment it performs, Lehman's journey eastwards clearly recalls Akerman's *D'Est*, but also differs from this antecedent voyage in significant ways. In the making of her own engagement with the afterlives of personal and collective history in the haunted landscapes of Eastern Europe, Akerman had staunchly resisted the lure of what she presented as 'a "back to my roots" kind of film' (Akerman 1995: 22). This is, however, exactly the kind of film that Lehman — enthusiastically receptive to the full associative and punning power of the vocabulary of hair — seeks to make. In consulting the archive of his hair, following it back to its root, Lehman moves directly in search of his own roots. In contrast to Akerman's refusal to film in the specific Polish village where her mother had grown up, accessing his capillary archive carries Lehman on a much more direct autobiographical route to the remains of the liquidated Lwów ghetto in search of traces of his father. Not only does this urban space not yield anything that might attest to his father's former presence, but everything he finds speaks of the systematic erasure of Jewish culture and history from this region. Lehman explains how those relatives who did not flee the region as his parents had done were all exterminated. This is a space of ruins.

Lehman's journey across Eastern Europe is also framed more explicitly as reenactment than was the case in *D'Est*. If, as Alisa Lebow suggested, Akerman's reverse reconstruction of the trajectories of exile functioned as a kind of 'embodied rehearsal' that allowed her to make this journey her own (2016: 57), this *rehearsal* was developed through montage and the positioning and movements of the camera, with the filmmaker permanently concealed behind her recording equipment. This is similarly the case in certain sequences of *Histoire de mes cheveux*, but Lehman also chooses to recreate the movements of bodies from the past with those of his own body in front of the camera, physically replicating the journeys that once led millions to their deaths in these same landscapes. In contrast to the earlier search for self in Lausanne, these reenactments no longer entail *witnessing* the recreated past, but rather actively participating in it.

Lehman's voice-overs at points acknowledge the fear he feels as he moves through landscapes that appear so durably haunted by the spectre of the gulag, the ghetto, the death camp. They simultaneously emphasise the embodied physicality of his journey, the weightiness of the replicated footsteps that lead him ever onwards:

Il a fallu beaucoup de temps, beaucoup d'effort pour que je me décide à entrer dans ces contrées qui ont vu la mort de tant de gens, des camps à profusion et des prisons. J'allais marcher dedans, dans les parcs et sur les quais de gare, dans les usines, dans les forêts, ici et là, et encore là. Cinquante millions de prisonniers, d'offensés et d'humiliés, travailleurs déportés construisant villes et tunnels, routes et canaux, maisons et camps. J'étais en train de marcher dedans, je marchais sur les morts, sur mon père et sur ma mère, et toute ma famille. Voilà pourquoi je suis ici à ne rien chercher que l'ombre de moi-même ou la cendre qui sait, à refaire sans m'en rendre compte le trajet des condamnés, jusqu'à loin dans les mines, dans la neige et le froid.

[It took a long time, a lot of effort, for me to make up my mind to enter these regions that have seen the deaths of so many people, camps as far as the eye can see and prisons. I was going to walk within them, in the parks and on the station platforms, in the factories, in the forests, here and there and there again. Fifty million prisoners, wounded and humiliated people, deported workers building towns and tunnels, roads and canals, houses and camps. I was walking within these regions, I was walking on the dead, on my father and on my mother and my whole family. This is the reason why I am here looking for nothing but the shadow of myself or the ashes, who knows, or retracing the journey of the condemned without realising it, far into the mines, the snow, the cold.]

We watch as Lehman retraces an eastern march of death along abandoned railway lines or down deserted roads that disappear into the horizon. With a roadmap in his hands and luggage by his side, he appears almost as a tourist setting out on the route to past atrocity.

Whereas Akerman had avoided the actual sites of historical atrocity in the regions she visited, Lehman journeys through landscapes scarred by the atrocities of Bełżec and Janowska, through the crumbling ruins of Siberia's Solovetsky gulag as they are slowly reclaimed by nature. Composed in rhythms of montage that seemed always on the verge of collapse and through which resolution was continually deferred, Akerman's *D'Est* was, as we saw, a film that adamantly refused all telos. This is definitively not the case with *Histoire de mes cheveux*: as Lehman copies the movements of the countless other bodies that preceded him on this *trajet des condamnés*, his reenacted journey seems always fated to arrive at its ultimate destination. Towards the conclusion of the film, his camera lingers on an abandoned camp, fragmenting it into segments and details. Our attention is drawn to the crumbling and flaking of plaster and to the rusting of metalwork. A parallel is established in these images between the disintegrating textures of this site of historical trauma and the physical ravages of age that we saw etched onto the filmmaker's body, onto his greying and thinning hair and elsewhere. The archive of his hair allows Lehman to trace back his own personal history in search of his roots, but also to inscribe this within a much larger European history which the filmmaker presents as an unstoppable process of disappearance and annihilation. At the end of a journey of reenactment, Lehman claims a place in history, a history that threatens to swallow him.

A taste for deliberate provocation lies behind everything that we see and hear throughout *Histoire de mes cheveux*: it informs Lehman's encounters with a series of increasingly bewildered hair professionals, it guides the film's wilful and sometimes jarring mix of styles, tones and subjects, and it is of course inherent to the alignment made between individual experiences of natural hair loss and much larger histories of mass genocide. In Lehman's reenacted death march through Eastern Europe, so much of this provocation stems from issues of choice, from the activeness of Lehman's decision to experience something obscene for himself. As Lehman continues his journey inside sites of historical trauma, claiming a place within them, this provocation reaches its point of greatest intensity. Skirting along the camp's external wall, he presents the terms of his own internment: 'Je ne suis pas libre, vous comprenez, je me suis constitué prisonnier. Prisonnier volontiers. Je fais, j'ai fait le trajet du prisonnier' [I am not free, you understand. I have handed myself in. A willing prisoner. I am making, I have made the journey of the prisoner]. What he presents here as the willing, voluntary nature of his internment is particularly unsettling: this confinement within a space of collective trauma is elective. Lehman appears again, this time from inside the camp, his face criss-crossed by the barbed wire of its fence — a *prisonnier volontiers* spurred not by a guard or kapo but by his own inescapable desire. He moves further inwards, appearing on one of the camp's sparse wooden bunks. Emphasising the telos of this reenacted journey, the words Lehman utters whilst sitting on this derisory bed are perhaps the most provocative of the entire film: 'Je suis content d'être arrivé!' [I am happy to have arrived!]. The threat of being swallowed by a history of annihilation is one that he seemingly embraces.

The sheer provocation of these words — delivered by the son of parents who escaped internment, by a man who, through the circumstances of his birth in Lausanne, escaped annihilation in a camp much like this one, a man who, in the present day, now gladly chooses destruction, who inserts himself physically into the charnal sites of history, who finds pleasure and contentment in the inevitable telos of his journey, who presents this bunkbed as the logical endpoint to which his whole life (and maybe the lives of all Jews) has led — is startling. If the commemorative injunctions of *lest we forget* or of a post-war *devoir de mémoire* impose ethical responsibilities to the dead that demand that we remember their suffering as a means of ensuring, via a collective commitment to *never again*, that history does not repeat itself, Lehman here tests a mode of remembrance that actively does repeat history, that deliberately makes it happen again, that confronts us with a potentially discomforting identification with, even appropriation of, the suffering of others. That Lehman refrains from diverting the uncomfortableness of this image — one of a twenty-first-century Jew interned in a death camp — into anything as recognisably 'useful' as a political message or a warning to the present from history of course does nothing to diminish his provocation.

Vitally, the fact of carrying a reenacted journey to its painful endpoint, of embracing the startling provocations that this journey brings with it, of seeking embodied knowledge of history for himself, grants Lehman a form of escape. From the haunted landscapes of the East, the shot changes abruptly to show Lehman, now far from his camp, kissing a friend. This sudden transition registers as a watershed and the tone of this new image is radically different from those it displaces. On the

FIG. 3.9. *Histoire de mes cheveux: de la brièveté de la vie* (2010), Boris Lehman
© Boris Lehman/Dovfilm (with: RTBF/Arte/CBA/Good and Bad News).

film's soundtrack we hear a Russian folk song that speaks optimistically of spring and the emergence of new life. Lehman's image of intimate contact is the direct counterpart of Akerman's Moscow cellist; but it is an image that, unlike the one found in *D'Est*, seems to promise closure and release, a hopeful turning towards the future. Throughout his film, Lehman plunges headfirst into what he had described in relation to the work of his compatriot as the haunting 'musique des morts et des mots ressassés', but nevertheless finds a way of breaking free, of coming back to the surface for air. Lehman stages himself as a post-holocaust Odysseus, escaping annihilation by the siren call of history, or as a version of Lot's wife who turns to gaze upon past destruction but continues her journey onwards as flesh not salt.[8]

Compared with Lehman's discoveries in Lausanne, *Histoire de mes cheveux* travels yet deeper, yet more frontally into the traumas of history, inhabiting them; so doing, it reiterates the hope that reenactment might offer a means of negotiating loss that holds out the possibility of forging more positive relationships with the past. This does not here entail an antidote to or a reversal of loss, whether that be the loss of youth, the losses of family history or those of a whole continent: certainly the ruins that Lehman traverses on his journey eastwards and the unstoppable physical decline that he simultaneously foregrounds on the ageing surfaces of his own body lead us away from such an interpretation. Rather, it offers an important route towards making one's peace with the ghosts that haunt us as we go on living. Lehman's attempts to find closure and to disentangle himself from the burden of the past as a means of moving forward to the future, to the time that remains to live, are developed yet more explicitly (and yet more definitively) in my final case study.

Embracing Effacement, Staging Disappearance: *Funérailles (de l'art de mourir)*

Although he has made other films in the intervening years, Lehman's 2016 film *Funérailles (de l'art de mourir)* (henceforth *Funérailles*) in many ways follows on directly from *Histoire de mes cheveux*. *Funérailles* is the final instalment of Lehman's *Babel*, the monumental film project he began in 1983; but it is also to be understood as a conclusion more broadly. Throughout his life, Lehman has sworn off filmmaking on numerous occasions, often bemoaning the weighty burden of his cinematic vocation, with instances of renunciation scattered across his work. Such forswearing appears, however, more final in *Funérailles*. Lehman has stated clearly that this will be the last film he ever makes (although subsequent endeavours have meant that this promise has not been entirely kept since). As he insists in the film's closing sequence: 'Et bien, c'est la fin. C'est la dernière fois que je me filme, que j'apparais à l'écran. C'est la dernière fois que vous me voyez. Il faut bien finir un jour' [And so, it's the end. This is the last time that I'm going to film myself and appear on screen. This is the last time that you're going to see me. You have to stop sometime]. Presenting the film in March 2016 at the same Cinémathèque Suisse previously visited in *A la recherche du lieu de ma naissance*, he reiterated this pledge, reinforcing its finality: 'C'est donc, on peut dire, un film testament. C'est mon dernier film, je n'en ferai pas d'autres' [You could say it's a farewell film. It's my last film, I'm not going to make any others].[5] *Funérailles* was filmed against the backdrop of the abdication of the Belgian King Albert II: an early sequence contains an extract from the monarch's televised address to the nation where he explains that age and illness prevent him from exercising his state duties as he would wish. Lehman's final film sees the self-appointed king of Belgian cinema ironically stage his own parallel abdication.

In a revealing article published the same year in the journal *Trafic*, Lehman picks apart his decision to definitively abandon filmmaking, whilst also recognising the scepticism he knows it will inevitably provoke in those familiar with him and his work:

> [P]our moi qui n'ai cessé d'accumuler films après films depuis mon plus jeune âge, au point que ma vie s'est confondue avec mes œuvres, cela ressemble à un canular. Pourquoi cette décision? Mon âge? Une certaine lassitude? La fin de la pellicule? La mort d'un certain cinéma que j'ai pratiqué? Le sentiment d'avoir bouclé mon œuvre? La disparition de proches qui furent mes muses et mes inspiratrices?

> [[F]or someone like me who right from the very beginning has never stopped piling up film after film, to the point that my life has blurred with my work, this seems like a hoax. Why this decision? My age? A certain weariness? The end of analogue film? The death of a certain kind of cinema that I have practised? The feeling of having wrapped up my work? The disappearance of loved ones who were my muses and my inspiration?] (2016: 52).

Through a vocabulary framed particularly in terms of *fin*, *mort* and *disparition*, the majority of the motives cited by Lehman evoke forms of decline and disappearance. And yet, as was also the case in the sudden shift in perspective sparked at the conclusion to *Histoire de mes cheveux*, even as Lehman finds himself drawn to unavoidable vanishing points, confronting the irreversible losses that litter the way, possible glimmers of optimism still emerge. I interpret *Funérailles* in terms of a motive that stands out from those listed above for its notably different, arguably more positive tone: *le sentiment d'avoir bouclé mon œuvre*. *Funérailles* resumes and indeed concludes a process developed in the previous case study through which Lehman divested himself of the weight of the past. This process allows Lehman to attain a sense of closure not only for his work and the questions that drive it, but also for the life to which this work is so inextricably bound, laying obsessions and anxieties to rest, taking control over how the story ends.

When Lehman appears on screen in *Funérailles*, the effects of ageing depicted in *Histoire de mes cheveux* have seemingly accelerated: his greying hair appears yet thinner, his pate now almost entirely bald. The threat of disappearance explored so extensively in the previous case study appears here yet more palpably imminent. The film opens with Lehman breaking land, Odysseus-like once again, to be recognised by a lone dog. Lehman's wandering Jew here returns from his journey into the past for one final voyage into the future. *Funérailles* closes with an epilogue in which Lehman appears sitting in front of towering stacks of film canisters — the remnants of his personal filmic archive — offering his final farewells, his last will and testament, directly to camera. He reflects upon his life and work, but also on what lurks just around the corner: 'Je me retire, je m'efface, je disparais' [I retreat, I fade, I vanish]. Via a dissolve, Lehman's body disappears from the screen, leaving behind an empty chair: 'peu à peu, l'image s'estompe et je disparais' [Little by little the image fades and I disappear]. If, in what was undoubtedly the strangest sequence from Lehman's search for himself in Lausanne, the filmmaker reenacted his own birth, *Funérailles* depicts an opposing but equally impossible autobiographical gesture as the filmmaker now imagines his own death.

Writing in the introduction to a 2005 special issue of *Forum of Modern Languages Studies* devoted to the literature of 'autothanatography', Susan Bainbrigge considers the various ways in which death, and particularly its unavailability to the self, inflects autobiographical practice. As Bainbrigge recognises, whilst the term autothanatography might initially appear a contradictory one, insofar as death can never be known to the self, the concept has nevertheless proved productive for theorisations of the relationship between art, the self and death, providing a framework for examining the personal engagements of writers and artists with their own mortality (2005: 359). Bainbrigge draws particular attention to the important investigations offered by Jacques Derrida and Louis Marin into the possible applications of the term in their analyses of writers and philosophers as varied as Montaigne, Nietzsche, Stendhal, Blanchot and Barthes. She highlights both Derrida's exploration in his *Otobiographies* (1984) of how the practices of authors who write about their own death confront us with questions surrounding the coherence of subjectivities, and Marin's considerations in *La Voix excommuniée* [*The Excommunicated Voice*] (1981) and *L'Écriture de soi* [*Writing Oneself*] (1999) of how the unknowable aporias of both birth and death might be negotiated through writing (359–60). These are autothanatographical stakes in which Lehman's film is also deeply invested.

Lehman has imagined elsewhere what his own death might look like. *Histoire de ma vie racontée par mes photographies* had, for instance, shown him pierced with arrows in a modern and deliberately masochistic martyrdom of Saint Sebastian, whilst *Mes sept lieux* had shown him collapse at the end of his peripatetic wanderings like an exhausted Pheidippides at Marathon. Such experimentation is developed much more extensively in *Funérailles*, a work that is entirely preoccupied with this death and with how it might be represented. If, in a shift from the retrospective to the prospective, the strategies of self-scrutiny and self-representation Lehman here uses can no longer be understood as *re*enactment, but necessarily as a form of *pre*-enactment, these strategies nevertheless exist in close dialogue with techniques seen in the previous case studies. As he imagines his own death, Lehman continues in particular to fundamentally deconstruct oppositions of truth and fiction: the sequences we watch are, of course, fabrications, but they also offer an authentic distillation of the filmmaker's wants, needs and fears as he approaches the end of his life — a personal mise-en-scène of desire. Through an autothanatographical pre-enactment, Lehman again seeks to experience something for himself and thus to gain embodied knowledge and understanding of it. In so doing, he further expands the already enlarged parameters of his autobiographical practice to encompass the entire span of a life, from its very beginning to its very end. Pre-enactment allows Lehman to make death, that unknowable margin of human experience, suddenly available (and so controllable) to the subject of autobiography.

In recent years, attention has increasingly been paid both in artistic practice and scholarly discourse to the notion of pre-enactment, often in ways that acknowledge the complex dialogues it maintains with reenactment. Writing in the proceedings of a 2017 conference whose very title — P/Re/Enact! — emphasised the dense temporal entanglements frequently at play in such experiments,[6] curator Francesca Laura Cavallo offers an account of pre-enactment that is helpful for our understanding of *Funérailles*. Surveying its varied appearances in contemporary art, Cavallo identifies in pre-enactment a possible tool for the management of future risk, citing a fire drill as paradigmatic illustration of such a function (2019: 179–98). In rehearsing gestures to be adopted in the event of a future conflagration, such drills perform the work of habituation, acknowledging threat but, so doing, mitigating and bringing it under control, making it familiar, a function we also see in *Funérailles*. Importantly, as it leads Lehman to assume ownership over what awaits him, pre-enactment enables him to elect the particular death he desires, a *good* death, one far removed from those myriad losses evoked in the previous case study. *Funérailles* becomes, as Lehman himself suggests, '[e]xercice thérapeutique, exorcisme sans doute, qui peut mener vers un apaisement' [therapeutic exercise, exorcism probably, that can lead towards calm].[7] By taking control over his own death and its representation, by embracing and taming the threat of definitive disappearance that this death carries with it, Lehman's final film sustains a therapeutic form of catharsis, a deliberate letting go of life.

Funérailles depicts the shedding of weight, both concrete and affective, in a figurative and literal cleansing. Throughout so much of the film, we watch as Lehman undertakes careful preparations for his death, seeking in particular to divest himself of the baggage — the archive — that he has accumulated so painstakingly across his life. As Lehman himself writes:

> Au cours de ma vie, j'ai accumulé pas mal de traces, d'éléments constitutifs de mon existence. Je me suis en quelque sorte interdit d'oublier et me voici encombré d'une mémoire colossale que je n'ai pas voulu effacer [...] Aujourd'hui tout cela m'encombre, est devenu étouffant. C'est ma camisole de force, mon boulet, ma chaîne. Un trop-plein qui me dévore et m'écrase. Je veux m'en débarrasser, m'évader de cette prison que je me suis construite, entrer en pauvreté.

> [During my lifetime, I have accumulated quite a few traces, constituent elements of my existence. In a way, I didn't allow myself to forget, and so here I am lumbered with a colossal memory that I couldn't erase [...] Today it all weighs me down, and it's become suffocating. It's my straitjacket, my millstone, my chain. An excess that's devouring and crushing me. I want to get rid of it, escape from this prison I built for myself, enter into poverty] (2016: 59–60).

In extended sequences, Lehman clears out his overstuffed living and work spaces, throwing away the piles of objects littering every surface that were enumerated in works such as *Mes sept lieux* and *Choses qui me rattachent aux êtres*. Elsewhere, Lehman sits atop an abandoned concrete artillery bunker on a Belgian beach, surrounded by stacks of film canisters. He kicks and throws his films down onto the sand before setting them alight. His camera closes in on the surface of the depleted film stock as it is gradually consumed by flames. *Funérailles* contains no more definitive statement of a desire to let go than the destruction of the film stock that has always been so dear to Lehman and that has accompanied him so faithfully through life, binding him to it. Boris the Memorious finally allows himself to forget.

In another sequence of destruction, a pile of books upon which sits a piece of paper bearing Lehman's name is ignited. The camera again zooms in on these images of combustion, highlighting the material processes of decay these objects are subject to. In a clear act of self-staging on the part of Lehman, the majority of these books are by Franz Kafka, a writer who famously requested that his writing be entirely destroyed after death. In destroying his own personal archive *before* death, Lehman apparently seeks to ensure that no Max Brod can ever ignore his comparable desires. At the same time, the choice of Kafka of course once more strongly frames Lehman's identity in terms of its Jewishness. Elsewhere again, Lehman sets fire to his clothes: these garments are initially arranged in a smouldering pile; but these clothes are then arranged into the shape of a body, reinforcing a parallel drawn throughout *Funérailles* between disappearing objects and a man on the point of his own disappearance.

There is a ritual, ceremonial quality to so much of *Funérailles*, a quality that becomes particularly apparent in certain sequences. The filmmaker visits an undertaker's showroom to choose a coffin for himself, selecting woods and finishes. We witness the striking image of the filmmaker trying out his chosen coffin for size, seemingly comfortable as he lies down inside, inserting himself physically within a site of disappearance very different from the concentration camp bunk of *Histoire*

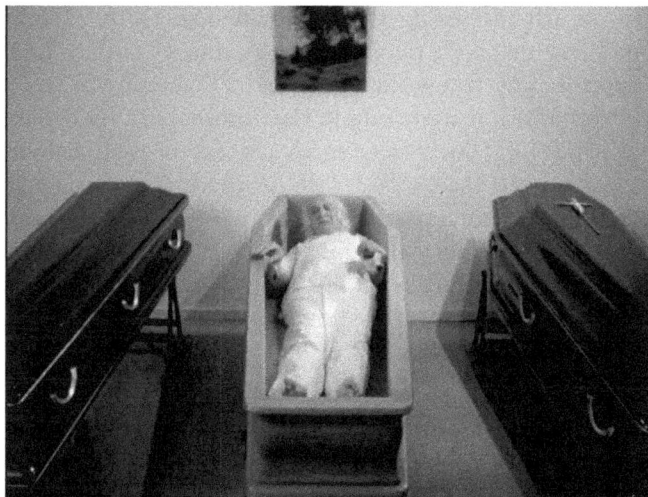

FIGS. 3.10 and 3.11. *Funérailles (de l'art de mourir)* (2016), Boris Lehman
© Boris Lehman/Dovfilm (co-production: Les Films du Centaure/Bandits-Mages).

de mes cheveux. Whilst, in contrast to the reenactment of birth from *A la recherche du lieu de ma naissance*, *Funérailles* never depicts the precise moment of Lehman's death, attention is paid to the loving posthumous care shown to his dead body. Kaddish, the Jewish prayer of mourning, is said for him. In a particularly peaceful sequence, bathed in natural light, the body of the filmmaker is washed: the camera zooms in on his naked feet, face, torso and penis as they are gently cleansed with a sponge. As the camera moves in on Lehman's face, the lids of his closed eyes quiver — not yet dead, but also strangely not entirely alive. In staging his own death, Lehman foregrounds the rites of mourning; these are, importantly, rites that, throughout *Funérailles*, seem wholly removed from melancholy and pain.

The processes of self-mourning that Lehman depicts are instead presented as celebratory, something that is particularly clear in images of the filmmaker's funeral cortege as it makes its way across the battlefield at Waterloo (a key site of Belgian nationhood and the location from which the filmmaker's own meandering *Babel* project originally began). These sequences are filled with colourful garments, people holding hands, and the joyous blare of instruments, as a state funeral-like commemoration is held for an artist who has always occupied the margins. A hole is dug in the earth into which Lehman carefully lowers himself, lying immobile. The ladder is removed, the filmmaker is covered with a shroud and the hole is filled in, one shovelful at a time. All that marks his final resting place is a small mound of disturbed earth. As Lehman writes in his *Trafic* article:

> Se mettre dans le trou et ne pas bouger, sentir la terre en dessous et au-dessus, c'est tout de même éprouvant. Mais c'est aussi un apaisement. J'ai toujours cru aux vertus thérapeutiques du cinéma.

> [Getting into the hole and not moving, feeling the earth below and above you, it's still hard. But it's also calming. I've always believed in the therapeutic virtues of cinema] (2016: 57).

In staging Lehman's definitive disappearance and the destruction of his archive, *Funérailles* offers therapeutic forms of mourning that hold out the comforting possibility of release, peace, even acceptance in the face of death. The relationship with mortality explored in *Funérailles* is not that of the attempts to resist the passing of time that we saw in the opening to *Histoire de mes cheveux*; rather, Lehman's film holds out the possibility of living consensually with death and of taking ownership of it. By *pre*-enacting his own disappearance, imagining what it might look like, Lehman is able to envisage death on his own terms.

Lehman's *Funérailles (de l'art de mourir)* invents an innovative *ars moriendi*, a celebratory *vanitas*, a therapeutic *memento mori* that reminds us that death and dying, loss and mourning, are inevitable, but that this inevitability does not necessarily need to be a source of sadness. Throughout *Funérailles*, Lehman confidently approaches death, embracing effacement and erasure, *choosing* them. Lehman's film confronts us with an image of inevitable disappearance, but one that also offers a final, defiant *image conforme de moi* to surpass all those that preceded it — an autobiographical image that he controls and that tells him both where he comes from and where he is headed. Lehman seeks to make knowable the unknowable zones of identity, but so doing puts that identity to rest. As I move into my final chapter and explore uses of reenactment in the work of Agnès Varda (another artist it is possible to speak of in relation to a continually reconfigured *archive of self*, albeit of a very different kind), certain qualities seen in my reading of Lehman will reappear. This will be the case, for instance, in her appetite for experimentation and play, as well as in the imaginative forms of fictional self-staging that her work frequently contains. But similarities maybe appear most clearly in the acceptance Varda displays of time's passing and the changes this passing inevitably brings. Varda's acceptance does not entail a disavowal of loss, pain or disappearance, nor an attempt to arrest time in its transformative onwards march; rather, and in perhaps yet more extensive ways than Lehman, it represents a means of *living with* these things.

Notes to Chapter 3

1. <http://www.borislehman.be/pages/bio.html> [accessed 9 March 2021].

2. <http://www.borislehman.be/pages/fondatio.html> [accessed 11 March 2021]. Lehman's search for a permanent home for his archives is explored further in the radio documentary 'Boris Lehman à la recherche du tombeau idéal', first broadcast on 15 November 2020 on *France Culture* as part of the series 'L'Expérience'. See <https://www.franceculture.fr/emissions/lexperience/boris-lehman-a-la-recherche-du-tombeau-ideal> [accessed 11 March 2021].

3. Quoted in <http://www.borislehman.be/soupage/naisse.html> [accessed 11 March 2021].

4. <http://www.borislehman.be/soupage/histoiredemescheveux.html> [accessed 12 March 2021].

5. 'Boris Lehman présente "Funérailles" à la Cinémathèque suisse' <https://www.youtube.com/watch?v=_OOxLCYhaWc&t=142s> [accessed 15 March 2021].

6. <https://www.ici-berlin.org/events/p-re-enact/> [accessed 15 March 2021].

7. <http://www.borislehman.be/soupage/Funerailles.html> [accessed 15 March 2021].

8. This possibility of escape has been reiterated in Lehman's 2020 addendum film *Une histoire de cheveux (Sibérie)* [*A History of Hair (Siberia)*].

CHAPTER 4

Agnès Varda — Stillness/Movement

Introduction — Revisiting Grief

There is a sequence from Agnès Varda's 2008 film *Les Plages d'Agnès* [*The Beaches of Agnès*] in which the filmmaker surveys the items on sale at a French flea market, with these disparate objects reminding her of past habits, of people she has met and of films she has made. She rummages through a box containing collectible cards of actors, directors and films from the long-running *Fiches de Monsieur Cinéma* correspondence series. From the mass of tightly packed cards, she finds one featuring her husband, fellow filmmaker Jacques Demy, captured in black and white with a flat cap firmly anchored on his head. Demy's card sits in its box adjacent to Varda's own entry in the series (separated only by a swiftly discarded Jean Cocteau). Reunited in the filmmaker's hands, these printed versions of Varda and Demy rub and slide against each other as they are fondled, fanned and restraightened, their faces momentarily aligned as if looking into each other's eyes. Inspecting these images of herself and of the man with whom, through phases of togetherness and separation, she spent so much of her life, Varda muses in voice-over: 'Je pense qu'avant d'être des fiches de cinéma avec des têtes en carton, nous avons été des êtres de chair et de sang, des amants comme ceux de Magritte' [I think that before becoming film cards with cardboard faces, we were beings of flesh and blood, lovers like Magritte's].

The sequence that immediately follows grants form to Varda's musing. A man and a woman, naked but for the crumpled fabric wound round their heads, walk backwards hand in hand through the courtyard of the home Varda and Demy shared on Paris's Rue Daguerre. Their covered heads nuzzle. The man's penis is erect. Right down to the blue sky and white clouds painted on the courtyard's rear wall, this is unmistakably a restaging of the 1928 series of paintings by René Magritte that Varda cites; but it is also clearly different, reworked to suggest something of the physical intimacy of a real relationship. Through the intermediary of the two shrouded forms that appear on screen, Magritte's unnamed *Amants* become Demy and Varda. What the sequences described above operate is the transition from the inertia of bodies captured on cardboard or canvas to the liveness of moving bodies, whose veins and engorged flesh house flowing blood. But this transition is only momentary: as the lovers complete their movement backwards, the image suddenly becomes saturated, freezes and turns to black and white. It is as if, from

FIG. 4.1. *Les Plages d'Agnès* (2008), Agnès Varda © Ciné-Tamaris/Arte France Cinéma.

the animation of bodies moving through space, we return to the flat fixity of the painting and the printed photograph, to the slumber of collectible relics stored in a box. This shift to black and white eases the transition to the images that follow: archive footage reveals the Rue Daguerre courtyard as it appeared four decades earlier. We watch as Varda works with actor Michel Piccoli and Demy works with composer Michel Legrand — all now dead. Whilst the lovers in the courtyard seemed for a moment able to resurrect something of the intensity of earlier contacts and attachments, they cannot ultimately dispel the sense of watching lives and loves now lost and definitively confined to the past.

Varda depicts her Rue Daguerre courtyard (or versions thereof) on a variety of occasions throughout *Les Plages d'Agnès*. After her flesh-and-blood citation of Magritte, she returns to this space in a later sequence for a very different artistic reenactment — one that seeks to communicate not the carnality of her relationship with Demy, but instead the raw potency of the grief she felt in the immediate aftermath of his death in 1990. The cropped remains of a tree standing in the courtyard fill the screen, severed branches and charred stumps seemingly offering a literalising metaphor for life cut short. Via a cross-fade, this tree merges with shots of waves lapping gently at one of the many titular beaches Varda's film contains. The shot changes and Varda herself appears on screen, her head hooded in cloth, the same lapping waves superimposed over her face. The camera moves outwards to show Varda seated at a table, funereally enrobed in white. She switches on the radio placed before her and music rings out amidst the silence. Once her arm is retracted, she settles into stillness, the twitches and quivers of her shoulders and head so slight as to be barely perceptible.

In this ascetic image of mourning, Varda uses her own body to recreate an installation piece by artist George Segal: *Alice Listening to her Poetry and Music* (1970).

Speaking in an episode of her 2011 television series *Agnès de ci de là Varda* [*Agnès Here and There Varda*], the filmmaker reflects further on this instance of artistic reenactment and what it meant to her, juxtaposing her copy against Segal's original on screen: 'Quand je ne savais comment filmer mon désarroi au moment de la mort de Jacques, je me suis toute emballée de blanc comme en plâtre, et j'ai imité Alice. J'ai écouté de la musique que nous aimions' [When I didn't know how to film my distress right after Jacques's death, I wrapped my whole body in white, as if in plaster, and imitated Alice. I listened to music that we loved]. After a pause, she adds, in a particularly touching line: 'Les artistes inventent pour nous comment exprimer nos émotions' [Artists invent for us ways of expressing our emotions]. Varda borrows the pallid forms of Segal's plaster sculpture, inhabiting them, as a means of sharing something of her own experience that she felt otherwise unable to express. Her reenactment stands as a record of a loss that seemed deadening and overwhelming to the point of inarticulacy, as well as of her need to wordlessly testify to the lacerating intensity of this felt reality.

These two artistic reenactments speak in different ways to a need to commemorate: the immediate impact of loss on the one hand, and the nature of what has been lost on the other. Taken as they appear chronologically in the film, both instances together communicate something of what it is to live, to love and to lose: Varda hints at the sensuality of our exposure to others, at the interpenetration of lives and bodies, and at the mutual exchange of pleasures; but she also explores how this perhaps inevitably comes at the expense of future pains. Read in such a way, Varda's artistic reenactments suggest that to open ourselves to attachment is to accept the possibility of the wrenching anguish of later separation. Crucially, both of these reenactments perform the same gesture: they take a static image and remake it through the resources of cinema, restaging past art in the present and turning stillness into movement. In both examples, this shift from stillness into movement is a precarious one: sometimes, as we see in Varda's colourful reworking of Magritte, movement collapses back into stillness; sometimes, as we see in the grief-stricken immobilisation of her version of Segal, this movement never fully manages to break free from sculptural fixity.

As Shirley Jordan suggests in a particularly neat formulation, Varda's is a filmmaking practice that resolutely lets 'neither the still nor the moving be' (2016: 144). For Jordan, '[i]ntent on the temporal and spatial expansion of the still image, [Varda] fragments it, frays it and teases it into movement; intent on the moment, she slows or halts what moves' (ibid.). The uncertain tension between stillness and movement that works its way throughout Varda's work is one within which the diverse instances of autobiographical reenactment analysed in this final chapter are tightly entangled. Whilst appearing in very different contexts and in very different films, each of these instances will overlap in various ways with those reenactments described above, sharing their orientation and approach. In these carefully staged scenes, Varda will offer an imperfect recreation of something earlier, often shifting between the cinematic and the non-cinematic, with reenactment functioning as a way to elicit and explore the encounter between different time frames and media. In all of these examples, Varda will attempt to nudge stillness into movement through the gestures, poses and arrangements of bodies, both her own and those of others. In so doing, Varda simultaneously navigates a number of other connected tensions: between past and present, mortality and vitality, foreclosure and possibility, sadness and celebration, the definitive and the continually updated. In propelling stillness into movement, Varda will often seek to effect similar shifts towards the latter term in these associated oppositions, in pursuit of forms of presentness, vitality, possibility, celebration, and the means through which to continually update earlier representations and experiences. But, as exemplified by Varda's versions of *Alice* and the *Amants*, there always exists the risk of being drawn back towards stillness and so towards pastness, mortality, foreclosure, sadness and the fixity of definitive answers.

Over the following sections, I consider Varda's autobiographical use of reenactment through a series of pairings. From instances in which, as was the case in her treatment of Magritte's paintings and Segal's sculpture, she reenacts works by other artists (*Jane B. par Agnès V.* [*Jane B. by Agnès V.*]; *Les Glaneurs et la glaneuse* [*The Gleaners and I*]) we move to films in which she reserves the same treatment for her own previous artworks (*Ulysse*; *Agnès de ce de là Varda*), before finally examining instalments in which she applies techniques of reenactment to the experiences of youth, both her own and those entrusted to her by a cherished loved one (*Les Plages d'Agnès*; *Jacquot de Nantes*). As case studies develop, the central tension tested by reenactment will continue to concern literal forms of stillness and movement; but it will increasingly also provide a framework for thinking about Varda's distinctive treatment of questions of temporality, memory, knowledge, ethics, identity and filmic structure. These filmic pairings as well as the essential stakes they bring into focus are not necessarily new, having previously been explored to great effect by certain other commentators; but approaching them from the perspective of the mediations of reenactment can lead us to think in distinctive ways about them and to locate (sometimes latent) points of alignment and dialogue.

Approaching Varda from the perspective of reenactment indeed encourages certain interpretations of her work and of the preoccupations, intentions, and interactions that have filled it, from its origins to its final expressions. In a striking sequence from the unmistakably valedictory *Varda par Agnès* [*Varda By Agnès*], released shortly before the filmmaker's death in March 2019, trophies won by Varda and Demy appear side by side on a base of sand. This image, already used in *Les Plages d'Agnès*, here receives an additional layer of meaning. Against a sound effect of howling wind stirring up the sands upon which these trophies stand, the image gradually fades whilst Varda speaks in voice-over: 'Et depuis... vanitas, vanitatis...' [And since then... vanitas, vanitatis...]. This fading, buffeted image pre-empts the film's close: in conclusion to a string of scenes foregrounding forms of departure, erasure and decline, Varda sits on a windswept beach and slowly fades to nothing. Through an image that recalls Lehman's final farewell from *Funérailles*, Varda says her goodbyes and allows herself to be swept away for good.

When Varda's very different reenactments of Magritte and Segal were considered together, concerns they shared were brought out with added force. These are shared concerns that are also thrown into sharp relief by the grouping of further examples I propose in this chapter. Considered individually but yet more powerfully so in aggregate, the films I explore urge us to see in Varda's work a composite form of vanitas: an extended meditation on the certainty of time's passing, the transience of life, the ephemerality of the earthly pleasures this life contains, the inevitability of death and disappearance. As poignantly resumed by those sequences from *Varda par Agnès* described above, Varda's work is acutely concerned with experiences of loss, both those that have already come to pass and those still to come. As they repeat something from the past in the present, variously striving to retrieve an earlier original in sameness or embracing the creative, interpretive, transformative possibilities of repetition, Varda's uses of reenactment are implicated in her engagements with loss in particular ways, as we will see. Whilst her responses to loss expose her as much to frustration and disappointment as to jubilation, her work in many ways represents the culmination of a development witnessed across preceding chapters, whereby the pleasures of reenactment gradually win out over the pains.

Thinking Varda through reenactment also encourages us to bring her work usefully into proximity with that of very different filmmakers. The artists analysed in the three previous chapters stand in close dialogue with one another, with their conversations sustained in particular by the common occupation of certain cultural spaces and by the chains of aesthetic and thematic influence that are often proudly announced in their work. Varda is not immediately identifiable as a participant in these specific dialogic exchanges, and comparisons with any of the other three filmmakers would not necessarily be the most instinctive. Whilst, as we will see frequently in the following sections, Varda actively positions herself in relation to a wide range of other artists, Akerman, Dieutre and Lehman would not be amongst her most obvious interlocutors. And yet, thinking Varda through the unifying thread of reenactment nevertheless brings grounds for possible comparison into clearer focus. In the pairings that follow, I seek to introduce Varda as a participant into the dialogues I established between Akerman, Dieutre and Lehman. In so doing, I propose distinctive readings of Varda's films, position these films as potential points of comparison to my earlier analyses, and further develop my exploration of autobiographical reenactment and of the varied effects it produces.

Reenacting Art History: *Jane B. par Agnès V.* and *Les Glaneurs et la glaneuse*

As strikingly emblemised by a 1962 photographic self-portrait in which she replicates the poses and postures of the Venetian noblemen from Bellini's *Miracle of the Cross at the Bridge of S. Lorenzo* (1500), Varda is a filmmaker who positions herself, both figuratively and literally, in relation to other kinds of image. Initially trained in photography and art history, Varda confesses in interviews from *Les Plages d'Agnès* to having been largely indifferent to the filmic medium before she turned to making her own films in the early 1950s — an oft-repeated narrative that the recent work of Rebecca DeRoo (2018) has done much to complicate. Even after her eventual move into cinema, Varda's filmmaking remains drawn towards other kinds of image-making and other histories of artistic representation. The effect produced by much of her filmmaking resembles a sequence from *Visages Villages* [*Faces Places*] (2017): in a playful gibe at a Godard who otherwise remains conspicuously absent, Varda traverses the Louvre in a wheelchair, reenacting the record-breaking dash of *Bande à part* [*Band of Outsiders*] (1964). Pushed at speed through the Grande Galerie by her collaborator JR, she exclaims her unabashed, almost ecstatic delight at the artworks she passes. Varda's beatific expression and enraptured gestures encapsulate something of what these images are to her: beloved friends with whom she is here reunited.

The significant, often reverent and loving space that Varda makes in her filmmaking for other art histories and other kinds of image nourishes the tension between stillness and movement that pervades her work, as the visual lexicons and signifying mechanisms of the filmic and the non-filmic are brought into frequent, generative interaction. As Jordan suggests, these interactions belie not conflictual battles between different media fighting for prominence, but rather 'a spirit of cooperation, an investigative coaxing of each away from what appears intrinsic to it' (2016: 144). Reenactment offers Varda a potent tool through which such coaxing cooperations are both orchestrated and questioned as well as a platform for very personal engagements with histories of representation. It allows her to explore what Rebecca Schneider presents as the possibility of 'transgenerational conversation' between artists, artworks and historical moments, and those ways in which precedent art is held in an ongoing relation of 'call and response' with the art that follows (2011: 111). In this opening section, I examine two films in which Varda stages reenactments of artworks taken from across multiple centuries of visual culture. Compared with what we have seen over preceding chapters, these instances of artistic reenactment most closely resemble Dieutre's baroque recreations, with Varda filming her body and the bodies of others in ways that explicitly replicate much earlier artworks (even if the tensions drawn out between originals and their copies will here be explored very differently). Whilst she shares with the director of *Leçons de ténèbres* a concern with what it might mean to recreate certain works of art from the past in the present moment, Varda is perhaps more critical about the multiple artistic lineages in relation to which she situates herself, claiming a position of both aesthetic continuity and rupture. These artistic reenactments grant important insight into the desires and identifications that bolster Varda's self-conception and self-construction as an artist and into the kinds of art she seeks to make.

Varda's 1988 film *Jane B. par Agnès V.* investigates the power of images and the relationships of power that undergird them. This investigation is developed through an avowedly fragmentary, often contradictory study of the English actor, singer and model Jane Birkin, then one of France's most prominent stars. An early sequence corroborates this star-status: Birkin walks confidently past the bright lights of the Champs-Elysées, tracked by a recording camera and pursued by the interested gazes of countless bystanders. After this consummate image of modern celebrity, Varda will seek to excavate beyond the surface of such instantly recognisable

FIG. 4.2. *Jane B. par Agnès V.* (1988), Agnès Varda © Ciné-Tamaris.

representations: to explore the anxieties, dreams and uncertainties that lie beneath, and to generate a more intimate, complex likeness of her subject. Reflecting three decades later on this collaboration with Birkin and the burgeoning friendship that surrounded it, Varda explains in *Varda par Agnès* how the idea for her film first developed:

> On marchait et soudain elle a dit: C'est terrible, je vais avoir quarante ans! J'ai sursauté: C'est idiot, c'est un âge magnifique! C'est le moment de faire ton portrait! Et c'est comme ça que ça a commencé. Je lui ai proposé, à elle qui était si vivace, si vivante, de faire le contrario des hommages aux actrices décédées, où l'on diffuse des extraits des films qu'elles ont tournés et des entretiens. Je lui ai dit: On va faire des extraits de films que tu n'as pas joués, on va les inventer, et des entretiens un peu fabriqués.

> [We were walking and suddenly she said, 'It's terrible, I'm going to be forty!' I was surprised and replied 'That's silly, it's a magnificent age! It's the moment to do your portrait!' And that was how it started. I suggested to her — she who was so hardy, so alive — that we did the opposite of those tributes to dead actresses, where you show extracts of the films they've been in and interviews. I said to her, 'We'll make extracts of films that you haven't been in, we'll invent them, and made-up interviews'.]

The portrait that Varda devises of her sitter as she apprehensively approached her fortieth birthday seeks to craft what Emma Wilson refers to as 'an imaginary archive of Birkin [...] a repertory to meet Birkin's desire and to release her possibilities' (2019: 75). In paying tribute *pre*-mortem, Varda's alternate star hagiography aspires to capture the resilient liveness of a woman both *vivace* and *vivante*, to assuage nagging fears at the onwards march of time, to devise a multifaceted resemblance that knowingly moves between fact and fiction, reality and imagination, as well as to offer Birkin a beautiful birthday gift made just for her.

From start to finish, Varda will compere, encourage, reassure, coax and cajole Birkin through their invented interviews and extracts, remaining a more or less discernible presence within her film, a presence that she repeatedly interrogates. An early sequence depicts Birkin in front of a suspended mirror, with Varda reflected within its rounded surface — an image that deliberately recalls artworks such as Van Eyck's famous Arnolfini newlyweds (1434). Replicating the same stance as her artistic forebears, Varda stages herself in the role of canonical portraitist, one who, as we will see, remains always attentive to the rights and responsibilities that bind her to her sitter within a work of art that bears her signature.

In building her imaginary Birkin archive, Varda gleefully raids what Alison Smith presents as the abundantly recognisable, sometimes even clichéd images of the 'Western cultural bank' (1998: 18), using them as the source material for her invented film extracts. Throughout *Jane B. par Agnès V.*, Birkin assumes a dizzying array of fictional roles, guided by Varda's associations and impressions of her (of her name, her accent, her origins, her shyness, her warmth, her sensuality, her beauty, her eagerness to please and desire to be found pleasing) as well as by her own feelings, tastes and aspirations (actors she would like to play alongside; dream acting parts that, she suggests, she would never be offered in real life; her occasional ambivalence towards fame and the demands it places on her). We watch as Birkin appears as an ethereal muse draped over the tomb of Rousseau at Ermononville; a slapstick pastiche of Stan Laurel throwing cream pies in a Rue Daguerre bakery; an elderly widow scattering her husband's ashes over a Montmartre vineyard; a Dickensian mother threatened with eviction; an English-accented Joan of Arc burnt at the stake; Calamity Jane in the Wild West; Ariadne in the labyrinth; a recalcitrant flamenco dancer; the lover of a Jean-Pierre Léaud taken straight from Truffaut. In the staging of many of these roles, Varda nods towards art history, with Birkin appearing as a sympathetic croupier in Magritte's Knokke casino; as the Virgin Mary in an annunciation modelled on Fra Angelico's frescos (c. 1450); as the leopardskin-clad Jane to a muscular Tarzan, standing in front of the forest of Rousseau's *Le Rêve* [*The Dream*] (1910); or as a corrupt art dealer in a segment that lists painterly references as varied as Picasso, Hockney, Dali, Munch, Manet, Monet and the School of Fontainebleau.

In certain of the roles that Varda leads Birkin to play in *Jane B. par Agnès V.*, this reference to art history is developed through forms of reenactment. Citing art-historical tradition, an early voice-over introduces a point of anchorage for the portrait Varda offers of her sitter: 'Et si on commençait par un portrait officiel, à l'ancienne, à la Titien, à la Goya' [Let's start with an official portrait, in the old-fashioned style, in the style of Titian or Goya]. The image that appears on screen, as if summoned by Varda's invocation of art history, faithfully reproduces the setting of Titian's *Venus of Urbino* (1538): in the background of this tapestry-lined space, servants lean over a chest, whilst in the foreground a dog hovers upon a couch strewn with rumpled pillows and sheets. Birkin reclines in front of this dog, her raised arms resting gently on her head, her knees slightly bent. She is clothed in a translucent gown, a sash at her waist, gold slippers on her feet. Whilst the

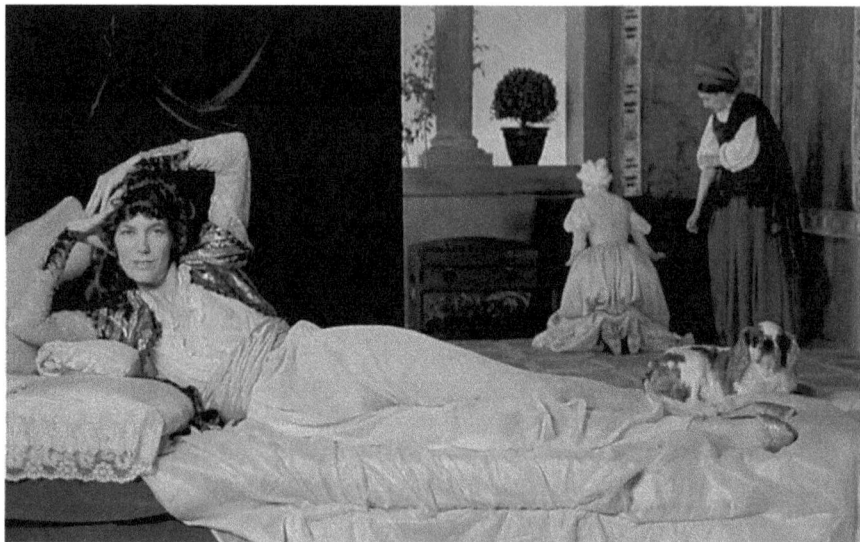

FIG. 4.3. *Jane B. par Agnès V.* (1988), Agnès Varda © Ciné-Tamaris.

space in which Birkin finds herself is Titian's, her pose and attire is instead that of Goya's *La maja vestida* [*The Clothed Maja*] (1800–1807). A cut reveals Birkin in the same pose but now naked, with Varda's art-historical reference shifting to Goya's corresponding pendant, *La maja desnuda* [*The Nude Maja*] (1795–1800). Moving from this frontal view, the camera skirts slowly along Birkin's unclothed form — from toe, to leg, to knee, to thigh, to hip, to nipple, to armpit, to face — tracing a path between freckles, moles and folded flesh. As it traces the outline of Birkin's body, this tracking shot captures the gentle heaving of ribcage before settling on the faint darting of her eye as it unblinkingly meets the camera's gaze. Birkin recreates past art in the present with her living, breathing, responsive body, but this remains an image of enduring stillness.

The stillness of Varda's art-historical copy differs significantly from Dieutre's attempts to recreate the sensuous immersion of baroque chiaroscuro through the visual resources of analogue film, where intertwined bodies were captured in caressing, fondling movement. In its appearance and composition, in the thick atmosphere of stillness that pervades it, Varda's blended reenactment of Titian and Goya more directly recalls the tradition of the *tableau vivant*. This novelty of the eighteenth- and nineteenth-century salon through which living actors reproduced the poses of iconic artworks is of course entirely predicated on the kind of tension between stillness and movement that I identify throughout this chapter. Insofar as this pre-cinematic representational mode allowed the flat images of art history to be animated and spatialised, the *tableau vivant* takes on a particular significance when, as here, it is captured on film, with frozen images intervening within a representational space of moving images. As the filmic medium both acknowledges its inheritance from earlier artforms and explores the terms of its own specificity, there is a meta-cinematic dimension to such on-screen uses of the *tableau vivant* that produces particular effects in the viewer.

As Steven Jacobs suggests, through the 'aestheticisation of immobility' that characterises them, the *tableau*'s on-screen appearances create blockages in the narrative flow of a film that can foster an enigmatic quality inviting decipherment (2011: 95). Such filmic uses simultaneously serve to amplify an inherent morbid uncanniness (96). As Michael Goddard writes in relation to Raúl Ruiz's *L'Hypothèse du tableau volé* [*The Hypothesis of the Stolen Painting*] (1978), a film that contains some of the most famous (albeit imaginary) examples of cinematic *tableaux vivants*, the introduction of this representational strategy within a filmic framework amplifies the oppositions of stasis and mobility, vitality and mortality that are inherent to this very particular mode of art-historical engagement: 'What is a *tableau vivant* if not an impossible exchange between a dead, past representation and living bodies, who sacrifice their present liveliness in order to re-animate the dead past [...]?' (2013: 50). Varda's enigmatic, *tableaux*-like reenactments illustrate the 'impossibility' of this artistic exchange: Birkin revives the dead representations of art history across her own body but does so at the expense of sacrificing the very perennial liveness that Varda first sought to commemorate in her portrait.

Jane B. par Agnès V. opens with a prologue in which Birkin, assuming the guise of one of the servants from the background of Titian's painting, describes the misadventures surrounding her thirtieth birthday from a decade earlier. The voice-over with which Varda introduces this image emphasises how the stillness of the *tableau vivant* seems to render the passage of time more acute: 'C'est une image très calme, hors du temps, tout à fait immobile. On a l'impression de sentir le temps qui passe, goutte à goutte. Chaque minute, chaque instant, les semaines, les années' [This is a very calm image, timeless, totally still. You can almost feel time passing, drop by drop. Every minute, every instant, the weeks, the years]. References to the transience of life and to the inevitability of loss are woven throughout the film, from the taxidermy animals and wilting lilies found inside Birkin's Paris home to a fleeting glimpse of an elderly women seen laboriously pushing a seaweed-draped Zimmer frame along a beach. Within an experiment with filmic portraiture that sought from its outset to offer the contrary of a post-mortem tribute, as these artistic reenactments lead Birkin to sacrifice the mobility of her living body in order to restage the immobility of historical images, they might be seen to invite an unavoidable death in prematurely.

This impression is yet more pronounced when Varda reenacts an image from a very different location in the archives of visual culture. Questioning what she sees as Birkin's contradictory desire to be both known and unknown, famous and anonymous, adored and ignored — to be what the filmmaker jokingly terms an 'inconnue célèbre' [famous unknown] — Varda likens the actor to the late-nineteenth-century case of the *Inconnue de la Seine* [unknown woman of the Seine], the unidentified drowning victim whose death mask (and the ambiguous smile it bore) inspired generations of authors, artists and ordinary Parisians. Varda confesses to having herself bought a plaster copy of this face in her youth, suggesting that it became the site for people to project their own divergent fantasies. On screen, an image of this death mask slowly merges with Birkin against a backdrop of flowing water. Varda transforms Birkin into a late-twentieth-century death mask, her face directly aligned with the inert plaster of the *Inconnue*, the scooped curve of her neckline closely replicating the edges of the original mortuary casting. Birkin opens her eyes, as if resuscitated from drowning and delivered back to life; but as she gazes directly at the camera this remains an image held in the fixity of rigor mortis.

My reading here differs from that of Sarah Cooper, who refutes the idea that such images of immobility should automatically be equated with death and stasis (2006: 82). But my consideration of what happens when cinema replicates the *tableau vivant* is by no means incompatible with Cooper's wider account of the film, one that has considerably shaped a great deal of subsequent Varda scholarship as well as my own understanding of the filmmaker's work. The instances of artistic reenactment described above provide isolated interludes of stillness within a film that, once it begins to expand outwards from its pictorial anchoring *à l'ancienne*, moves through a kaleidoscopic, enlivening succession of sketches and impressions that pauses only ever momentarily before setting out anew in search of ever more facets to add to an increasingly complex portrait. The *tableaux*-like sequences of artistic reenactment described above are facets amongst countless others. Through the assemblage of such facets, *Jane B. par Agnès V.* produces a likeness that is never allowed to fully rest or settle, that works to deliberately undo and disarm fixity. This is a likeness that, as Cooper suggests, plunders myriad sources in an attempt to avoid confining Birkin within a single image (78). The tension between stillness and movement negotiated in Varda's film involves not only the literal states at stake in the bodily mediations of the *tableau vivant*, but also more broadly the ethical questions that govern the art of portraiture and the artist's relationship to their sitter.

In a fascinating study of the cultural reverberations of the *Inconnue de la Seine* that acknowledges the belated resurfacing described above, Anne-Gaëlle Saliot argues that a Gradiva complex governs any work where the figure of this unknown woman is evoked (2015: 278). The risk of projecting an immobilising ideal image onto the subject of art is one that Varda acknowledges and indeed tests throughout the portrait she produces. Resisting certain earlier commentaries that had diagnosed in Varda and Birkin's interactions the violence of a distorting power struggle won by the all-powerful artist (2006: 79, 90 no. 1), Cooper presents the film as an ethical, egalitarian dialogue between the desires of artist and sitter. Whilst I ultimately agree with Cooper's reading, it sometimes risks underplaying the position of control that Varda here knowingly adopts — a position that sees her flex her representational muscles and that entails a certain capacity for violence. As Varda experiments with her role as canonical portraitist, as cinematic Van Eyck, she repeatedly announces her own potential power to mould, to coerce, to prod, to bully, to project upon her sitter, to use her as a vessel for breathing life into her fantasies, to kill into art. Wilson usefully draws attention in her analysis of the film to striking sequences where Serge Gainsbourg dictates and modulates Birkin's singing, roughly pushing her towards the microphone with a hand placed firmly on the nape of her neck

(2019: 94). Varda never conceals those moments where what she demands of Birkin might entail comparable degrees of forcefulness. Varda describes in the film how Birkin has been 'revealed' by the various men who have used her as muse in their work and who have moulded her in line with their fantasies; she recognises her own capacity do the same (even choosing to retain the indelible *Jane B.* label penned by Gainsbourg in a 1969 song). But this is a capacity that is announced to then be interrogated, to be diverted into a different kind of portrait.

At the heart of *Jane B. par Agnès V.*, Varda seeks to construct a space of artistic representation in which the desires of the artist encounter those of the sitter; in which imbalances of power are acknowledged and consent actively sought for representational experiments and exchanges; in which Birkin is free to reject the fantasies she is asked to embody; in which the terms of engagement of artistic inspiration and creation are repeatedly revisited. Varda crafts a portrait that, as it deliberately avoids confining Birkin within a single, fixed image, makes no more claims to definitive knowledge of its subject than this subject does of herself, a puzzle that will never be definitively solved. Shown so frequently in fragmentation and refraction within the mise-en-abyme of reflective surfaces, Birkin refuses to be definitively pinned down — a refusal that Varda respects. This multi-faceted portrait aspires to draw out Birkin's endless possibilities, to reveal these to her and convince her of them; to show her as beautiful, loving and loved, as full of variations and contradictions, as constantly changing.

Jane B. par Agnès V. closes as it opens: with Birkin in the guise of renaissance servant, reflecting upon the unstoppable passage of time that is thrown into sharp relief by a milestone birthday and amplified by this concluding image of stillness. The composite, deeply subjective portrait Varda creates is her gift to her sitter on the eve of her fortieth birthday and her response to her apprehensions. This gift denies neither time's passing nor the ineluctability of loss; instead, it offers an encouragement to Birkin to embrace and enjoy the earthly pleasures that life continues to offer as it unfurls, to remain alert to new and changing possibilities, those that lie within her and those that are released when shared with others. It indeed asks her to take pleasure in change, pleasure in the fact that, as she suggests at one point, 'le temps laisse des traces' [time leaves traces]. Fleeting moments of stillness inserted within *Jane B. par Agnès V.* allow these encouragements to reverberate all the more strongly.

As it touches upon the destitution of individuals who, for the most part, live lives outside of the spotlight, the case study I pair with *Jane B. par Agnès V.* is in many ways far removed from Varda's portrait of one of France's most successful and prominent celebrities. And yet, the varied instances of artistic reenactment they contain bring these two films into useful proximity. *Les Glaneurs et la glaneuse* (2000) explores the activity of gleaning — the millennial practice of collecting material left behind after the harvest — and its various cultural, historical and legal framings. It combines a study of the apparently endemic waste that occurs within industrialised food production with a reflection on the lives of people who depend in various ways upon what others overlook and discard. In another anchoring appeal

FIG. 4.4. *Les Glaneurs et la glaneuse* (2000), Agnès Varda © Ciné-Tamaris.

to pictorial tradition *à l'ancienne*, Varda's film takes as its point of departure what undoubtedly remains the most famous artistic representation of this activity: Jean-François Millet's 1857 painting *Les Glaneurs*. This painting is shown in the film's introduction first in the entry on gleaning from the Larousse dictionary and then in the flesh in Paris's Musée d'Orsay, where the stillness of the canvas contrasts with the accelerated motion of some of the many thousands of visitors who pass before it each year. From this initial point of definitional anchorage in the still images of art history, Varda's film expands beyond the confines of the dictionary and the museum — these privileged repositories of official, institutionalised cultural memory and knowledge — drawing the image into movement with bodies in the present in a way that exemplifies what Wilson identifies as the film's staunch refusal of the 'ossification (or exhibition) of the past' (2005: 106). Seeking to expand, update and animate the cultural archive of gleaning's representations, Varda moves outwards both physically and thematically towards an engagement with the activity that emphasises in particular its most unofficial, provisional, makeshift and marginal expressions at the threshold of the twenty-first century.

Varda's demands on the modern bodies she films in early sequences differ from what we saw in the previous case study. *Les Glaneurs et la glaneuse* in many ways reveals a Varda yet more aware and wary of the artist's power to project an ideal image onto their subject matter, to mould into imposed shapes, to assume what Cooper presents as totalising knowledge of lives and identities that confound knowability (2006: 84–90). These early sequences resemble less those Old Master recreations described above than another of Birkin's reenactments. In a recent return to *Jane B. par Agnès V.*, Cooper draws attention to Birkin's vivid account of her dreams and nightmares (2019: 60–64). In the sequence Cooper highlights, Birkin is juxtaposed

— both physically and through montage — with the female caryatids of a Parisian Wallace fountain, her raised arms recalling her recreations of Titian and Goya from elsewhere but also directly aligned with those of these cast-iron figures (61). Moving in search of modern gleaners, Varda's early intervention in *Les Glaneurs et la glaneuse* is comparable: one of establishing alignments and juxtapositions, of teasing out and amplifying gestural echoes. She films first a woman who collects sticks to illustrate memories of gleaning from her youth. Through montage, this woman's pose is aligned with those shown in grainy black-and-white footage of historical gleaning and in details of Jules Breton's 1859 painting *Le Rappel des glaneuses* [*Calling in the Gleaners*], in a juxtaposition that frames her as inheritor to these earlier representations. Varda goes on to assemble a further succession of individuals who glean not to recreate memories of youth, but as a means of immediate survival: in filming these unnamed bodies as they stoop to pick up food left behind in fields or after markets, Varda deliberately teases out visual echoes between their bent spines and extended arms with the foreground figures of Millet's famous painting.

For Isabelle McNeill, the stooping motion of these modern gleaners, along with the cultural and political significance that immediately attaches to it, functions as a kind of 'mobile monument' within Varda's film, recalling the past whilst being continually reinscribed in a changing modern context (2010: 79). In filming this gesture as it is performed by numerous bodies in the closing years of the twentieth century, *Les Glaneurs et la glaneuse* indeed contests the temporal siting proposed by certain early interviewees: 'glaner, c'est l'esprit d'antan ça' [gleaning, that's how things were done back in the day]. In filming contemporary iterations, Varda confronts us instead with an unbroken continuity of destitution and need that perdures into the present. As she suggests in a voice-over characteristically dense with playful assonance and rhyme: 'si le glanage est d'un autre âge, le geste est inchangé dans notre société qui mange à sa satiété' [If gleaning is from another era, the gesture remains unchanged in a society where people have enough to eat]. Insofar as they embody the *presentness* of gleaning and thus the continuity of the political and cultural conditions that promote gleaning's modern persistence, the men, women and children who appear on screen in early sequences of *Les Glaneurs et la glaneuse* are not entirely dissimilar to the expectant commuters, snow-bound trudgers (and indeed potato pickers) from Akerman's *D'Est*. In repeating an action that has not been confined definitively to history (as might be convenient to believe), these modern gleaners challenge the triumphalist narratives of progress that so abounded at the turn of the millennium and that inform agro-industrial production methods in which, as Varda shows, wastage is deliberately programmed. As resumed sarcastically by a gleaner rescuing misshapen, under- and oversized potatoes left to rot in a field: 'on arrive à l'an 2000, c'est ça le plus beau' [it's nearly the year 2000, that's the best bit].

In moving outwards from nineteenth-century painting, Varda explores how the art of the past can provide a framework, a vocabulary, an iconographic and gestural repertory for thinking about very present concerns, whilst also showing how these present concerns then urge us to continually review and reimagine past art in

FIG. 4.5. *Les Glaneurs et la glaneuse* (2000), Agnès Varda © Ciné-Tamaris.

return. As she expands and updates gleaning's possible referents and representations, consciously resisting the lure of the picturesque in her depiction of the suffering of others, Varda stages a transition from the stillness of oil paints towards a diverse succession of living, moving, often underfed and worn, bodies, that refuse to collapse back into immobility or settle into fixed images anew.

As she extends her definitional chain outwards from nineteenth-century painting across late-twentieth-century France, Varda encourages a capacious understanding of the practice of gleaning: an understanding that combines the forms of urban and rural subsistence described above, the actions of those who scavenge food more for enjoyment or through ethical conviction, the practices of artists who draw upon recuperated materials in their work, as well as an increasingly figurative parsing — 'ce glanage-là, d'images, d'impressions, d'émotions' [that kind of gleaning, of images, impressions, emotions] — in which she recognises her own filmic methodology. Indeed, whilst exploring how earlier artworks such as Millet's both frame and are reinscribed by later realities, Varda simultaneously shows how the art of the past can also offer an iconography and a vocabulary for understanding thoroughly modern acts of artistic creation.

This is announced in particular through a reenactment that, as an instance of artistic self-staging and a declaration of creative intent, shares something with Varda's earlier imitation of Van Eyck. This reenactment also reflects how her willingness to mould and arrange is here much greater when the gleaner she films is herself. Breton's 1877 painting *La Glaneuse* is, like Millet's work before it, introduced within the officialising spaces of the dictionary and the museum, to then be brought into life and movement, inscribed with new meaning and relevance. Varda travels to the northern town of Arras to visit the painting's original: she stands side-by-side with Breton's gleaner, replicating this lone woman's stance, a similar bundle of wheat resting upon her shoulder. Two gallery assistants suspend a patterned cloth behind her, lending a certain theatrical quality, an avowed artifice to her performance of artistic precedent. Speaking in voice-over, Varda explains: 'L'autre glaneuse, celle du titre du documentaire, c'est moi' [The other gleaner, the one from this documentary's title, is me]. She holds her pose in perfect stillness for a moment before breaking into movement, dropping the bundle of wheat and bringing a handheld digital video camera to her eye. Through this reenactment, Varda lays claim to her own status as gleaner — one who collects new memories, encounters and sensations through the lens of her camera — whilst also positioning her creative practice as a point of both continuity and rupture within the history of image-making.

Varda's lightweight recording technology allows her to get closer to the varied lives of others as she tracks gleaning's modern declensions; but it also allows her to get closer to herself in a way that both reenacts and updates another gesture that predates her, as we see in a sequence that directly addresses her film's autobiographical charge. As she surveys souvenirs brought back from a trip to Japan, Varda inspects postcard reproductions of Rembrandt paintings, caressing their glossy surface before moving her hand to fill the frame. She lifts her fingers to reveal the face of one of Rembrandt's self-portraits, her voice-over reinforcing the alignment created visually on screen: 'C'est la même chose en fait. C'est toujours un autoportrait' [It's the same thing, you know. It's always/still a self-portrait]. Tracing a continuity of the autobiographical in art, Varda explores how both she and Rembrandt perform the same gesture of self-scrutiny: the Dutch master turning his gaze upon himself with paintbrush and palette in painterly flatness in the seventeenth century, the French filmmaker doing so at the dawn of a new millennium with a DV camera that allows her to penetrate the grain and furrows of her ageing flesh in its living three-dimensionality. Aligning herself with one of the most famous of all self-portraitists, Varda executes a compelling kind auto-canonisation, proudly and confidently claiming her place in art history.

In foregrounding her tools of (self-)portraiture and how they differ from those of her illustrious forebears, Varda also interrogates her place in the ongoing transformations of *film* history. A visit to a vineyard formerly owned by physicist Étienne-Jules Marey leads Varda to reflect upon the origins of cinema and the relationships of stillness and movement these origins negotiated. Integrating samples of the 'chronophotographic' images that allowed Marey to break down human and animal locomotion into consecutive photographic frames, Varda claims a link of filiation: 'Il est l'ancêtre absolu des cinéastes, on est fier de faire partie de sa famille' [He is the ancestor of all filmmakers, we're proud to be part of his family]. This is a cinematic descendance that, importantly, accommodates variation and innovation. Immediately after her reenactment of Breton's lone gleaner, Varda extols the virtues of the digital camera substituted for the bundle of wheat. As she praises the 'effets stroboscopiques [...] narcissiques, et même hyper-réalistiques' [stroboscopic [...] narcissistic, hyper-realistic effects] granted by this new technology, the screen is filled with ghosted, pixelated, rasterised footage filmed with the same camera. This camera allows Varda to film herself in close-up, to investigate the puckered, wrinkled skin of her hands and face, her greying and thinning hair as she combs it. In showing the decomposition of this digital footage, revealing its most basic elements to be no longer chemically produced frames displayed one after another, but rather countless bytes and discrete pixels, Varda presents a form of cinematic movement that has negotiated a different relationship with stillness.

This reading of digital movement is particularly relevant if we accept that, through what Mireille Rosello presents as a powerful, albeit unspoken connection between death and gleaning (2001: 35), *Les Glaneurs et la glaneuse*, like *Jane B. par Agnès V.* before it, functions as a form of *vanitas*. From the early gleaner who intends to die in the house in which she was born to the liver-spotted hands that remind Varda that 'c'est bientôt la fin' [it's nearly the end], references to the proximity and inevitability of death litter the film. Like Varda's portrait of Birkin, her study of gleaning begins with a movement away from stillness that, as it is prolonged through endless variations on themes first introduced through historical painting, refuses to collapse back into the immobility of fixed definitions and representations. Ultimately, what this film urges in many ways resembles the lessons of the previous case study: not a denial of time's passing or an attempt to halt it, but an encouragement to take pleasure in the changes that time brings (the rot, the damp, the benign horror of ageing, shifting forms of beauty so often rejected or overlooked) as we go on living. But in this digital *vanitas*, where cinematic motion both plays tribute to its birth in the still and announces its departure from it, the risk of a premature sacrifice of present liveness is lessened yet further.

Photographic Afterlives: *Ulysse* and *Agnès de ci de là Varda*

The two previous case studies saw Varda expand the cultural repertory of visual representations surrounding her subject matter, be that Jane Birkin or the act of gleaning. As part of this expansion, Varda extracted much earlier images from the archives of visual culture to then reimagine this past art in the present, sparking proliferating chains of associative reinterpretations. The new representations thus generated of course simultaneously serve to expand Varda's own representational archive, enlarging the diverse portfolio of images that bear her signature. As resumed particularly neatly by a 2015 post on the Instagram account of artist JR[1] where she thumbs her nose at the younger version of herself from the 1962 self-portrait with which I opened the previous section, in the later decades of her life Varda increasingly chose to revisit and rework the images of her own artistic past. Describing Varda's tendency towards self-reflexive retrospection, Wilson foregrounds an intense investment in the 'afterlife' of her projects (2012: 22). Refusing to let past works rest or to be definitively *done*, Wilson suggests, Varda repeatedly adds belated supplements and variations in pursuit of a relationship with her own art that is conceived of as 'ongoing' (ibid.).

In this section, the images Varda retrieves from her representational archive and with which she seeks an ongoing relationship are both works of photography — the medium that witnessed her debut as a creator of images. As an instant of arrested action and as the element that, when viewed in rapid succession, permits the illusion of cinematic motion, the photographic medium is of course tightly bound within the tension between stillness and movement that frames my analysis in this chapter. As she returns to photographs taken decades earlier, interrogating the circumstances of their production and asking what they mean for her now, we encounter a Varda who, as Jordan suggests in a vocabulary that overlaps usefully with Wilson's, is concerned 'less with what Henri Cartier-Bresson famously referred to as the "decisive moment" in photography than with what Geoff Dyer has called the "ongoing moment", and with opening photographs up afresh to time' (Jordan 2016: 144; see also Dyer 2005). Through two very different attempts at photographic reenactment, Varda will again explore time's passing and the losses it brings, whilst questioning the access an image can grant to what is no more.

The photograph that Varda seeks to open afresh in her 1982 short, *Ulysse*, is held on screen for a protracted moment at the film's opening. Like Birkin's *tableaux*, the stillness and silence of this introduction issues an invitation to contemplation and decipherment; but this photographic enigma will more consistently withhold the keys to its own interpretation, refusing the pleasures of even tentative resolution and understanding. Towards the film's conclusion, Varda will acknowledge the sphinx-like qualities of a photograph that shares the name of her film. Taken on the afternoon of 9 May 1954 on the beach at Saint-Aubin-sur-Mer in Normandy, it shows a man standing by a seated child on the rocky shoreline, both stripped naked; the man gazes towards the sea whilst the boy looks towards a dead goat in the photograph's foreground. In an echo of the riddle given to Oedipus, this photograph lends itself to being read as a reconfiguration of images such as Titian's *Three Ages of Man* (c. 1512–1514), where the evocations of *vanitas* seen in the previous case studies reappear. Returning to an image in which the unavoidable passage of time is graphically delineated and in which death is literally foregrounded, Varda will indeed navigate the embalming, mortifying force many have found in the immobilising art of photography (Barthes 1980; Bazin 1971; Mulvey 2006).

Varda revisits each of the photograph's protagonists in turn. She encounters first the man — Egyptian photographer Fouli Elia — in the offices of *Elle* magazine where, in the intervening years, he has become artistic director. At Varda's behest, Elia stands naked behind his desk, replicating but reversing his former stance gazing out to sea. Varda hands him a print of the original photograph as well as a fistful of pebbles that, she suggests, have come from the same rocky beach on the Normandy coast captured in 1954. As an investigative reenactment of an earlier photograph that is grounded in materials taken from a beach, this sequence shares something with Simon Fujiwara's mixed-media installation *Studio Pietà (King Kong Komplex)* (2013). But Varda's attempted reenactment will here go no further. Despite the prompts Varda offers, Elia confesses to having limited memory of the photograph and of what it depicts beyond partial impressions, failing to recognise the likeness of himself in this image or in others from the same era: 'Je me souviens pas de cette personne-là [...] je ne veux pas me souvenir' [I don't remember that person [...] I don't want to remember].

FIG. 4.6. *Ulysse* (1982), Agnès Varda © Ciné-Tamaris.

Failures of recognition and recall appear yet more pronounced as Varda revisits the boy from the photograph, the eponymous Ulysse, son of exiled Spanish Republicans who once shared the same Rue Daguerre courtyard, now a bookseller with children of his own. Reviewing multiple photographs of her and the infant Ulysse in tender embrace, Varda describes the intense emotional connection that once bound her to this boy: 'Il a été mon premier enfant. Mon premier enfant favori' [He was my first child. My first favourite child]. These intimate images of past closeness and love contrast with the guarded diffidence, even sternness, of the adult Varda meets in the present and who, like Elia, claims to have limited memory of the photo or of that particular Spring day in 1954: 'J'ai réellement aucun souvenir' [I really have no memory]. Interviews with his mother, Benvenida, another of Varda's former repeat sitters, reveal that when the photograph was taken Ulysse was suffering from Legg-Calvé-Perthes Disease and had visited the coast for a seaweed cure. His mother's spontaneous tears resume the difficulty of this time for the family and the worry that accompanied it. Pressed by Varda, Ulysse explains that he still remembers the pain of his necrosing hip joint, exposing an embodied connection to the sensations of the past that he is perhaps reluctant to amplify through the kinds of reenactment in which Elia more willingly participates. This adult seems totally removed from the suffering little boy he once was. In discussions that recall her negotiations with Birkin, Varda coaxes and cajoles Ulysse, urging him to lower his guard and remember. Ultimately, however, the work of recall is shown to be no more productive with Varda's human interlocutors than with the live goat to which she turns to complete the photograph's trio, and which calmly chews the image of its caprine predecessor.

One of the first on-screen manipulations to which the photograph is subjected sees it inverted, lightened and superimposed with framing grids, in an attempt to recreate what Varda herself would have witnessed that afternoon on the ground-glass viewing screen of her plate camera. Here and elsewhere, however, Varda struggles to gain renewed access to her own past experiences and perspective on them. Such hampered processes of recall contrast with the relative ease with which Varda apparently summons details of other events from a similar period. This is most notably the case for the initiatory production of *La Pointe Courte*, filming for which would begin only two months later in July 1954. As Varda brings traces of her debut film within *Ulysse* through visual and auditory cues, she falteringly situates her image of a man, a boy and a goat within this transitional stage in her life and creative practice; but she also strives to situate her enigmatic photograph within a broader history.

In sequences that bear a striking resemblance to scenes from *A la recherche du lieu de ma naissance* where Lehman lists events that occurred on the day of his birth, Varda integrates newsreel footage, newspaper headlines, archival extracts of what was taking place far from a Normandy beach on that May afternoon in 1954: the immediate aftermath of the Battle of Dien Bien Phu and the beginning of the withdrawal of French colonial forces from Vietnam; progress reports on the Geneva Conference peace talks; coinciding Gaullist and scooter rallies on the streets of Paris; clips of films showing in cinemas at that time. Varda admits in voice-over that she herself has no memory of these events and was forced to research them. These broader world events are cited in an avowed appeal to verifiable reality: Varda lists them as if in the hope of lending additional historical consistency to her photograph, of anchoring it in *official* time. But these public events seem impossibly removed from the stony beach, the figures it once housed and the feelings of a private, intimate reality. Rendered inaccessible, Varda's photographic relic slips further and further into an almost mythological timelessness and indecipherability (see Handyside 2016: 136–39; Smith 1998: 47–48, 157–58).

From the known and unknown faces of history that emerge from the official archival traces she consults, Varda turns back to the image taken from her own photographic archive and reflects: 'Les acteurs de l'Histoire, ceux qui font la mémoire officielle, passent comme les ombres vues depuis la caverne de Platon' [The agents of History, those who make official memory, pass like the shadows seen from Plato's cave]. *Ulysse* explores how all images — be they photographic, cinematic or other — are partial, often illusory representations, each no more definitively true than the next, never entirely reality itself. The same holds, Varda suggests, for memory, understood as an imaginary, subjective representation unable to grant privileged access to the past as it really happened. As a product of the traces left by light passing over a photochemical surface, the image Varda examines offers indexical proof that these three specific bodies indeed once occupied these specific positions on this specific beach. But as the past reality her photograph indexes remains tantalisingly out of reach, Varda continually grapples with the impossibility of restoring earlier events and experiences in sameness to the present through memory. I disagree with Jordan when she suggests that Varda's photograph is revived in the film through being repeatedly shared, held and touched (2016: 147–48); from this perspective, a useful point of comparison to *Ulysse* is found in

Lehman's *Histoire de ma vie racontée par mes photographies*, where the rekindling, tactile force Jordan identifies is discernible to a much greater degree. Whilst Varda clearly takes pleasure in filming the unguarded readings offered by the neighbourhood children to whom she goes on to distribute her images, these supplementary layers of visual interpretation carry her yet further from the love, care and concern that once linked her to a different child at a particular moment in time. Against the backdrop of time's unstoppable passing so emphasised by Varda's quotations from poets Li Bai and Lamartine, the photograph at the heart of *Ulysse* remains frozen and inert as a connection to what it captures is seemingly lost forever.

As we see in a work that encourages comparison with *Ulysse*, Varda continued to look backwards to such earlier moments. In the very different photographic investigation I juxtapose with *Ulysse*, a form of reenactment is much further and much more pleasurably developed. Attempting to open up another frozen moment afresh to time, Varda here approaches phenomena registered in *Ulysse* as obstacles (the ambiguities of pictorial decipherment, the separation of reality and representation, failures of recognition and the incommensurability of past and present identities, the irretrievability of past realities through memory) as spurs to enthusiastic and generative artistic experimentation.

Varda's five-part television series *Agnès de ci de là Varda*, first shown on the ARTE network in December 2011, in many ways functions as a kind of follow-on piece to *Les Plages d'Agnès*, offering a compendium of offshoots, offcuts, reframings and addenda. As signalled by its title, the series displays a yet greater degree of multi-directional itineracy than the 2008 film, with Varda travelling the globe to meet friends, acquaintances and other creatives. It reflects Varda's continued curiosity for the work of artists she admires, as well as her attentiveness to possible points of encounter between her own creative practice and that of countless others across multiple media. The first episode in particular offers valuable insight into the enduring draw of the photographic within Varda's work. Towards this episode's conclusion, Varda visits a rain-soaked Lisbon, explaining in voice-over how she and her assistants had amused themselves during the editing process by freezing footage of passers-by leaping over puddles. 'C'est le moment décisif dont parlait Cartier-Bresson' [It's the decisive moment Cartier-Bresson spoke of], narrates Varda, reinforcing a comparison with her photographic confrère by superimposing his famous Saint-Lazare puddle jumper (1932) over her own image. Such images of interrupted motion inspire what Varda presents as a digression on a subject close to her heart — 'le mouvement ou pas, le cinéma et la photographie, l'instant et la durée' [movement or otherwise, cinema and photography, the instant and duration] — in which reenactment will pay a vital role.

A series of Varda's own photographs and film clips appear on screen, including a number previously seen in *Ulysse*. From a freeze-frame taken from *Les Cent et une nuits* [*One Hundred and One Nights*] (1994) to an extract of the dynamic photomontage of *Salut les Cubains* [*Hey Cubans*] (1963), these sequences evoke both photography's capacity to capture an instant and its status as the original building block of cinematic movement. One of these photographic images in particular allows Varda to explore the issues at play in her thematic digression more directly. This black-and-white photograph was taken shortly after that scrutinised in *Ulysse*, in the summer of 1955 whilst Varda was preparing a photographic feature on Le Corbusier's then recently completed *Cité radieuse* housing block in Marseille. It shows an unknown family group with a baby loosely arranged on the roof of the building, starkly delineated against the paleness of the *brut* concrete wall behind them. Varda describes her photograph and confesses that she had always wondered who these people were and what had happened in the moments leading up to this particular moment or immediately afterwards. Once again, she announces a stance of non-knowledge, drawing our attention to her photograph's enigmatic charge; but the challenge of decipherment and understanding is here approached very differently from what we saw in *Ulysse*.

Varda explains: 'L'envie m'a prise d'imaginer un scénario — faire de ces personnes inconnues les personnages d'une scénette' [I decided to imagine a script: to turn these unknown people into the characters in a little scene]. She describes how — 'comme au cinéma' [like in cinema] — she chose a filming location, transferring her imagined scenario and the *scénette* that grew from it some 200 kilometres further down the Mediterranean coast, to the roof of the Théâtre de la Mer in Sète, a stone's throw from La Pointe Courte. The filmmaker appears on screen, standing in front of the brand-new concrete wall she has had built, 'en décor' [as a set], to mimic the backdrop to the original photograph. As was the case with the patterned backdrop suspended by two museum assistants for her reenactment of Breton's *La Glaneuse*, Varda here foregrounds the constructedness, the theatrical mise-en-scène of the illusion she seeks to create. The similarity is yet closer with certain sequences from *Jane B. par Agnès V.* where Birkin weaves her way through the painted backdrops, dividers, studio lights, technicians and cameras of the film sets used for her reenactments of Titian and Goya. Speaking in voice-over, Varda enumerates the successive steps necessary to the production of her imagined Mediterranean scene. She assembles a crew, hires equipment, recruits local actors, installs tracking rails for her camera, writes a script and sits back to observe the staged recreation of a relic excavated from her own artistic past: 'J'ai mis en scène en 2007 le scénario improbable d'une photographie prise en 1955' [In 2007 I staged the improbable story of a photograph taken in 1955]. We in turn watch as the successful, celebrated artist looks back at a now distant stage in her career, mobilising the full representational apparatus of cinema to answer a riddle she has set for herself.

Varda's actors play an imagined version of the moments that led up to the original Marseille photograph. The scene is wholly ordinary, depicting the everyday affections and tensions at the heart of an extended family. Their acting is slightly awkward, betraying its origin in Varda's written text: we are never allowed to forget that these are *personnages* scripted and arranged in 2007 and not the selfsame *personnes* once captured in 1955. When the actors that Varda directs in the twenty-first century slip into the positions and poses once held by their forebears in the 1950s, the screen flashes to black and we hear a shutter click sound effect. A position of viewing is recreated, and we are invited to observe alongside Varda as if through

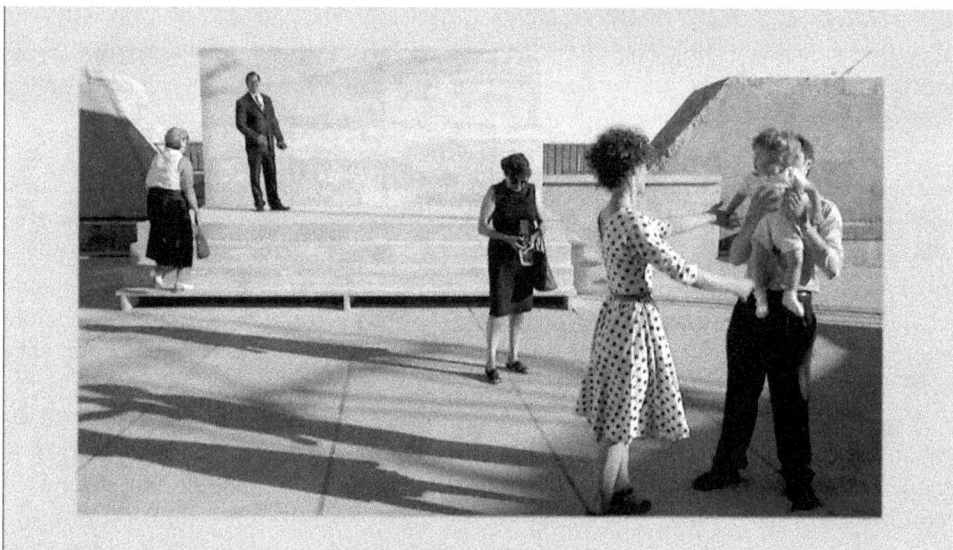

FIG. 4.7. *Agnès de ci de là Varda* (2011), Agnès Varda © Ciné-Tamaris/Arte France.

the lens of her original camera at the very instant a shutter opened and closed. The reimagined scene is frozen for an instant then compared with the original photograph: even with knowledge of the artificiality, the fiction, that underpins this reenactment, the resemblance between colour copy and its original in black and white is here striking. Varda asks us to accept this frozen image as another, newer photograph of the very same moment in time. Herein lies part of the *improbable* dimension Varda describes: how, after all, might it be possible to photograph in the present an event that took place in the past? This 'photograph' is offered as an avowedly artificial index, as hypothetical, fictive proof of what *might have happened* on a summer's afternoon fifty-two years earlier. Both true and false at the same time, both reality and merely one possible representation amongst others, this kind of evidential trace with the ambiguities it fosters is familiar to us from the proof-making experiments of Dieutre and Lehman. Varda's scene is brought back into movement as she imagines the moments that succeeded the instant captured on the roof of the *Cité radieuse*, in turn freezing this action into an entirely new image. Through reenactment, Varda makes the choice of the ongoing over the decisive, opening up a moment once frozen in time to investigate its possible margins and witness them for herself.

It is interesting to note that Varda's ongoing relationship with her own artistic past has been extended yet further by subsequent engagements with her *Cité radieuse* photograph: as part of a 2013 art residency in Aix-en-Provence, Varda revisited the roof of Le Corbusier's actual building once again, photographing some of its current female residents in the same location where she herself had stood, camera in hand, in 1955. None of these revisitations seek to restore an earlier instant in pristine identicality, exactly as it was; but rather allow Varda the possibility of creating an expanding series of new images, using the traces of the past as the material for continuing creative and imaginative interventions. In such a way, the *Cité radieuse* reenactment, whilst fleeting and confined to what is recognised as a bracketed digression, offers an illuminating illustration of Varda's understanding of memory and of the access it grants to the past. Varda's reenactment lays bare how, rather than permitting unmediated access to historical reality itself, memory is a question of imperfect, artificial representation that takes place, crucially, always in the present. Whilst the embalmed irretrievability of the 'real' past captured in a photograph was registered in *Ulysse* as an experience of loss, here it functions more powerfully as a stimulant to creativity, to fun, to play, to possible *what ifs*; as a vehicle for new inventions, satisfactions and pleasures. Juxtaposed in this way, an impression of embalmed immobility contrasts with one of resilient and productive liveness. Such stakes will be particularly important in my final pairing of case studies, where Varda turns from reenacting artworks to more directly reenacting lived experience, both her own and that of her husband. Through reenactments that replicate and inflect effects seen above, Varda will seek what we might think of as an ongoing relationship with herself and with those who have shared her life, exploring the possible afterlives that might be found for encounters, discoveries, sensations and attachments.

Moving Memorials: *Les Plages d'Agnès* and *Jacquot de Nantes*

Behind both *Jacquot de Nantes* and *Les Plages d'Agnès* there lies an impulse towards retrospection through which two artists, sensing that they are nearing the end of their lives, look backwards and take stock. The circumstances of these acts of retrospection are, of course, very different: on the one hand, there is Demy, hurriedly scribbling his memories down on paper when confronted with the stark certainty of his own death from AIDS; on the other, there is Varda who, staging herself in the guise of 'petite vieille' [little old lady], sums up her life from the perspective of advancing old age and of the multiple losses the passage of the years has heaped upon her. The two films deliver a form of cinematic tribute that in certain ways resembles the *contrario* act of portraiture undertaken in *Jane B. par Agnès V.*, where a composite likeness of a *pre*-mortem subject is sought. In contexts where the proximity of mortality appears yet more pronounced than was the case on the eve of Birkin's fortieth birthday, at stake in these two films will be the question of how our memories can comfort and accompany us as we approach inevitable disappearance as well as how these memories might allow something of life to endure beyond death.

The two films are composed of comparable elements. Both contain footage of Demy or Varda in the present, the former with the material symptoms of disease etched onto his moribund skin, the latter as she revisits the many people and places she has known in her life, returning to past encounters and forging new ones. Alongside this footage, both films also contain quotations from Demy and Varda's many films as well as varied reenactments of episodes from childhood and youth. The reenactments staged in *Jacquot de Nantes* and *Les Plages d'Agnès* initially produce very different effects; but in the end, these two films lead us to a very similar place. In the combination of the elements they contain, both *Jacquot de Nantes* and

Les Plages d'Agnès construct memorials to the life and art of their subjects. These twin memorials are of a very specific kind: refusing the concrete stillness of the commemorative monument, they seek to keep the memories of a life mobile and live, subject to belated acts of reinvention and open to new possibilities. Both films mourn for losses — those that have already occurred and those that are still to come. This mourning is developed not through melancholic or nostalgic longing for something out of reach, but rather through present, ongoing gestures of joyful celebration.

As it retraces Varda's journey through life, revisiting the geographical locations and human exchanges that have shaped her, *Les Plages d'Agnès* clearly announces itself as a film about remembering. The act of remembering is figured at various sites throughout the film as both pleasurable and unpleasant; as a puzzle that can never definitively be solved; as like clawing through a disordered swarm of uncertain, sometimes contradictory recollections that besiege and submerge us. But the film is simultaneously very much also a film about forgetting. On a number of occasions, Varda meets or describes individuals who have experienced the symptoms of dementia and memory loss, whilst also admitting to the increasing haziness of her own powers of recall. The instances of autobiographical reenactment that Varda stages with her own body and the bodies of others throughout *Les Plages d'Agnès* participate in these atmospheres of forgetting in distinctive ways. They staunchly refuse a form of memory work that would seek to retrieve the past intact and instead choose to reinvent it in the present, foregrounding the transformations and distortions, the forms of experimentation and play that this process brings. These reenactments seek not to *undo* forgetting, but rather to *redo* memory.

As was the case in both *Ulysse* and the *Cité radieuse* sequence from *Agnès de ci de là Varda*, a black-and-white photograph propels the first instance of reenactment found in *Les Plages d'Agnès*. Varda appears on screen, reclining amongst the dunes of one of the Belgian beaches of her childhood, looking through photographs of herself as a child, alone or with her parents and siblings. Asked by her cameraman whether she feels an attachment to the childhood these images represent based in nostalgia, she replies, pointedly: 'Non, pas du tout. Mais j'ai du plaisir à en voir les images' [No, not at all. But it's nice to look back at the pictures]. She carefully arranges these childhood mementos in an almost shrine-like configuration, inserting their corners into the damp sand. The stillness of photographs contrasts with the gentle movement of wild grasses in the breeze, captured blurrily in the foreground. Looking at photographs of herself paddling in the sea, Varda says that she fantasises about seeing modern little girls wearing the same old-fashioned swimming costumes. As if summoned into being by the filmmaker's words, the sequence that immediately follows reveals little girls playing in the beach's sand in the present, dressed in similar striped and strapped bathing suits to the ones that Varda herself had worn in her photograph, with the frozen past suddenly reanimated in the present day. Mobilised in such a way, reenactment is framed from the outset of *Les Plages d'Agnès* as a form of memory work responsive to the subject's curiosities and desires. Explicitly rejecting nostalgia, Varda pursues a more live, more present, more transformative connection with her own past.

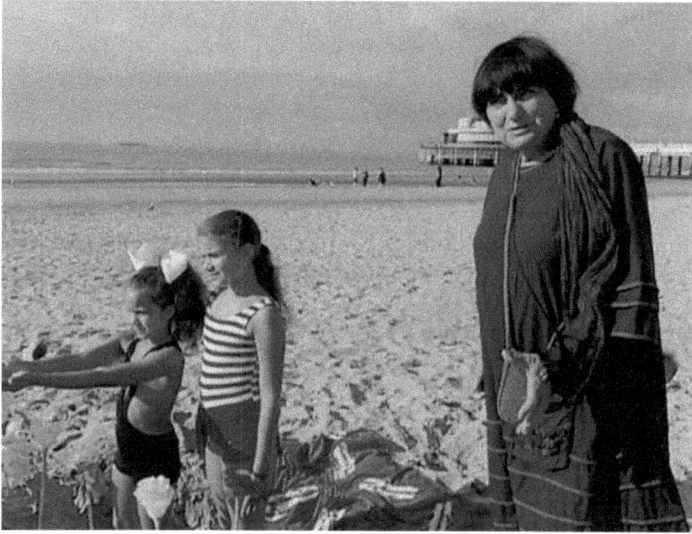

FIG. 4.8. *Les Plages d'Agnès* (2008), Agnès Varda © Ciné-Tamaris/Arte France Cinéma.

The filmmaker appears on screen to observe this reconstruction, seemingly bemused at the autobiographical scene she has willed into existence. If Varda confessed to feeling pleasure at reviewing her photographs, the avenues for such pleasures are here expanded, as the decisive moment captured in childhood relics is opened afresh to exploration and interaction in time and in three-dimensional space. This instance of Varda witnessing 'Varda', of old age witnessing youth, replicates something of the disorientating strangeness of Lehman's childhood reconstructions from *A la recherche du lieu de ma naissance*. But this sense of strangeness is amplified yet further by a more pronounced effect of 'doubling' than was seen in Lehman's film: Varda's reenactment lays bare the multiplication of selves which occurs as soon as we direct our attention inwards, literalising the essential alterity of the autobiographical encounter with oneself, uncovering its fictions. Through reenactment, the filmmaker shares the frame with a version of herself who really *is* an other. Varda's encounter with 'herself' refuses to conceal the gulf between past and present selves, the perceiver and the perceived, that lies, often concealed or disavowed, at the heart of autobiography, and instead makes it visible, physical, navigable, denying conflation or elision. As she gazes upon this recreated beach scene, Varda muses: 'Je ne sais pas ce que c'est de reconstituer une scène comme ça. Est-ce que ça fait revivre ce temps-là? Pour moi, *c'est du cinéma, c'est un jeu*' [I don't know what it means to reenact a scene in this way. Does it let us relive that moment in time? For me, *it's cinema, it's a game*] (emphasis mine). Her assessment recalls the *comme au cinéma* uttered on the recreated *Cité radieuse* rooftop. In both instances, Varda taps into the resources offered by cinema for the production of convincing artifice and illusion, developing imaginary, playful representations of identity and experience, to be both witnessed and enjoyed.

In this opening instance as elsewhere in *Les Plages d'Agnès*, reenactment throws open a fantasy space for the exploration and reinvention of the filmmaker's self. As Claire Boyle suggests, this is not a space which tries to cover over the gaps of self-knowledge that both Varda and we encounter as she attempts to tell us who she is, but rather one which makes these gaps decidedly more visible (2013: 165). Foregrounding their approximate, interpretive nature, the scenes that Varda stages alert us to 'the transformations inherent to the operation of memory, and to the fictionalisations of the past self that may result' (Boyle 2012: 65). As Kelley Conway rightly suggests, it becomes quickly apparent that in her reenactments Varda is concerned less with apprehending some definitive, coherent, even totally accurate, version of herself from the past than she is in staging new, installation-like artworks that bring her memories and fantasies into physical form (2015: 113). As Dominique Bluher argues in an analysis explicitly framed in terms of reenactment, the laying bare of the autobiographical mise-en-scène at play in these installation-like sequences does not represent a 'demystification' but rather an explicit acknowledgement of the inevitable mediation of the past by the present through memory (2013: 64). Emphasising both the fragmentary doubling of the autobiographical self and the artifice of this particular engagement with the personal past, the opening reenactment of *Les Plages d'Agnès* establishes characteristics that will reappear more or less prominently in the instances that follow it. From her opening reenactment onwards, Varda does not seek to bring *ce temps-là* back intact and unchanged within reach of the present: the little girls she watches are never exactly, never entirely her. What her reenactments consistently and consciously brings forth is not the past with the lives it once contained as it really was *then*, but rather as it is imperfectly remembered and remade *now*.

At a later point in the film, Varda sails from Sète to Paris, moving along the river Seine as she recounts her arrival in the capital some six decades earlier. She describes her enrolment as an art student at the École du Louvre and recalls how, during the stresses of her first-year studies, she would often retire to the nearby riverbanks to devour books on art history. As she evokes these memories, Varda sails past another reenactive avatar who appears as if conjured from the filmmaker's memory into life. From the sharply bobbed haircut that has become the filmmaker's trademark, this youthful figure is easily recognisable as an imagined version of Varda. Varda gazes at 'herself', a wistfully contented expression on her face. As the eighty-year-old Varda gazes towards the riverbank, eighteen-year-old 'Varda' looks up from her book and returns the filmmaker's cross-temporal gaze. As Varda watches 'herself' struggling to adapt to her new life as a student, she does not nostalgically long for a past moment that she recognises as having been difficult; instead, she takes enjoyment from watching mental images thrown into movement in the present in this improbable encounter across time and between selves.

Varda uses her recreated Rue Daguerre courtyard as the site for several of the film's reenactments, often drawing our attention in particular to the artifice of this space. The space that Varda has once again recreated 'en décor' is filled with electric cables, boom microphones, stage lighting, wooden frames, the hands of

FIG. 4.9. *Les Plages d'Agnès* (2008), Agnès Varda © Ciné-Tamaris/Arte France Cinéma.

a cameraman, clearly painted brickwork, in ways that recall the varied behind-the-scenes sequences seen in the examples discussed above. Varda's courtyard reconstruction is made to resemble the artificial backdrops of stage scenery, creating an almost caricature-like quality that persists in the increasingly stylised reenactments developed within this space. In comical sequences, modern Varda puts on versions of the improvised winter clothes she had worn when she first moved into the courtyard, or carefully manoeuvres a cartoon-like cardboard cut-out car through the fictive courtyard's narrow passageways. In their marked exaggeration, such sequences reveal a taste for self-parody as Varda experiments gleefully with her own image.

Touches of the exaggerated, the parodic and the caricatural inflect many of the film's other reenactments, lapsing occasionally into the grotesque. This is the case, for instance, in a sequence devoted to the years Varda spent with her mother and siblings on a houseboat during WWII. The filmmaker appears in the foreground of the frame, dangling her legs over the edge of the dock, gazing beyond the camera, a contented smile on her lips. Another of her avatars appears behind her playing hopscotch. This childhood 'Varda' is marked out by the billowing bow that she wears in her hair, similar to that seen in the Belgian beach photographs. The cameraman and boom operator appear within the frame, alerting us once again to the constructedness of these images. In the background, a flasher exposes himself to passers-by, pulling back his overcoat to reveal a garish pink, clearly rubber penis, flopping from his open fly. As a brightly-coloured prosthesis, as something that is clearly false but also believable, as an artefact created in the present that imperfectly recalls the past, the flasher's rubber appendage also offers a perhaps unexpectedly relevant synecdoche for the kinds of memory work performed by Varda's autobiographical reenactments throughout *Les Plages d'Agnès*.

There will be no such exaggerated adornments in the film I juxtapose with *Les Plages d'Agnès*. As Varda applies techniques of reenactment not to her own autobiography but to the autobiography of her husband, restaging it at his behest and on his behalf, the prevailing tone of *Jacquot de Nantes* will be very different from the luminous scenes described above. In her short documentary *Agnès V. raconte l'histoire triste et gaie du film Jacquot de Nantes* [*Agnès V. Tells the Sad and Happy Story of the Film Jacquot de Nantes*], included as an extra to the titular film's 2012 DVD rerelease, Varda describes the genesis of her project. She explains how in the closing months of 1989 Demy grew increasingly ill and began to spend most of his time indoors. He had also begun to note down reminiscences of his childhood and adolescence in the city of Nantes, taking pleasure and succour in this act of autobiographical recollection. Varda's documentary is filled with images of Demy sitting at his desk writing: close-up images of his distinctive, scrawled handwriting, with pages covered in lines and arrows as he organised the segments of his memories. These images ground Varda's descriptions in Demy's act of writing, in the materiality of his signature. Varda explains that Demy would regularly pass these pages to her to read, inviting her to share in the memories of his past. She confesses to taking similar pleasure in reading the sparse limpidity of these descriptions, seeing within them the germ of a possible film. Lacking the strength to make this film himself, Demy invites Varda to bring his youth back to life on screen in his place: '*Fais-le!*' [*Do it!*].

With Varda thus appointed by her ailing husband, *Jacquot de Nantes* reconstructs Demy's memories of childhood and adolescence in sequences that constitute the majority of the film's running time. From details of costume and prop to snippets of period music, Varda brings a convincing rendering of mid-century Nantes to the screen. Three of the city's modern residents take turns to reenact successive chronological chapters of the filmmaker's early life. These three versions of 'Jacquot' participate in recreations of Demy's experiences of wartime destruction and evacuation; his first communion; his early flirtations; his boredom with his technical college and dissatisfaction with provincial life; his multiple clashes with his mechanic father and rejection of the life that Demy Sr had chosen for his son. In these reenactments, Varda foregrounds above all else the development of her husband's nascent cinephilia, the seeds of his later vocation, his growing fascination with and then mastery of the varied techniques of cinematic image-construction. There is a teleological force to these depictions, as Varda uses her reenactments to demonstrate the specific experiences that would lead Demy to devote himself to cinema and the obstacles he overcame on the path he had chosen for himself. Whilst the majority of Varda's reenactments appear in crisp black and white, recalled moments of heightened spectacle, of performance, of sensory excess and immersion occasionally usher in fleeting glimpses of rich colour. Emphasising in such a way those critical points where the filmmaker's visual imaginary and personal inventory of fantasies were forged, Varda carefully traces the transition from the little *Jacquot* greedily gazing at film posters at local cinemas to the *Jacques Demy* whose name would eventually appear on film posters of his own.

Jacquot de Nantes represents, as Smith suggests, 'the explicitly autobiographical film that Demy himself never made, and the complex transfer of memory which presided over its making is also the subject of the film' (1998: 160). This transfer elicits a particular stance from Varda, as she seeks to do justice to the trust and belief placed in her. Useful as a point of comparison here is a sequence from *Jane B. par Agnès V.* where Birkin appears in front of a fairground mirror: the camera zooms in to inspect the actor's reflected face, as it bulges and undulates in the mirror's curves. This is a form of distortion which Birkin seemingly accepts as an inevitable product of the act of portraiture, albeit with an important caveat:

> Moi, si j'accepte qu'un peintre ou qu'un cinéaste fait mon portrait, oui je veux bien être déformée [...] l'important c'est l'œil derrière la caméra, la personne derrière la brosse à peinture. Je m'en fous un peu de ce que tu fais avec moi du moment que je sens que tu m'aimes un peu.

> [If I agree to a painter or a filmmaker doing my portrait, I don't mind being deformed [...] the important thing is the eye behind the camera, the person behind the paintbrush. If I feel that you love me, I don't really care what you do with me.]

In contrast, the yet greater love that Varda feels for her sitter in *Jacquot de Nantes* translates instead into a staunch refusal of distortion across the reenactments we see on screen. Whereas *Les Plages d'Agnès* joyfully laid bare and amplified the mediations of memory, the distorting effects of the multiple degrees of mediation to which the remembered past is subject in *Jacquot de Nantes* (from Demy's original act of writing to Varda's translation of these childhood reflections from page to screen) are concealed underneath the careful mimesis of Varda's historical reconstruction. In the production of her film, Varda assigns herself a role of custodianship. She strives to not betray or corrupt the gift of memory Demy had entrusted to her, to not lessen the importance of these memories to him, their formative power.

Throughout the reenactments of *Jacquot de Nantes*, Varda attempts to ground the memories she recreates in a verifiable reality external to her own (potentially distorting) authoring subjectivity. In the development of this autobiography by proxy, she employs a variety of authenticating strategies in order to reinforce the accuracy of her reenactments. This is seen, for instance, in the film's casting, with actors chosen for the closeness of their resemblance, both physical and behavioural, to their real-life equivalents. It is seen also in Varda's decision to use the very same working garage in which Demy had grown up. So many of Varda's reenactments take place in the garage's repair pit where Demy's own father had worked, its workshop where the real Demy had tentatively experimented with his first films, the communal courtyard where the real Demy family had once participated in the daily life of the busy neighbourhood that surrounded them. In *Agnès V. raconte l'histoire triste et gaie du film Jacquot de Nantes*, Varda describes how she had insisted upon this spatial anchoring, despite both the difficulty encountered in securing the filming location and the ready availability of another similar garage nearby: 'J'ai dit: Non, moi je crois trop aux murs, à la matière, à tout ce qui reste d'un lieu où on a habité' [I said, 'No, I believe too much in the walls, in the substance, in everything that remains of a place you've lived in']. Privileging what she saw as the concrete authenticity of a lived environment, the materiality of its affective atmospheres, Varda doggedly fought to secure the right to film there. From the same documentary, we learn that the scenes of *Jacquot de Nantes* that take place in the interiors of the Demy family apartment above the garage were actually filmed inside a film studio in Paris. It is telling that as spectators we do not at any point register this shift between real and artificial, experiencing sequences recorded in this fictive decor as similarly authentic to the sequences filmed inside the space of the garage. The contrast between these painstakingly accurate studio recreations and the openly fake studio recreation of Varda's courtyard from *Les Plages d'Agnès* is, in this regard, striking.

Though in increasingly frail health, Demy would regularly come to the garage to witness the filming, to watch Varda's version of his autobiography, her version of him. Looking back at this uncanny situation in which Demy was brought face to face with versions of 'himself' and of his past, Varda has described her apprehension at her husband's judgement and the reassurance she sought from him:

> Quand Jacques venait au garage — son garage d'autrefois — et qu'il s'installait dans mon fauteuil en toile pour regarder évoluer un garçon qui était supposé être lui, 'son père' bricolant dans un moteur et 'sa mère' servant l'essence en actionnant la manette de la pompe-même qui n'avait jamais été enlevée du mur depuis 1938, il me semblait que c'était inouï. Une fois je suis venue près de Jacques: *Est-ce que c'est ça? Est-ce que ça ressemblait à ça? Est-ce que les gestes sont justes? Et les mots? Qu'est-ce que tu vois? Qu'est-ce que tu ressens? Dis-moi.* Il m'a répondu: *J'y suis.*

> [When Jacques would come to the garage — his old garage — and sit down in my director's chair to watch a boy who was supposed to be him grow up, 'his father' fiddling with an engine and 'his mother' serving petrol with the same pump that had not been taken down from the wall since 1938, it seemed incredible to me. One time, I went up to Jacques and asked him 'Is that it? Was it like that? Are the movements right? And the words? What do you see? What do you feel? Tell me.' 'I'm there,' he replied] (1994: 206–07).

Varda recounts the relief she felt at Demy's lapidary response, the acceptance and approval, the presence and adherence it entailed: 'Ce mot très simple m'a fait plaisir et confirmé que moi aussi j'étais là. En voyage dans la mémoire d'un autre, en chemin avec lui. Revivant un autre temps' [This very simple reply made me happy and confirmed that I was there too. Travelling in someone else's memory, travelling with him. Reliving a different time] (207). As Varda's carefully crafted reenactments are delivered back to their source and designated judge, their recognisable veracity is formally approved.

Varda's response here once again encourages comparison with *Les Plages d'Agnès*. In describing it as *inouï*, Varda acknowledges the disorienting strangeness of Demy's cross-temporal encounter with 'himself' and with his youth on the film set, a strangeness so prominent in the autobiographical doublings of the previous case study. But this strangeness is not actually replicated within the final film itself and in our experience of watching it. Varda's suggestion that she found herself *revivant un autre temps* contrasts particularly strongly with the appraisal made on a Belgian beach that reenactment does not *fait revivre ce temps-là*. The reenactments of *Jacquot de Nantes* consciously seek to relive the past *as it really was*, to restore it in verbal and gestural sameness to the present. The emphasis Varda places on literalness and identicality produces something of an embalming effect upon the images that appear before us: what we most forcefully encounter in watching Varda's reenactments of her husband's youth is the *pastness* of the past that is reconstructed, its completion and fixity in time.

These reenactments leave Demy as he relocates to Paris, finally crossing the threshold of the film school he had dreamed of so ardently and for so long: a moment of discovery and becoming. But when we witness it, the possibility and promise of this moment feels long passed, closed to access and activation in the present, spent. This is a sensation that Varda's decision to record her reenactments predominantly in black and white (a choice taken, she has suggested, in homage to films of the late 1930s and early 1940s) does nothing to lessen. From this perspective, the effect produced by such sequences contrasts strongly with experiences of watching Akerman's *Portrait d'une jeune fille*, where the intense sensations that adhere to moments of transition seem to linger on long after those moments have ended. Viewing these reenactments with knowledge of Demy's death, a mere ten days after filming was completed, amplifies the sense of loss and irretrievability — of youth, of health, of life, of possibility — that hangs over them. In an early sequence of the film, Varda reenacts a visit to the grave of Demy's paternal grandfather, whose name he shared — a scene that resembles Varda's later visit to her husband's own graveside in *Les Plages d'Agnès*. The reenactments of *Jacquot de Nantes* leave us with the distinct impression of bearing witness to the evolution of a young life that has already irrevocably ended, to a death foretold that has already come to pass.

The reenactments described above are not, however, the film's only components: Varda consistently introduces other elements amongst them that fundamentally transform the effect they produce. As the varied elements of *Jacquot de Nantes* are brought into interaction, Varda draws out a force of fiction and interpretation that works to dispel the impression of deathly fixity that emerges from her carefully staged reenactments when they are considered in isolation, granting new mobility to memory. Speaking in *Agnès V. raconte l'histoire triste et gaie du film Jacquot de Nantes*, Varda identifies another layer to the film and acknowledges the question that informed it: 'Peut-on trouver dans la vie de Jacquot des scènes qui ont généré des scènes de film?' [Can we find scenes in Jacquot's life that gave rise to scenes in his films?]. Faced with another puzzle she sets for herself, Varda will once again seek answers to her own curiosities and desires.

Varda's reenactments of Demy's youth are frequently intercalated with quotations from Demy's work. The positioning of these images within Varda's montage establishes direct lines of generative influence from Demy's lived experience to the varied films he would later go on to make in adulthood, from his feature debut with *Lola* (1961) to the joyous effervescence of *Les Demoiselles de Rochefort* [*The Young Girls of Rochefort*] (1967) to the fairy-tale spectacle of *Peau d'âne* [*Donkey Skin*]

(1970), for instance. As quotations from Demy's work rub up against reenactments of his youth, the montage of *Jacquot de Nantes* becomes increasingly heterogeneous, collage-like. The contrast between these juxtaposed images is often stark, most strikingly so when the quoted films are in full colour and Varda's reconstructions are in black and white. Varda renders such contrasts explicit, refusing to smooth out their edges within her montage, drawing our attention to the transitions she stages between contiguous layers of representation. These transitions are often signalled by the use of graphic intertitles: the typographic manicule mark, pointing first right then left, foregrounds such shifts. By quoting these works, Varda changes them, charging them with an autobiographical valency in a way that Demy himself had never done, inscribing these films with new meaning through reference to the reenacted events of the filmmaker's life.

Less a distortion of memory than an augmentation, Varda's treatment allows the past to be reconfigured and recontextualised, granted new relevance, an *afterlife* even, through the resources of cinematic montage. These new meanings and connections are doubly complex when the generative influences that link life to art are reversed. In her documentary presentation, Varda suggests that alongside the above instances where Demy's childhood experiences are shown to have potentially generated scenes in his films, there are also instances where the influence worked in the opposite direction: where she chose an extract from one of Demy's films and oriented her script towards this reference point. Here we encounter not life generating art but, rather, art being used as a fictional script with which to reimagine, to rewrite life.

Effects of movement across layers of time and representation are replicated in the sequences of *Jacquot de Nantes* where we encounter an ailing Jacques Demy in the filmic present. There are instances where, through the effects of montage, elements seem to persist across temporal frames: reenacted sequences of young Jacquot operating one of his early cameras in the 1940s are, for instance, immediately followed by images of Demy in 1990 holding the same device; in another sequence, the music that accompanies close-up images of Demy's wrinkled, stained skin recorded in the present is shown to originate in the reconstructed past, emanating from the record player that young Jacquot receives as a communion gift, seemingly echoing across time and across borders of fact and fiction. Elsewhere, the direction of this trans-temporal reverberation is reversed as a physical gesture originating in the present — Varda's hand placed on Demy's frail shoulder — appears to *pre-empt* the same gesture of loving comfort in the reenacted scene that immediately follows.

To borrow a vocabulary Wilson used to describe the portrait the filmmaker had earlier gifted to Jane Birkin, *Jacquot de Nantes* sees Varda craft an 'imaginary archive' of Demy that seeks to release his untold possibilities. When combined with the elements of temporal ambiguity described above, the film's reenactments move beyond the embalming effect that, alone, they can be seen to foster. In such a way, this film as a whole and the composite portrait it constructs propels stillness into movement, establishing an ongoing relationship with the past. This is a relationship that refuses ossification and that instead holds out the possibility of

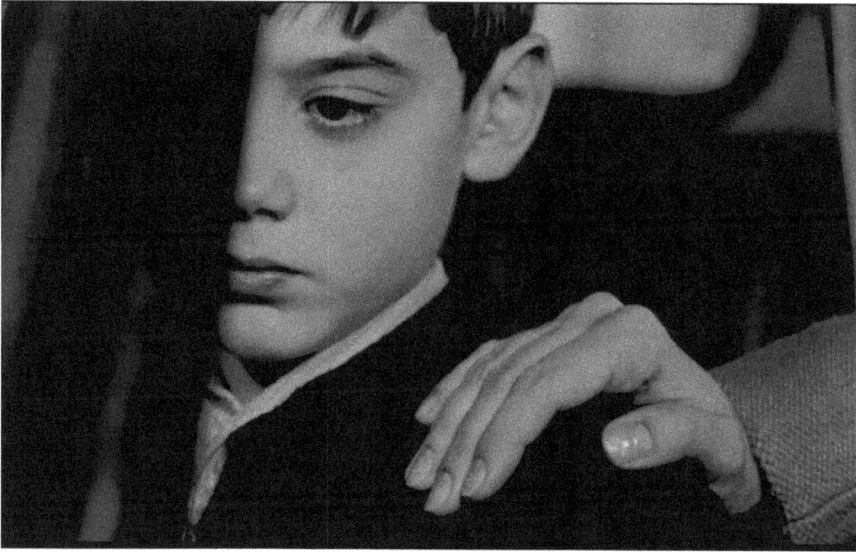

FIG. 4.10. *Jacquot de Nantes* (1991), Agnès Varda © Ciné-Tamaris.

persistence and change across time. This relationship does not seek to deny death but offers a mode of living with loss in the present that encourages us to envisage imaginary afterlives for the inspirations, encounters and intimacies of the past. As we have seen across this chapter, these imaginary afterlives can provide the basis for relationships with the past potentially grounded in pleasure and enjoyment. As perhaps best emblemised by the image of a hand placed lovingly on a shoulder that reverberates strangely across temporal borders, in *Jacquot de Nantes* this is an ongoing relationship with what has disappeared that can be a source of support and comfort as we carry on living.

It is in this way that the memory work performed in *Jacquot de Nantes* moves into closest proximity with what we saw of the fantasy-drenched reenactments of *Les Plages d'Agnès*. Varda's 2008 film closes with an epilogue in which the filmmaker is surprised by a spontaneous celebration for her eightieth birthday. The day after this party, Varda reflects upon the memory that it leaves behind: 'Tout ça est arrivé hier et c'est déjà du passé. La sensation s'est mélangée instantanément à l'image qui en restera. Je me souviens, pendant que je vis' [It all happened yesterday and it's already the past. The feeling mixed instantly with the image left behind. I remember, while I'm alive]. Varda appears on screen, a mirror on her lap. Her likeness reappears inside the mirror's gilt frame, held within a specular mise-en-abyme. As corroborated particularly clearly by both *Les Plages d'Agnès* and *Jacquot de Nantes*, this is what memory means for Varda: a continual, almost palimpsestic series of new images, produced in the present, that reimagine, rework and reinscribe the feelings and sensations of the past. Even if they announce themselves explicitly as fictions, for Varda, these images are just as real as the original experiences that inspire them. *Je me souviens pendant que je vis*: memory, for Varda, is a force that can

FIG. 4.11. Memorial Graffiti, Paris 2019 © The Author.

create something new, something active, something positive, that we can carry with us as we move forward into whatever future awaits us.

Of course, a little over a decade after her declaration of intent to go on living and remembering, Varda too died. This is a death that, as seen in the varied nods to time's relentless passing that rise to the surface in all of the films considered in this chapter, Varda herself openly recognised as unavoidable. But the films explored over the preceding pages also urge us to refuse the idea that this death should necessarily represent the point at which everything stalls and stops; at which movement falls definitively into stillness. The day after Varda's death, I was walking in Paris towards the banks of the river, near to the Pont des Arts (the bridge identified in *Les Plages d'Agnès* as Varda's favourite). On the wall of the short passageway that leads between the Rue de Seine and the Place de l'Institut, someone had spray-painted: 'Il faut qu'on vive pour Agnès Varda' [We must live for Agnès Varda]. When I returned later, this text had already been modified. This piece of graffiti participated in a wave of spontaneous memorials to Varda that sprung up at various locations in the wake of her death, most noticeably in the neat rows of flowers, hearts and potatoes left on the Rue Daguerre. I think that Varda would have approved of the message left and updated by anonymous graffiti artists — one that also seems compatible with the instances of autobiographical reenactment I have assembled above.

In this chapter, reenactment has assumed a large variety of forms and has appeared in a wide range of contexts. It is the technique through which Varda developed deeply personal engagements with the images of art history and through which she sought to bring these images to life. It allowed her to develop similarly intense engagements with the images of her own creative archive and to attempt to access the frozen memories these images contained anew. It offered the representational strategy through which Varda explored memories of childhood and youth — both her own and those lovingly entrusted to her. I framed each of these distinctive examples in relation to a tension between stillness and movement. In Varda's negotiations, this tension has sometimes been literal, with different media brought into conversation; but it has often also entailed more figurative questions of memory, knowledge, ethics, time and identity. These very different case studies conspire to show how, as Smith suggests, Varda conceives of the past as 'something which has an active role in the present and which can be put to creative use as an inspiration, not something to be nostalgically desired' (1998: 168). Throughout so much of Varda's work, the past issues continual invitations to very present acts of revisitation and reworking: in Varda's handling, it frequently becomes the material for experimentation, play and creative possibility. Varda's work acknowledges that experiences of loss, of things moving irretrievably out of reach, can be painful; but it also suggests that loss can sometimes provide a spur to new kinds of pleasures. This is of course something recognised by the three other filmmakers considered in this book; but it is perhaps Varda who seems to be having the most fun whilst putting it to the test.

Note to Chapter 4

1. @JR 24/03/2015.

CONCLUSION

❖

The Adequate Art of Mourning

As they question what might remain and continue to evolve after a death framed as anything but a definitive end point, Varda's attempts to imagine possible afterlives for the life and work of one she loved from the previous chapter in many ways bring this book full circle. And so, I conclude where I began: with a filmmaker looking for his wife. Seeking a point of entry into this book's subject, my Introduction surveyed the increasingly strange experiments Alain Cavalier staged in *Irène*. We saw him allow the affective atmospheres still clinging to revisited spaces to swell and swirl around him; arrange a variety of inanimate objects into shapes and configurations that seemed to suggest bodies or parts thereof; audition live surrogates and evaluate their ability to credibly mimic something of the titular Irène he so desperately sought to invoke; and restage both a birth and an abortion with kitchen utensils and a watermelon. I want now to think about another instance of autobiographical reenactment from *Irène* and about how it relates to the hopes and fears that motivate Cavalier's film more broadly.

In two separate sequences of the film, Cavalier reenacts his last moments with his wife. He explains how on that January afternoon in 1972 the couple had argued: she had wished to go for a walk in the forest whilst he had grumpily asked her to wait a while. The argument had led to Irène driving off alone in frustration towards the accident that would cause her death. Filming from the same window from which he had seen her alive for the last time, leaning over the balustrade and asking us to share this point of view, Cavalier adopts a position he had occupied nearly four decades earlier and repeats the couple's parting exchange:

> Oui, je me suis penché. Elle était là, en bas.
> — *Et non, pas maintenant, attends un peu, on n'est pas pressé!*
> Elle a dit: *J'y vais, j'y vais!*
> — *Bah, vas-y, vas-y!*
> C'était peut-être un tout petit peu plus rude que ça. Et j'ai bien vu la voiture démarrer là, bien bien vu. Et la place vide après. Je me souviens très bien.

> [So I leant out. She was there, down below.
> 'No, not now, wait a bit, we're in no rush!'
> 'I'm off, I'm going!' she said.
> 'Fine, go on then, go!'
> It was maybe just a little bit harsher than that. And I clearly saw the car start up, saw it quite clearly. And the empty space afterwards. I remember very clearly.]

FIG. C.1. *Irène* (2009), Alain Cavalier © Caméra One/Pyramide Productions/
Arte France Cinéma.

In reviving this precise moment through an immersive form of reenactment that resembles a number of other examples found in previous chapters, Cavalier resuscitates the complicated feelings that have attached to this instant over the years and plunges us directly within them. Such sequences foreground feelings that we have not really seen in the work of the other four filmmakers assembled in this book (or at least not seen quite so starkly). What emerges most forcefully here is the guilt, regret and self-hatred that adheres to Cavalier's angry *Vas-y, vas-y*, to his failure to stop his wife from leaving and to the impossibility of changing what happened. Cavalier's camera lingers on the empty space, *la place vide*, outside the window. This is an emptiness that Irène had left behind as she drove off on that afternoon in 1972 but that seems yet more irreparable as Cavalier replays a final dialogue in 2009 to a vacant patch of grass. As Jacques Mandelbaum (2009) wrote in a contemporary *Le Monde* review: 'Combien de courage, d'impudeur, de délicatesse faut-il pour filmer cela!' [How much courage, indecency, delicacy do you need to film that!].

This particular example of autobiographical reenactment revives difficult feelings not to exorcise them: what we watch here is not an atonement or an attempt at self-forgiveness. It instead confronts us with how Cavalier is still haunted by this moment, with how regret and guilt can lead us repeatedly through memory to nodal points of past experience and force us to endlessly ask ourselves *what if?* Other instances of autobiographical reenactment encountered in *Irène* do, however, appear as attempts at atonement, as expiations of past failures and of the guilt and regret that bind to them. Whilst the autobiographical reenactment described above reinforced the painful permanence of loss, the desolation of an unfillable void, the film as a whole seems convinced of the possibility of forging other relationships with the past and with what from it cannot be fully regained in the present.

Towards the end of his film, Cavalier admits that he had not been able to bring himself to go to identify Irène's body before it was sealed into a coffin. As he ponders: 'Si j'étais allé voir son visage mort, peut-être que je n'aurais pas fait ce film' [Maybe if I'd gone to see her dead face, I wouldn't have made this film]. In many ways, the bewildering experiments through which Cavalier seeks to access or reconstruct something of his wife in *Irène* and turn her absence into presence represent attempts to atone for this earlier failing, to improvise a means of reaching out to her beyond death, to fill a hole left behind by loss, to build a new image of her that he might, this time, be able to view. It is from such a perspective that *Irène* offers a counterpoint to Cavalier's decidedly better-known *Ce répondeur ne prend pas de message* — a film made in the earlier rawness of grief in which, as the filmmaker obscured his own face with bandages and painted everything around him pitch black, he seemed intent on definitively withdrawing and on destroying all possibility of image, all possibility of healing. *Irène* seems, in contrast, to offer an opening up to the world and to the hesitant possibilities it still contains, as well as a strident reaffirmation of belief in the power of art.

As I suggested in this book's Introduction, Cavalier's exasperated admission when faced with the limits of an actor's resemblance to Irène that '*Elles* ne sont jamais *elle!*' [*They* are never *her!*] announced the impossibility of fully regaining his wife through the varied attempts he makes to locate something of her. I suggested that Cavalier's exasperation encapsulates something of what documentary theorist Bill Nichols, writing in a survey of on-screen uses, presents as the 'impossible task' of all reenactment: to retrieve or return to a lost object in its original and genuine form even as the act of retrieval and return inescapably produces a new object, one that can never exactly or entirely be that which is longingly sought. I questioned whether — insofar as each successive attempt at repetition further drives home the irreversibility of loss (without quelling the desire for that which has moved out of reach) — the impossibility of reenactment's task aligned such undertakings with the painful cycles of melancholy. But I also asked whether *Irène* might hint at possible ways in which, as Nichols indeed suggests, reenactment can help to make good and come to terms with losses, precisely through those new objects, new pleasures it brings forth.

Freud's 1917 essay 'Mourning and Melancholia' offered an attempt to differentiate between contrasting responses to loss that has remained durably influential in subsequent years as a point of reference to be developed or contested. Freud's own thinking on the matter was not, however, entirely unchanging. In a 1929 letter to a friend, for instance, Freud nuanced the stance he had assumed twelve years earlier, returning to the possibility (even desirability) of definitively overcoming loss:

> No matter what may fill the gap, even if it be filled completely, it nevertheless remains something else. And actually this is how it should be. It is the only way of perpetuating that love which we do not want to relinquish (Freud 1961).[1]

As demonstrated in *Irène* and indeed in many of the films explored in the chapters of this book, autobiographical reenactment leads us to see a transformative force in this excessive, supplementary 'something else' — a force that can be powerfully awakened in response to an array of losses of differing natures, sources and scales.

In a discussion of what he terms 'the art of mourning', psychotherapist Thomas Ogden encourages an understanding of mourning as a process critically involving the 'experience of making something, creating something adequate to the experience of loss' (2000: 66). What we make and create in mourning, Ogden suggests, can assume a range of forms — a thought, a feeling, a gesture, a perception, a memory, a dream, a work of art (65–66). As he argues:

> What is 'made' and the experience of making it — which together might be thought of as 'the art of mourning' — represent the individual's effort to meet, to be equal to, to do justice to, the fullness and complexity of his or her relationship to what has been lost and to the experience of loss itself (66).

Crucially, for Ogden, *equal to* is not to say *identical to* (86), but it is to seek to create something that replicates the complex power of what has been lost and of its importance to the individual. As they negotiate various forms of loss, the French and Belgian filmmakers examined in this book often mobilise autobiographical reenactment as part of their own creative arts of mourning. In exposing themselves and us to what Rebecca Schneider referred to as the curious 'inadequacy of the copy', reinforcing that what returns to the present through reenactment is not the past itself, unchanged and identical, these filmmakers frequently acknowledge the irreversibility of loss. And yet, through the intense new pleasures that they can unleash, these 'inadequate' autobiographical reenactments sometimes produce effects that prove adequate to the filmmaker, adequate to their relationship with what has been lost or with the idea of loss more generally — something not the same but equally potent that can open dialogues across time.

In the very varied reenactments Cavalier staged at points throughout *Irène*, what he sought to bring forth sometimes was a new, avowedly imperfect version of the cherished loved one he had violently lost; but in other instances, the filmmaker was also concerned with the meaning and significance of this loss more generally, with those complex ways in which experiences of loss had shaped his life and identity and indeed continued to do so. The same is true of the autobiographical uses of reenactment found in the work of Akerman, Dieutre, Lehman and Varda. Over previous chapters, we have seen these filmmakers use autobiographical reenactment directly or indirectly in connection and response to a wide range of occasionally intersecting losses: bereavement; memory loss and failures of recall; the dimming of certain affective connections or intensities; the rupture of continuities of culture and knowledge linking present lives with lives that came before; the countless losses of global history or the multiple transformations inevitably brought by the passing of time; physical processes of erosion, ageing and decline with the material symptoms these processes produce. We have sometimes seen these filmmakers make autobiographical use of reenactment to generate imperfect versions of that which has been lost; but we have also seen them use such varied techniques of self-investigation and self-representation to offer broader interrogations of what loss means to them as they go on living, loving and discovering, of how experiences of loss (both those that have already come to pass and those that are still to come) spur them to test multiple possible ways of being in and of the world, ways that activate the latent potentials residing in and between past, present and future. None of these filmmakers ever deny that losing something or someone can be profoundly painful and disorienting; but, like Cavalier, they also manage in places to tap into more pleasurable feelings of varying types and potencies that coexist with (and sometimes manage to distract from or even overwhelm) painful feelings: 'la joie pure, la sensualité, l'amour' [pure joy, sensuality, love] (Mandelbaum 2009).

Note to the Conclusion

1. I came to this later text and to the inflection it suggests in Freud's thinking via Jennifer Rushworth's *Discourses of Mourning in Dante, Petrarch, and Proust* (See Rushworth 2016: 5-6).'

FILMOGRAPHY

❖

A bout de souffle (Jean-Luc Godard 1962)
The Act of Killing (Joshua Oppenheimer 2012)
A la recherche du lieu de ma naissance (Boris Lehman 1990)
Agnès de ci de là Varda (Agnès Varda 2011)
Agnès V. raconte l'histoire triste et gaie du film Jacquot de Nantes (Agnès Varda 2012)
Allah Tantou (David Achkar 1992)
Also Known as Jihadi (Eric Baudelaire 2017)
The Angelic Conversation (Derek Jarman 1985)
Les Années 80 (Chantal Akerman 1983)
The Arbor (Clio Barnard 2010)
Bande à part (Jean-Luc Godard 1964)
Die bitteren Tränen der Petra von Kant (Rainer Werner Fassbinder 1972)
Blue (Derek Jarman 1993)
Bonne Nouvelle (Vincent Dieutre 2001)
Le Camion (Marguerite Duras 1977)
Caravaggio (Derek Jarman 1986)
Casting JonBenet (Kitty Green 2017)
Les Cent et une nuits (Agnès Varda 1994)
Ce répondeur ne prend pas de message (Alain Cavalier 1979)
Choses qui me rattachent aux êtres (Boris Lehman 2008)
Confessions to the Mirror (Sarah Pucill 2016)
Demain on déménage (Chantal Akerman 2004)
Les Demoiselles de Rochefort (Jacques Demy 1967)
D'Est (Chantal Akerman 1993)
Dreams of a Life (Carol Morley 2011)
EA1 Les Accords d'Alba (Exercice d'admiration 1: Naomi Kawase) (Vincent Dieutre 2004)
EA2 (Deuxième exercice d'admiration: Jean Eustache) (Vincent Dieutre 2007)
EA3 (Troisième exercice d'admiration: Jean Cocteau) (Vincent Dieutre 2010)
EA4 Viaggio nella dopo-storia (Quatrième Exercice d'Admiration: Roberto Rossellini) (Vincent Dieutre 2015)
EA5 Frère Alain (Cinquième exercice d'admiration: Alain Cavalier) (Vincent Dieutre 2017)
L'Ellipse (Pierre Huyghe 1998)
Entering Indifference (Vincent Dieutre 2001)
Le Filmeur (Alain Cavalier 2005)
La Folie Almayer (Chantal Akerman 2012)
Fragments sur la grâce (Vincent Dieutre 2006)
Funérailles (de l'art de mourir) (Boris Lehman 2016)
Les Glaneurs et la glaneuse (Agnès Varda 2000)
Histoire de ma vie racontée par mes photographies (Boris Lehman 2001)
Histoire de mes cheveux: de la brièveté de la vie (Boris Lehman 2010)
Histoires d'Amérique: Food, Family and Philosophy (Chantal Akerman 1988)

L'Hypothèse du tableau volé (Raúl Ruiz 1978)
I Don't Belong Anywhere: The Cinema of Chantal Akerman (Marianne Lambert 2015)
Illibatezza (Roberto Rossellini 1963)
Irène (Alain Cavalier 2009)
Jacquot de Nantes (Agnès Varda 1991)
Jane B. par Agnès V. (Agnès Varda 1988)
Jaurès (Vincent Dieutre 2012)
Jeanne Dielman, 23 Quai du Commerce, 1080 Bruxelles (Chantal Akerman 1975)
The Jinx: The Life and Deaths of Robert Durst (Andrew Jarecki 2015)
Là-bas (Chantal Akerman 2006)
Landscape (Sergei Loznitsa 2003)
Landscape Suicide (James Benning 1986)
Leçons de ténèbres (Vincent Dieutre 1999)
Lehre deutsch mit Petra von Kant (Ming Wong 2017)
Lerne deutsch mit Petra von Kant (Ming Wong 2007)
Lola (Jacques Demy 1961)
Magic Mirror (Sarah Pucill 2013)
La Maman et la putain (Jean Eustache 1973)
Mes entretiens filmés (Boris Lehman 1995–2012)
Mes sept lieux (Boris Lehman 2001)
The Missing Picture (Rithy Panh 2013)
Mon voyage d'hiver (Vincent Dieutre 2003)
My Winnipeg (Guy Maddin 2007)
News From Home (Chantal Akerman 1976)
No Home Movie (Chantal Akerman 2015)
Le Paradis (Alain Cavalier 2014)
Peau d'âne (Jacques Demy 1970)
Perestroika (Sarah Turner 2009)
Perestroika: Reconstructed (Sarah Turner 2013)
Les Plages d'Agnès (Agnès Varda 2008)
Poesía sin fin (Alejandro Jodorowsky 2016)
La Pointe courte (Agnès Varda 1954)
Porto da Minha Infância (Manoel de Oliveira 2001)
Portrait (Sergei Loznitsa 2002)
Portrait d'une jeune fille de la fin des années 60 à Bruxelles (Chantal Akerman 1993)
Rear Window (Alfred Hitchcock 1954)
Les Rendez-vous d'Anna (Chantal Akerman 1978)
Revisiting Solaris (Deimantas Narkevicius 2007)
La Ricotta (Pier Paolo Pasolini 1963)
Ro.Go.Pa.G. (Roberto Rossellini, Jean-Luc Godard, Pier Paolo Pasolini and Ugo Gregoretti 1963)
S-21: The Khmer Rouge Killing Machine (Rithy Panh 2003)
Salut les Cubains (Agnès Varda 1963)
Scénario du film Passion (Jean-Luc Godard 1982)
Sherman's March (Ross McElwee 1986)
Shoah (Claude Lanzmann 1985)
Stages of Mourning (Sarah Pucill 2004)
Stories We Tell (Sarah Polley 2012)
Sud (Chantal Akerman 1999)
Tentatives de se décrire (Boris Lehman 2005)

The Thin Blue Line (Errol Morris 1988)
Thus A Noise Speaks (Kaori Oda 2010)
Toute la mémoire du monde (Alain Resnais 1956)
Ulysse (Agnès Varda 1982)
Une histoire de cheveux (Sibérie) (Boris Lehman 2020)
Il Vangelo secondo Matteo (Pier Paolo Pasolini 1964)
Varda par Agnès (Agnès Varda 2019)
Viaggio in Italia (Roberto Rossellini 1954)
Vincent Dieutre, la chambre et le monde (Fleur Albert 2013)
Visages Villages (Agnès Varda and JR 2017)

BIBLIOGRAPHY

❖

AGNEW, VANESSA. 2004. 'Introduction: What is Reenactment?', *Criticism*, 46 (3): 327–39

——.2007. 'History's affective turn: Historical reenactment and its work in the present', *Rethinking History: The Journal of Theory and Practice*, 11 (3): 299–312

AGNEW, V., J. LAMB, and J. TOMANN. 2020. 'Introduction: What is Reenactment Studies?', in *The Routledge Handbook of Reenactment Studies: Key Terms in the Field*, ed. by Vanessa Agnew, Jonathan Lamb and Juliane Tomann (Abingdon; New York: Routledge), pp. 1–10

AKERMAN, CHANTAL. 1995. 'On *D'Est*', in *Bordering on Fiction: Chantal Akerman's 'D'Est'*, ed. by Kathy Halbreich and Bruce Jenkins (The Walker Art Centre: Minneapolis), pp.14–45

——.2004. *Chantal Akerman: Autoportrait en cinéaste* (Paris: Editions du Centre Pompidou/ Editions Cahiers du Cinéma)

ANDERSON, BEN. 2009. 'Affective atmospheres', *Emotion, Space and Society*, 2 (2): 77–81

BAINBRIGGE, SUSAN. 2005. 'Introduction: Autothanatography', *Forum for Modern Language Studies*, 41 (4): 359–64

BAL, MIEKE. 1999. *Quoting Caravaggio: Contemporary Art, Preposterous History* (Chicago: University of Chicago Press)

——.2011. 'Baroque Matters', in *Rethinking the Baroque*, ed. by Helen Hills (Farnham: Ashgate), pp. 183–202

BALDACCI, CRISTINA. 2019. 'Reenactment: Errant Images in Contemporary Art', in *Re-: An Errant Glossary*, ed. by Christoph F. E. Holzhey and Arnd Wedemeyer (Berlin: ICI Berlin), pp. 57–67

BALDWIN, JAMES. 1979. *Just Above My Head* (London: Michael Joseph)

BARTHES, ROLAND. 1980. *La Chambre claire: Note sur la photographie* (Paris: Gallimard)

BAZIN, ANDRÉ. 1971. 'The Ontology of the Photographic Image', in *What is Cinema?*, Vol. 1, trans. and ed. by Hugh Gray (Berkeley: University of California Press, 1967; 2005), pp. 9–16

BECKETT, SAMUEL. 1954. *Waiting for Godot: a tragicomedy in two acts* (London: Faber & Faber)

BERGSTROM, JANET. 2003. 'Invented memories', in *Identity and Memory: The Films of Chantal Akerman*, ed. by Gwendolyn Audrey Foster (Carbondale: Southern Illinois University Press), pp. 94–116

BERSANI, L., and U. DUTOIT. 1998. *Caravaggio's Secrets* (Cambridge: MIT Press)

BEUGNET, MARTINE. 2007. *Cinema and Sensation: French Film and the Art of Transgression* (Edinburgh: Edinburgh University Press)

BLACKSON, ROBERT. 2007. 'Once More... With Feeling: Reenactment in Contemporary Art and Culture', *Art Journal*, 66 (1): 28–40

BLUHER, DOMINIQUE. 2013. 'Autobiography, (re-)enactment and the performative self-portrait in Varda's *Les Plages d'Agnès / The Beaches of Agnès* (2008)', *Studies in European Cinema*, 10 (1): 59–69

BOYLE, CLAIRE. 2012. 'Self-Fictions and Film: Varda's Transformative Technology of the Self in *Les Plages d'Agnès*', *Revue critique de fixxion française contemporaine/Critical Review of Contemporary French Fixxion*, 4: 60–71

——.2013. '"La vie rêvée d'Agnès Varda": Dreaming the Self and Cinematic Autobiography in *Les Plages d'Agnès*', in *L'Autobiographie entre autres: Écrire la vie aujourd'hui*, ed. by Fabien Arribert-Narce and Alain Ausoni (Oxford: Peter Lang), pp. 149–66

BOYM, SVETLANA. 2001. *The Future of Nostalgia* (New York: Basic Books)

BROWN, WENDY. 2001. *Politics Out of History* (Princeton: Princeton University Press)

BRUNO, GIULIANA. 2016. 'Passages through Time and Space: In Memory of Chantal Akerman', *October*, 155: 162-67

BRUSS, ELIZABETH W. 1980. 'Eye for I: Making and Unmaking Autobiography in Film', in *Autobiography: Essays Theoretical and Critical*, ed. by James Olney (Princeton: Princeton University Press), pp. 296–320

BRUZZI, STELLA. 2020. *Approximation: Documentary, History and the Staging of Reality* (London; New York: Routledge)

BUTLER, JUDITH. 2009. *Frames of War: When is Life Grievable?* (London: Verso)

BUTLER, KRISTINE. 1995. 'Bordering on Fiction: Chantal Akerman's *D'Est* (Review)', *Postmodern Culture: An Electronic Journal of Interdisciplinary Criticism*, 6 (1) DOI <10.1353/pmc.1995.0042>

CAPP, ROSE. 2000. 'Akerman Resists Southern Comfort', *Senses of Cinema* <http://sensesofcinema.com/2000/feature-articles/south/> [accessed 19 March 2021]

CARRIGY, MEGAN. 2021. *The Reenactment in Contemporary Screen Culture: Performance, Meditation, Repetition* (New York: Bloomsbury Academic)

CARVAJAL, RINA. 2008. 'Visions in Passing: *From the East (D'Est)*', in *Chantal Akerman: Moving Through Time and Space*, ed. by Terrie Sultan (Houston: Blaffer Gallery, The Art Museum of the University of Houston), pp. 10–17

CAVALLO, FRANCESCA LAURA. 2019. 'Rehearsing Disaster: Pre-Enactment Between Reality and Fiction', in *Performance zwischen den Zeiten: Reenactments und Preenactments in Kunst und Wissenschaft*, ed. by Adam Czirak and others (Bielefeld: Transcript), pp.179–98

CIORAN, E. M. 1986. *Exercices d'admiration: Essais et portraits* (Paris: Gallimard)

CLIFTON, LUCILLE. 2000. *Blessing the Boats: New and Selected Poems, 1988–2000* (Rochester: BOA Editions)

COMOLLI, JEAN-LOUIS. 2012. 'Mots et Images', <https://cesfilmsapart.wordpress.com/2012/10/05/mots-et-images/> [accessed 19 March 2021]

CONWAY, KELLEY. 2015. *Agnès Varda* (Chicago: University of Illinois Press)

COOPER, SARAH. 2006. *Selfless Cinema? Ethics and French Documentary* (London: Legenda)

——.2019. *Film and the Imagined Image* (Edinburgh: Edinburgh University Press)

CRIMP, DOUGLAS. 1989. 'Mourning and Militancy', *October*, 51: 3–18

CUTHBERTSON, TOM. 2022. 'Europe Wounded? Politics of Hope and Resistance in Vincent Dieutre's *Orlando Ferito* (2013)', in *The Routledge Companion to European Cinema*, ed. by Gábor Gergely and Susan Hayward (Abingdon; New York: Routledge), forthcoming

CVETKOVICH, ANN. 2003. *An Archive of Feelings: Trauma, Sexuality, and Lesbian Public Cultures* (Durham: Duke University Press)

DAVID, CATHERINE. 1995. '*D'Est*: Akerman Variations', in *Bordering on fiction: Chantal Akerman's D'Est*, ed. by Kathy Halbreich and Bruce Jenkins (Minneapolis: The Walker Art Center), pp. 56–63

DEROO, REBECCA J. 2018. *Agnès Varda between Film, Photography, and Art* (Oakland: University of California Press)

DERRIDA, JACQUES. 1984. *Otobiographies: L'Enseignement de Nietzsche et la politique du nom propre* (Paris: Galilée)

——.1993. *Spectres de Marx: L'État de la dette, le travail du deuil et la nouvelle Internationale* (Paris: Galilée)

——.1996. *Archive Fever: A Freudian Impression*, trans. by Eric Prenowitz (Chicago: University of Chicago Press)

DIEUTRE, VINCENT. 2003. 'Abécédaire pour un Tiers-Cinéma', *La Lettre du cinéma*, 21: 75–85

——.2004. 'Sud', in *Chantal Akerman: Autoportrait en cinéaste*, ed. by Chantal Akerman (Paris: Centre Pompidou/Cahiers du Cinéma), p. 211

——.2005. 'Lettre d'un tiers-cinéaste' <https://www.pointligneplan.com/document/lettre-dun-tiers-cineaste-vincent-dieutre-2/> [accessed 19 March 2021]

——.2014. 'Vincent Dieutre: "L'amour tient-il de l'admiration?"' <https://www.universcine.com/articles/vincent-dieutre-l-amour-tient-il-de-l-admiration> [accessed 19 March 2021]

DIEUTRE, V., and G. COLLARD. 2010. *(07/09)X2* (Paris: Les éditions ah!)

DINSHAW, CAROLYN. 1999. *Getting Medieval: Sexualities and Communities, Pre- and Postmodern* (Durham: Duke University Press)

DURAS, MARGUERITE. 1977. *Le Camion: suivi de Entretien avec Michelle Porte* (Paris: Minuit)

DYER, GEOFF. 2005. *The Ongoing Moment* (London: Little, Brown)

FLITTERMAN-LEWIS, SANDY. 2019. 'A Tree in the Wind: Chantal Akerman's Later Self-Portraits in Installation and Film', in *Chantal Akerman: Afterlives*, ed. by Marion Schmid and Emma Wilson (Cambridge: Legenda), pp. 13–25

FOSTER, HAL. 1996. *The Return of the Real: The Avant-Garde at the End of the Century* (Cambridge: MIT Press)

——.2004. 'An Archival Impulse', *October*, 110: 3–22

FOX, ALBERTINE. 2019. 'Sounding queer collaborative acts: Chantal Akerman films Sonia Wieder-Atherton', *Studies in French Cinema*, 20 (3–4): 243–64

FRADENBURG, L., and C. FRECCERO. 1996. *Premodern Sexualities* (New York; London: Routledge)

FRECCERO, CARLA. 2006. *Queer/Early/Modern* (Durham: Duke University Press)

——.2011. 'Queer Times' in *After Sex? On Writing Since Queer Theory*, ed. by Janet Halley and Andrew Parker (Durham: Duke University Press), pp. 17–26

FREEMAN, ELIZABETH. 2010. *Time Binds: Queer Temporalities, Queer Histories* (Durham: Duke University Press)

FREUD, SIGMUND. 1957. [1917]. 'Mourning and Melancholia' in *The Standard Edition of the Complete Psychological Works of Sigmund Freud*, Vol. XIV, ed. by James Strachey and Anna Freud (The Hogarth Press: London), pp. 243–58

——.1961. [1929]. 'Letter to Ludwig Binswanger' in *Letters of Sigmund Freud*, ed. by Ernst L. Freud (The Hogarth Press: London), p.386

——.1962. [1899]. 'Screen memories' in *The Standard Edition of the Complete Psychological Works of Sigmund Freud*, Vol. III, ed. by James Strachey and Anna Freud (London: The Hogarth Press), pp.301–22

GODDARD, MICHAEL. 2013. *The Cinema of Raúl Ruiz: Impossible Cartographies* (London: Wallflower Press)

HALBREICH, K., and B. JENKINS, (eds.). 1995. *Bordering on Fiction: Chantal Akerman's "D'Est"* (Minneapolis: The Walker Art Centre)

HALLAM, E., and J. HOCKEY. 2001. *Death, Memory, and Material Culture* (Oxford: Berg)

HANDYSIDE, FIONA. 2016. 'La mer, la mer, toujours recommencée: A Centrifugal Reading of the Beach in the Work of Agnès Varda', in *Agnès Varda Unlimited: Image, Music, Media*, ed. by Marie-Claire Barnet (Cambridge: Legenda), pp.127–42

HONOREZ, LUC. 1993. 'Chantal Akerman tourne son nouveau film dans les rues de Bruxelles, une jeune fille des sixties reveillera-t-elle le présent?', <https://www.lesoir.be/art/d-19930804-W3E08G> [accessed 12 August 2021]

HUYSSEN, ANDREAS. 1995. *Twilight Memories: Marking Time in a Culture of Amnesia* (New York; London: Routledge)

JACOBS, STEVEN. 2011. *Framing pictures: Film and the Visual Arts* (Edinburgh: Edinburgh University Press)

JARMAN, DEREK. 1984. *Dancing Ledge* (London: Quartet)

JONES, AMELIA. 2012. 'The Now and the Has Been: Paradoxes of Live Art in History' in *Perform, Repeat, Record: Live Art in History*, ed. by Amelia Jones and Adrian Heathfield (Bristol: Intellect), pp.11–25

JORDAN, SHIRLEY. 2016. 'Still Varda: Photographs and Photography in Agnès Varda's Late Work', in *Agnès Varda Unlimited: Image, Music, Media*, ed. by Marie-Claire Barnet (Cambridge: Legenda), pp. 143–56

KAHANA, JONATHAN. 2009. 'Introduction: What Now? Presenting Reenactment', *Framework: The Journal of Cinema and Media*, 50(1–2): 46–60

KRISTEVA, JULIA. 1992. *Black Sun: Depression and Melancholia*, trans. by Leon S. Roudiez (New York: Columbia University Press). Originally published as *Soleil noir, depression et melancolie* (Paris: Gallimard, 1987).

KWINT, MARIUS. 1999. 'Introduction: The Physical Past', in *Material Memories: Design and Evocation*, ed. by Marius Kwint, Christopher Breward and Jeremy Aynsley (Oxford: Berg), pp.1–16

LAVIN, IRVING. 1995. 'Why Baroque?' in *Going for Baroque: Eighteen Contemporary Artists Fascinated with the Baroque and Roccoco*, ed. by Lisa G. Corrin and Joaneath Spicer (Baltimore: The Contemporary and The Walters), pp. 5–8

LEBOW, ALISA. 2008. *First Person Jewish* (Minneapolis: University of Minnesota Press)

——.2016. 'Identity Slips: The Autobiographical Register in the Work of Chantal Akerman', *Film Quarterly*, 70: 54–60

LEHMAN, BORIS. 1985. 'Premiers films', *Revue belge du cinéma*, 13: 24–30

——.2004. 'Ma nuit avec toi', in *Chantal Akerman: Autoportrait en cinéaste*, ed. by Chantal Akerman (Paris: Editions du Centre Pompidou/Editions Cahiers du Cinéma), pp.190–91

——.2016. 'La fin de mon — du — cinéma (Confessions, 2)', *Trafic*, 98: 52–65

LEPECKI, ANDRÉ. 2010. 'The Body as Archive: Will to Re-Enact and the Afterlives of Dance', *Dance Research Journal*, 42(2): 28–48

LIÉNARD, MARIE. 2006. '*Sud* de Chantal Akerman ou une histoire de territoire et de terre: le Sud comme espace de mémoire', *Caliban*, 19: 131–38

LOVE, HEATHER. 2007. *Feeling Backward: Loss and the Politics of Queer History* (Cambridge: Harvard University Press)

LÜBECKER, NIKOLAJ. 2019. 'LANDSCAPE MEMORIES: Akerman's *Sud* and the spectator-environment', *Angelaki*, 24(6): 41–56

LÜTTICKEN, SVEN. 2005. 'An Arena in Which to Reenact' in *Life, Once More: Forms of Reenactment in Contemporary Art*, ed. by Sven Lütticken (Rotterdam: Witte de With, Center For Contemporary Art), pp.17–60

LYOTARD, JEAN-FRANCOIS. 1993. *Moralités postmodernes* (Paris: Galilée)

MACDONALD, SCOTT. 2005. *A Critical Cinema 4: Interviews with Independent Filmmakers* (Berkeley: University of California Press)

MANDELBAUM, JACQUES. 2009. '"Irène": Cavalier, au nom de la femme aimée', http://www.lemonde.fr/cinema/article/2009/10/27/irene-cavalier-au-nom-de-la-femme-aimee_1259328_3476.html [accessed 10 April 2018]

MARGULIES, IVONE. 1996. *Nothing Happens: Chantal Akerman's Hyperrealist Everyday* (Durham: Duke University Press)

——.2019. *In Person: Reenactment in Postwar and Contemporary Cinema* (New York: Oxford University Press)

MARIN, LOUIS. 1981. *La Voix excommuniée: Essais de mémoire* (Paris: Éditions Galilée)

——.1999. *L'Écriture de soi: Ignace de Loyola, Montaigne, Stendhal, Roland Barthes* (Paris: Presses Universitaires de France)

MARKS, LAURA U. 2000. *The Skin of the Film: Intercultural Cinema, Embodiment, and the Senses* (Durham: Duke University Press)

MARX, KARL. 1978. [1856]. 'Speech at the anniversary of the people's paper' in *The Marx-Engels Reader*, Second Edition, ed. by Rovert C. Tucker (London: Norton), pp. 577–78

MATSUDA, MATT K. 1996. *The Memory of the Modern* (New York; Oxford: Oxford University Press)

MAUROUX, JEAN-BAPTISTE. 1968. *Du bonheur d'être Suisse sous Hitler* (Paris: Pauvert)

MAYER, SO. 2019. 'Texas (is not Paris) is Burning: The Drag of Dis/Orientation in Chantal Akerman's *Sud*', in *Chantal Akerman: Afterlives*, ed. by Marion Schmid and Emma Wilson (Cambridge: Legenda), pp.102–14

MAYNE, JUDITH. 2003. 'Girl Talk: Portrait of a Young Girl at the End of the 1960s in Brussels', in *Identity and Memory: The Films of Chantal Akerman*, ed. by Gwendolyn Audrey Foster (Carbondale: Southern Illinois University Press), pp.150–61.

MCNEILL, ISABELLE. 2010. *Memory and the Moving Image: French Film in the Digital Era* (Edinburgh: Edinburgh University Press)

MODIANO, PATRICK. 1997. *Dora Bruder* (Paris: Gallimard)

———.2014. *Pour que tu ne te perdes pas dans le quartier* (Paris: Gallimard)

MULVEY, LAURA. 2006. *Death 24x a Second: Stillness and the Moving Image* (London: Reaktion)

MUÑOZ, JOSÉ ESTEBAN. 1996. 'Ephemera as Evidence: Introductory Notes to Queer Acts', *Women & Performance: A Journal of Feminist Theory*, 8(2): 5–16

NICHOLS, BILL. 2008. 'Documentary Reenactment and the Fantasmatic Subject', *Critical Inquiry*, 35(1): 72–89

O'DWYER, JULES. 2018. 'Histoire(s) de l'art: The Queer Curation of Vincent Dieutre', *Alphaville: Journal of Film and Screen Media*, 16: 53–66

OGDEN, THOMAS H. 2000. 'Borges and the Art of Mourning', *Psychoanalytic Dialogues*, 10(1): 65–88

PEREC, GEORGES. 1975. *W ou le souvenir d'enfance* (Paris: Denoël)

———. 1982. [1975]. *Tentative d'épuisement d'un lieu parisien* (Paris: Christian Bourgois)

RENOV, MICHAEL. 2004. *The Subject of Documentary* (Minneapolis: University of Minnesota Press)

REYNAUD, BÉRÉNICE. 2004. 'Histoires d'Amérique' in *Chantal Akerman: Autoportrait en cinéaste*, ed. by Chantal Akerman (Paris: Editions du Centre Pompidou/Editions Cahiers du Cinéma), pp.200–01

ROBERTS, ADAM. 2019. 'Laugh or Cry: Jewish Humour in Chantal Akerman's *Histoires d'Amérique*' in *Chantal Akerman Retrospective Handbook*, ed. by Joanna Hogg and Adam Roberts (London: A Nos Amours), pp. 202–03

ROSELLO, MIREILLE. 2001. 'Agnès Varda's *Les Glaneurs et la glaneuse*: Portrait of the Artist as an Old Lady', *Studies in French Cinema*, 1(1): 29–36

ROTH-BETTONI, DIDIER. 2007. *L'Homosexualité au cinéma* (Paris: La Musardine)

RUSHWORTH, JENNIFER. 2016. *Discourses of Mourning in Dante, Petrarch, and Proust* (Oxford: Oxford University Press)

RUSSELL, CATHERINE. 1999. *Experimental Ethnography: The Work of Film in the Age of Video* (Durham: Duke University Press)

SALIOT, ANNE-GAELLE. 2015. *The Drowned Muse: Casting the Unknown Woman of the Seine Across the Tides of Modernity* (Oxford: Oxford University Press)

SARLIN, PAIGE. 2009. 'New Left-Wing Melancholy: Mark Tribe's "The Port Huron Project" and the Politics of Reenactment', *Framework: The Journal of Cinema and Media*, 50(1–2): 137–57

SAUVAGE, BARNABÉ. 2018. 'Vincent Dieutre (2018): L'être aimé est la médiation entre les sphères', www.debordements.fr/Vincent-Dieutre-2018 [accessed 10 September 2019]

SCHMID, MARION. 2010. *Chantal Akerman* (Manchester: Manchester University Press)

SCHNEIDER, REBECCA. 2011. *Performing Remains: Art and War in Times of Theatrical Reenactment* (Abingdon; New York: Routledge)

SHERINGHAM, MICHAEL. 1993. *French Autobiography: Devices and Desires: Rousseau to Perec* (Oxford: Clarendon Press)

——.2005. 'Memory and the Archive in Contemporary Life-Writing', *French Studies*, 59(1): 47–53

SMITH, ALISON. 1998. *Agnès Varda* (Manchester: Manchester University Press)

TAYLOR, DIANA. 2003. *The Archive and the Repertoire: Performing Cultural Memory in the Americas* (Durham: Duke University Press)

UNGAR, STEVEN. 2012. 'Scenes in a Library: Alain Resnais and *Toute la Mémoire du Monde*', *SubStance*, 41(2): 58–78

VARDA, AGNÈS. 1994. *Varda par Agnès* (Paris: Cahiers du Cinéma)

WHITE, PATRICIA. 2008. 'Lesbian minor cinema', *Screen*, 49(4): 410–25

WILSON, EMMA. 2005. '*Les Glaneurs et la glaneuse*: Salvage and the Art of Forgetting', in *The Art of the Project: Projects and Experiments in Modern French Culture*, ed. by Johnnie Grafton and Michael Sheringham (New York; Oxford: Berghahn Books), pp.96–109

——.2012. *Love, Mortality and the Moving Image* (Basingstoke: Palgrave Macmillan)

——.2019. *The Reclining Nude: Agnès Varda, Catherine Breillat, and Nan Goldin* (Liverpool: Liverpool University Press)

WYLIE, JOHN. 2009. 'Landscape, absence and the geographies of love', *Transactions of the Institute of British Geographers*, 34(3): 275–89

YOUMANS, GREG. 2009. 'Ghosted Documentary: Chantal Akerman's *Là-bas*', *Millennium Film Journal*, 51: 71–80

INDEX

❖

www.ingramcontent.com/pod-product-compliance
Lightning Source LLC
Chambersburg PA
CBHW081131090426
42737CB00018B/3293